Performing Under Pressure

D1536938

Performing Under Pressure is an essential resource on improving sporting performance in high-pressure situations. Perry's work guides coaches and athletes through nine key elements of the sporting mindset to help athletes to perform at the highest standards, even under the most pressurized of situations.

This valuable read includes empirically-based advice on areas such as embracing competition; building confidence, concentration and focus; maintaining emotional control; learning from and coping with failure or injury; being braver; and being able to push harder. Perry also provides 64 strategies to support each sporting mindset, offering not just the evidence as to why they work but exactly how to implement them.

This book uniquely offers those supporting athletes a toolkit of sport psychology strategies and interventions in a way that is evidence-based, accessible and engaging, whether you are starting out studying sport psychology, on a sports science course, or are a coach of many years' standing, for both elite and amateur athletes.

Josephine Perry is a chartered sport psychologist based in London and Director of Performance in Mind, a Sport and Performance Consultancy. She is a member of the British Psychological Society and the Association of Applied Sports Psychology. Perry works with both novice and elite athletes to help them perform better under pressure so they can achieve their goals and enjoy their sport more.

Performing Under Pressure

Psychological Strategies for Sporting Success

Josephine Perry

Routledge
Taylor & Francis Group

LONDON AND NEW YORK

First edition published 2020
by Routledge
2 Park Square, Milton Park, Abingdon, Oxon, OX14 4RN

and by Routledge
52 Vanderbilt Avenue, New York, NY 10017

Routledge is an imprint of the Taylor & Francis Group, an informa business

British Library Cataloguing-in-Publication Data
A catalogue record for this book is available from the British Library

Library of Congress Cataloging-in-Publication Data
A catalog record has been requested for this book

ISBN: 978-0-367-33314-0 (hbk)
ISBN: 978-0-367-33317-1 (pbk)
ISBN: 978-0-429-31915-0 (ebk)

Typeset in New Century Schoolbook
by Swales & Willis, Exeter, Devon, UK

Contents

Introduction

Performing under pressure

When stood on a beach in Australia, watching the biggest waves you have ever seen, knowing that shortly you have to run into the sea to start an Ironman race, you tend to get anxious. And understandably so. What helped when I was in this position was hearing the commentator over the loudspeaker. He reminded us that we couldn't control the conditions, but what we could control was the way we felt about them. That was a lightbulb moment. It was when I realised that in competition my mind could be just as powerful as my body. That lightbulb helped me to adjust my mindset enabling me to perform under pressure. I jumped into the water. I swam. I set a new personal best for that distance and ever since I've been learning how to help myself and others use sport psychology to understand what is happening in our bodies and brains when we compete. Understanding this helps us feel more in control so we can select the right strategies for our own success.

This lightbulb moment switched on a whole new career. Two masters degrees and three years of supervised practice saw me become a chartered sport psychologist. I now run a thriving sport psychology consultancy and am privileged to be able to spend every day working with athletes helping them to perform under pressure.

This book helps explain why athletes react the way they do under pressure and how this impacts their thoughts and behaviours. From crises of confidence, fear of failure and nauseating nerves to a lack of focus, emotional control, frustration or pressure from expectations. It offers insight into nine key areas required to perform successfully in sport and offers accessible and practical strategies to those supporting athletes to help them develop strengths in these areas.

The nine key areas covered are those which arise most regularly in the athletes I work with; across all sports and at all different levels; from novices to world champions. It explains why the issues in each area so often occur and how overcoming them enhances both our enjoyment and our performance. It offers 64 practical strategies and techniques that can be implemented to overcome these issues. Once the athlete understands why they are struggling and is able to reflect upon their own reaction to it, we are usually able to identify the strategies that will support them in overcoming that barrier. Not every strategy works for every athlete but many of the 64 strategies that are included have benefited hundreds of athletes in thousands of competitions.

On the occasions I work alongside the coaches of the athletes I support I usually approach with trepidation. I fear they feel I will be stepping on their toes. Yet most are incredibly welcoming; not only delighted that someone else is supporting their athlete but keen to also learn the strategies themselves so they can be a more effective and psychologically informed coach. So this book is designed for these coaches, trainee sport psychologists and those working in sport who want to support the athlete they work with not just physically but also mentally. It can either be used when it is clear an athlete has a specific need such as a lack of confidence, being unable to concentrate or having maladaptive approaches to setbacks or as a way of developing and building the athlete's mental skills over time. For either purpose it is designed to help athletes set better goals, prepare well for competition, perform under pressure, identify the conditions under which they perform best and utilise effective support. Using the strategies should build up their coping mechanisms and ensure they will be better equipped to deal with any future setbacks or frustrations.

First, we look at how to positively embrace competition. Many athletes love their sport but fear the competitive element. The feeling of comparison and being judged can culminate in high levels of anxiety as the athlete translates the competition into an attack on their ego. We learn about the ways athletes can evaluate the stressors in their lives and ensure they have the coping mechanisms in place to meet them so, instead of perceiving competition as an anxiety inducing threat, they interpret it as an exciting challenge.

Chapter 2 focuses on confidence. This is probably the most common concern of athletes; that they don't have the confidence they feel they need and that this is holding them back. Often they are right. Their lack of confidence means they set goals which are not ambitious enough, talk themselves out of increasing their efforts or become so nervous in the build up to competition they skip essential elements of their preparation. Chapter 2 explains why confidence is so important and identifies 12 sources that can be used by athletes to make theirs more robust.

Strong support systems make up the next piece in the jigsaw of performing well under pressure. When helpful support is in place it can make a huge difference as to how comfortable an athlete feels, their level of wellbeing and their performance. When it goes wrong they may feel unable to be open and honest with their coach, scared to engage with their peers and nervous about being able to meet the expectations of others. As a result, Chapter 3 suggests various routes to building positive support and engagement and some ways to measure if the expectations that are being felt are real or imagined.

Sports all differ in the amount of time they require their athletes to concentrate and focus and Chapter 4 covers this. Some may literally require a few minutes of intense focus breaking up many hours of competing and others need almost continual concentration but for only short periods of time. Athletes who understand the concentration requirements of their sport can learn how to focus, how to avoid distraction and how to switch their attention on to the right things at the right time.

Alongside a lack of confidence the other standout reason athletes come to see sport psychologists is due to a lack of emotional control. Smashing tennis racquets on the ground or yelling at other players helps the athlete let off steam but it also earns them a poor reputation and means they are less likely to perform well. Their energy is going into anger about not doing well rather than performing the actions which will help them to win. Expectations, their own or from others, and high levels of perfectionism are often the cause here and Chapter 5 considers ways to cope with these better.

Chapter 6 is aimed at helping athletes get braver. Comfort zones are popular places to stay – for a very good reason – but if we want to do well and perform at a high level it is essential to step outside of them. Often athletes will self-sabotage to give themselves a controlled excuse for any failure, but if they understand their own motivation, how to build in some basic levels of psychological safety and are able to effectively attribute their successes or failures they should feel confident enough to stretch their comfort zones and get closer to reaching their goals.

They may now have got braver in their goals and training towards them but mid-competition bravery is required to work harder and push through tough times. Chapter 7 explains where physiology and psychology meet in setting our limits when we perform, and how we can increase motivation and decrease our perception of effort to be able to push harder and perform better.

No athlete can win every competition they enter. But they can all learn something from it. So Chapter 8 focuses on ensuring there is always a purpose to competing; either learning or improving. We look at how to analyse every event so there will always be a lesson to take or an action to implement and we consider the importance of celebrating and giving back once a big challenge or season is over.

Chapter 9 covers an area that every athlete will come up against at some point; setbacks and injury. Dealing with these well and following five steps to cope with them means athletes can benefit from stress-related growth so they return to full training and health in an improved position.

Each chapter ends by directing us to the strategies which will be most helpful to the athlete who is struggling to cope with the situation at hand. Altogether there are 64 strategies that can be used to support athletes to perform better when under pressure and they are located in the final five chapters. For each strategy we will learn how it works, the benefits of it and how to teach it to athletes so they can use it effectively.

The strategies sit within five areas of sport psychology that have been found to be so vital for success:

- Setting and sticking to the right goals.
- Preparing effectively.
- Developing a performance mindset.
- Building high levels of self-awareness.
- Having great support.

The strategies around goals and preparation should get the athlete to competition day feeling focused, confident and in control. Setting these foundations for their success should ensure they arrive at the competition armed with mental and physical strategic approaches in mind, having considered their fears and weaknesses as well as being confident they have planned or mitigated for them. The support they have built up around themselves should give them a comfort blanket so they do not feel alone and that even if the competition doesn't go to plan they can learn from it and pragmatically reflect that there is always another day, another competition.

This understanding and insight into the pressures of performance and these strategies to become a psychologically switched-on athlete means when they are in competition the athlete should have a huge toolkit of mental strategies at their fingertips and will feel comfortable enough to be able to pull out the right tactic, technique or strategy at the right moment. This means they can confidently perform under pressure.

1

Embracing competition

Focus on the challenge – not the trophy

The Latin root of 'compete' comes from 'com' and 'petere' meaning 'together' and 'seeking' suggesting that competing was not originally about beating others but working together to create something better. This is lost in most sport today where everything comes down to scores, results and trophies. And with those scores, results and trophies, comes lots and lots of pressure.

Some athletes love competing. But many don't. Enjoying the sport and the training but fearing competition is remarkably common. The score, speed, distance or height achieved can feel very final, very judgemental and very personal. Whether it is a weekly football match in the local league or a once in a lifetime Ironman challenge, the build up to and time within competition can see common sense decision-making and rational thought processes go out of the window, replaced with an athlete who is a bundle of nerves; withdrawn, grumpy and nauseous.

In these cases athletes are mentally assessing the competition as a threat rather than a challenge.

The sweet spot of nerves: turning a threat into a challenge

On competition day the nerves that take up residence in an athlete's stomach can feel consuming. They often talk about them as butterflies in their tummy but the more scientific term is 'increased arousal'. Athletes benefit from this arousal as it influences their performance by physically affecting their muscle tension, fatigue and coordination, raises their heart rate, adrenaline and cortisol levels and changes their attention, concentration and visual search patterns. This arousal gets the athlete psyched up, focused on what they are about to do, makes them fully aware of their surroundings and gets adrenaline pumping round their body.

It makes them alert and primed for action. Studies have found that athletes without any nerves perform poorly. One study asked basketball players to think about their mortality to increase their nerves and it worked – it improved their results.[1] The key though is getting the balance right so they only have nerves, not anxiety. Where the pre-competition nerves start to harm the athlete is when they move too far towards anxiety, making their muscles tight and their coordination and concentration poorer. This anxiety can cause headaches, nausea, a strong negative inner voice and pushes us to focus on tasks that are not related to the competition ahead of us. None of these are helpful to performance.

We want our athletes to be talking about these nerves as being butterflies gently fluttering about with excitement and anticipation rather than butterflies armed and ready for a full-on battle. The ideal level of arousal is different for each of us. We all have our own zone of optimal functioning where we can extract our best performance but either side of that, with too few nerves or too much anxiety, we will not be able to perform so well. To find their zone athletes need to become more conscious of how they are feeling before each event and to reflect afterwards how this impacted their performance. Once they spot some positive correlations they can incorporate these into their preparations.

The nerves we feel come about because when we are about to compete we unconsciously evaluate the demands and stressors of that event. The transactional theory of stress[2] suggests that it is not the actual demands and stressors which cause problems, it is how we each appraise them and the decision we then make as to whether we have the resources (ability, previous experience, skills or support) to meet them.

There are things that some athletes may see as a destructive stressor which would not even occur to others. Trying to capture every single potential stressor would be too huge a task as there are just too many, with too many variations, for coaches and athletes to realistically evaluate their potential impact. A 2012 study identified 339 distinct stressors[3] and many others will be unique to the individual athlete due to their own perceptions and expectations. Stressors can include the worry we will be judged, uncertainty about how we are doing or will do, the level of importance we or others have given to the competition ahead or when we have set high expectations for ourselves. Rather than trying to concentrate on every single stressor and counter it can be helpful for athletes to take an overarching approach to their competition and to any combination of stressors by focusing on preparation for each competition. Then, when they are evaluating the stressors they are able to appraise that they do have the resources to cope. This will put them into a challenge state; able to engage with the competition, focus well on their personal requirements and to employ positive and effective coping strategies for the elements which worry them. Instead of the nerves causing anxiety, they actually help the athlete to see that they really care about the challenge ahead and are excited about it.

If the athlete looks at the stressors, considers what they would need in place to deal with those stressors and appraises that they don't have the resources to deal with what they are confronting, they will find themselves in a threat state. This makes them feel as if they are putting themselves in some type of danger[4] and negatively impacts their sporting performance[5] as they start to feel anxious and question their abilities.

A stressor may be identical for two people (or a whole team) but the skills or techniques or preparation of each individual will impact whether they see it as a threat or a challenge. Take two athletes sitting next to each other in the changing room of a local derby football match on an unusually hot day. The established player who has just been training hard overseas in a hot country, feels safe surrounded by friendly teammates and feels like an important player in the team and so is able to see that match as an exciting challenge to be involved with. Sitting next to them is the new member of the team who has heard lots of scary stories about the abuse given by their rivals' fans, feels out of shape and is unprepared for the heat. They are going to interpret the demands of that match very differently. It is likely the new player sees the match as far more threatening. They are playing the same match, in the same venue, wearing the same kit, but yet one sees a threat and the other a challenge.

The interpretation we give though does not just come from skills, techniques and training. As shown in Figure 1.1 it is also based on our personality and mental approach. Studies have found that self-confidence, perceptions of control, levels of mental toughness or personality traits like extraversion, neuroticism and perfectionism can influence whether we are likely to perceive a situation as offering us a challenge or becoming a threat. Those habitually finding they have a threat mindset will often have lower self-belief, feel they lack control over their environment, focus on avoidance and find reasons not to compete. They will display poor focus, low self-confidence and no feelings of control. Their focus is on what can go wrong. The 'challenge' athletes are confident, approach their goals actively, feel in control of the situation[6] and have higher mental toughness.[7]

Having sifted each situation through their personal filters the state the athlete finds themselves in will influence their emotions, behaviours and the quality and speed of their cognitive functioning.

To move towards seeing each event as a challenge rather than a threat, athletes need to be using problem-focused coping (trying to resolve the problem itself) rather than the more negatively charged emotion-focused (such as venting) or avoidance (removing yourself mentally or physically) coping mechanisms that can become our go-to tools if we feel under threat. An athlete can also increase their perception of whether they can cope with the demands and stressors being thrown at them by building up their confidence, developing higher levels of mental toughness, aiming to be more goal-focused and being fully prepared. These tactics help them feel more in control. And control is something we will come back to regularly.

Potential stressors...

- **Performance** (Preparation, injury, pressure, opponents, self, event superstitions)
- **Environmental** (Selection, finances, training environment, accommodation, travel, competition environment, safety)
- **Personal** (Nutrition, injury, goals, expectations)
- **Leadership** (Coaches, coaching style)
- **Team** (Atmosphere, support, roles, communication)

On someone with...

Low confidence
Mental fragility
Low levels of preparation
Perfectionistic traits
Neurotic traits
Introversion

May perceive...

A competition as a threat

With a performance outcome...

Lower effort levels
Low motivation
Poor decision making
Lower physical functioning
Reduced performance capabilities

On someone with...

High levels of confidence
Mentally tough
High levels of preparation
Conscientious
Extroverted
Feels in control

May perceive...

A competition as a challenge

With a performance outcome...

Higher effort levels
Motivated to do well
Focused
Good quality decisions
High level of personal performance

Figure 1.1 How potential stressors can be interpreted

If the danger is physical, such as a steep and twisty downhill cycling or skiing course and the athlete feels they have weak handling skills then it is clear that additional physical and skill-driven preparation is required before the competition for the athlete to feel comfortable and able to enter a challenge state. More often though the danger is not a physical risk, but a threat to their ego, particularly those situations where athletes are worried they will be rejected by others or feel they have failed. They may fear being judged for poor performance, beaten by someone ranked lower than them or worried about missing publicly stated goals. In addition, the more an athlete's self-identity is built around their sport, the more their ego may feel at risk.

When the anxiety doesn't subside this sets off an uncontrollable feeling that overwhelms the athlete. Our brains were designed to cope with fairly rare, mainly physical threats which required physical responses, such as the release of chemicals that help us escape; cortisol and adrenaline. As humans though we are pretty poor at distinguishing a real physical threat from an ego threat so any strong physiological arousal will see our sympathetic nervous system send us into fight, flight or freeze mode. As society has developed and become mentally as well as physically competitive, threats arise more often and we are flooding our bodies with cortisol and adrenaline on a regular basis. Over time this has a negative impact on our health as high levels of cortisol suppress our immune system.

A great way to explain the process of what happens to us when under threat that has resonated very well with athletes is what Professor Steve Peters has called the Chimp Philosophy.[8]

Chimp philosophy

Chimp philosophy is a way of explaining the neuroscience behind our brain's response to threat. Peters, in giving it a visual identity, helps athletes to develop a clear comprehension of what is going on in their brain and what each part does so they can become more aware and better able to make different choices.

Peters' model highlights that we have three key areas in our brains which are used in emotional regulation and decision-making, all with different needs. They are labelled as the 'Human brain', the 'Chimp brain' and the 'Computer brain'. In understanding the agenda and needs of each element we can work with them to develop more positive behaviours.

At our core we have a 'Computer'. Sitting in the parietal region of our brain it behaves as a storage library for memories, values, automatic behaviours, experiences and habits so we can use them for future reference. Most of the time it works automatically using pre-programmed thoughts and behaviours (basically habits). This is essential as we are thought to need to make up to 35,000 decisions a day.

The more we can rely on our Computer the better we are able to perform as our Computer will make sub-conscious decisions helping us perform automatically. If we are able to let our Computer work away in the background then we are left with more mental bandwidth for other things; such as strategic thinking in a match or noticing what is going on around us in a competition. Trained behaviour helps actions become automatic. Athletes can think of it as: not doing something till they get it right. Doing it until they can't get it wrong. When we do this and also find ways to reduce our opportunities to feel under threat then we have more mental bandwidth when we compete to focus on doing well.

When something threatens us though, either physically or mentally, our emotions get ignited and our Chimp leaps into action. Our Chimp sits in the limbic region of our brain. It can be thought of as our base driver; following instinct, jumping to conclusions, getting paranoid and irrational. It is emotional and impulsive with decisions made incredibly quickly based not on logic or facts but on thoughts and feelings. Under physical threat our Chimp is very helpful – it prompts us to escape or fight. Under ego-driven threat we are more likely to make poor decisions and go into a self-destruct mode.

Alongside our Chimp we also have our Human. This sits in our pre-frontal cortex and is the rational, analytical part of our brain which searches for facts and context in order to make logical decisions. When under threat the

Human and Chimp work alongside each other and battle for dominance. The Chimp works five times faster than the Human though so will often win.

If we are able to teach athletes strategies to help their Human override their Chimp; by reducing the impact of the threat and increasing their likelihood of having challenge mindset, we can reduce the stress and pressure they feel ahead of competition.

A focus on the target and not the trophy is a way to do this. This involves shifting the athlete from outcome-oriented thinking towards mastery-oriented thinking; giving a huge amount of attention to process goals rather than outcome ones. The athletes then go into each competition with the aim of nailing a skill they have been working on, pushing through when they want to quit or wanting to learn something about themselves as an athlete so they can improve their performances in future. Each of these processes gives them a positive task to focus on, takes the pressure away from 'winning' and removes some of the stressors they are facing so will help an athlete be far calmer and more successful than if they are trying to win.

Comparing ourselves with ourselves

When an athlete focuses on the result they want or what will happen to them because of a good result, they remove some of their control from the situation. Focusing on results simply creates pressure, stress and anxiety and increases the athlete's risk of quitting if they start to see the score heading in the wrong direction. Focus should be on what will create a great outcome (the how to do it), rather than on the outcome itself.

The job of an athlete is to execute the processes of their sport as well as they can. If they focus on these activities they will do better (as they can control these) over focusing on things like winning, getting a specific score or keeping their coach happy. The elements an athlete can control; the effort they put in, the attitude towards their performance, the skills they use are the elements to help them focus on. This is an area where a coach, psychologist, manager or parents can really help to sway the conversation and thoughts in a positive way. Helping the athlete to focus on the processes, the day to day elements of their sport, keeps them grounded in good, strong technique. If the athlete gets this right often the results will follow.

Focusing on the process goals should feel very achievable but once the athlete enters the competition environment they become surrounded by other athletes, friends or family and their own inner voice reminding them they are in a competition and comparison takes over. In sport this atmosphere is particularly hard to avoid. There will always be numbers and scores ranking athletes, making it easy to compare. But these comparisons can be very harsh. Even multiple medal-winning Olympic athletes can get beaten. No-one can win everything. But not winning can feel very threatening when you feel you are expected to.

Technology and social media amplify these issues. Not only are athletes reminded about competitive aspects when they turn up to a race but every time they check their social media or online tracking feeds they can see other athletes looking fit on Instagram or read about their recent training session on Facebook. They go for a run and upload it onto tracking websites and see that a rival has gone faster, or longer and they feel like a failure.

A way to help athletes reduce the amount they compare and therefore reduce the level of threat they feel is to talk to them about who they are comparing themselves with. If it is others then an open chat about specific people and what they know of them can help them to realise that we are each too unique to compare fairly. Even identical twins will have different personality traits, different talents and different motivations. Not only is the other athlete's training history, amount of time to train, current fitness, race strategy and race schedule likely to be different but the physiological demands of events will vary considerably depending on their body type and physiology. Over time they should realise that an athlete can only compare effectively if they are starting from the same starting blocks as their rival. As this is very unlikely to happen the process of comparing is giving a focus on many elements the athlete has absolutely no control over, putting them in an unwinnable, and very frustrating situation. To help this process, educating athletes around impression management can be helpful so they can better control the information they give out about themselves, and interpret fewer elements of what they see from others as potential threats.

Summary

There are many potential stressors that athletes will come across prior to competition. The impact of these stressors is not usually due to the number or severity of the stressors but whether the athlete feels they have the resources and coping mechanisms in place to meet the required demands. If they do, then the competition should feel like an exciting challenge for them to get their teeth into. Without the resources in place an athlete will interpret that competition as a threat and perform below their abilities. Supporting athletes to build resources and develop coping mechanisms will be a worthwhile objective as it increases their enjoyment of the competition process and will improve their overall performance.

Key terms

- Challenge state – when we feel we have sufficient resources to meet the stressors we are facing.
- Chimp brain – a way of thinking about how our brain responds when under threat.
- Computer brain – a part of our brain used for storage of memories, values, automatic behaviours, experiences and habits.
- Coping mechanisms – the approach we take to handle difficult situations. Three key approaches are problem-focused coping (trying to resolve the problem itself), emotion-focused coping (venting or showing emotions) and avoidance (removing yourself mentally or physically).
- Human brain – a rational, analytical part of our brain which searches for facts and context in order to make logical decisions.

- Impression management – a process (often uncon-scious) where people attempt to influence how other people see them by controlling the information they share.
- Mastery-oriented thinking – a focus on learning and improving.
- Outcome goals – targets based on time, placings or a specific result.
- Outcome-oriented thinking – where the focus is on winning or achieving a specific result
- Process goals – targets based on mastery of a skill, practice or effort.
- Stressors – the events or situations which put demands upon us.
- Threat state – when we assess we do not have the resources required to deal with the situation in front of us.

Key messages to share with athletes

- Many athletes get really nervous ahead of competition.
- Some nerves are helpful as they get the body and brain primed for action.
- If we can see our competition as a challenge the nerves can be channelled effectively. If we interpret it as threatening the nerves become unhelpful. We see our competition as a challenge or a threat based on their evaluation of the demands and stressors of the event and whether they feel they have the resources to meet them.
- We all have a number of personality traits or mental skills we have developed which can impact whether we translate the competition as a threat or challenge.
- If we see the competition as a challenge many of our decisions during the competition can take place

on autopilot leaving our mental bandwidth free for high level tactics and strategies.
- If we see the competition as a threat our Chimp may come out and we will behave irrationally or make decisions based on emotion rather than logic.
- We can reduce our feelings of threat if we hold back from comparing ourselves with others and if we focus on process goals in competition rather than on the outcome.

Strategies to help athletes embrace competition

To help move athletes who have a threat mindset towards having more of a challenge one:

1 Identify the controllables through control mapping (Strategy 1) so the athlete is hyper-aware of which stressors they can impact, influence and ignore.
2 Ensure that goal setting (Strategy 2) has been followed so the athlete is reassured they have focused on the right mental, physical, logistical, technical and fitness skills.
3 Complete a strengths audit (Strategy 9).
4 Practise with some adversity sessions (Strategy 12) in the build up to competition.
5 Develop and follow competition planning (Strategy 21).
6 Complete a confidence booster (Strategy 22) before every competition.
7 Fill a confidence jar (Strategy 23).
8 Complete some familiarisation training (Strategy 24) ahead of competition.
9 Complete a 'what if' plan (Strategy 29) to prepare for and remove some stressors.
10 Design and implement a pre-performance routine (Strategy 37) to help them feel more in control.
11 Learn how to get into a pre-performance bubble (Strategy 40).
12 Develop and use a motivational mantra (Strategy 45) to help their inner voice focus on the challenge aspects of a competition.

13 Know their why (Strategy 49) to maintain their motivation to compete.
14 Become aware of key stressors by completing stressor identification (Strategy 54).

Notes

1 Zestcott, C. A., Lifshin, U., Helm, P., & Greenberg, J. (2016). He dies, he scores: Evidence that reminders of death motivate improved performance in basketball. *Journal of Sport and Exercise Psychology, 38*(5), 470–480.

2 Lazarus, R. S., & Folkman, S. (1984). Coping and adaptation. In W. D. Gentry (Ed.), *The handbook of behavioral medicine* (pp. 282–325). New York, NY: Guilford.

3 Fletcher, D., Hanton, S., Mellalieu, S. D., & Neil, R. (2012). A conceptual framework of organizational stressors in sport performers. *Scandinavian Journal of Medicine & Science in Sports, 22*(4), 545–557.

4 Blascovich, J., Mendes, W. B., Hunter, S. B., & Lickel, B. (2000). Stigma, threat, and social interactions. In T. F. Heatherton, R. E. Kleck, M. R. Hebl, & J. G. Hull (Eds.), *The social psychology of stigma* (pp. 307–333). New York, NY: Guilford Press.

5 Blascovich, J., Seery, M. D., Mugridge, C. A., Norris, R. K., & Weisbuch, M. (2004). Predicting athletic performance from cardiovascular indexes of challenge and threat. *Journal of Experimental Social Psychology, 40*(5), 683–688.

6 Jones, M., Meijen, C., McCarthy, P., & Sheffield, D. (2009). A theory of challenge and threat states in athletes. *International Review of Sport and Exercise Psychology, 2*(2), 161–180.

7 Kaiseler, M., Polman, R., & Nicholls, A. (2009). Mental toughness, stress, stress appraisal, coping and coping effectiveness in sport. *Personality and Individual Differences, 47*(7), 728–733.

8 Peters, S. (2013). *The chimp paradox: The mind management program to help you achieve success, confidence, and happiness.* London: TarcherPerigee.

2

Building confidence

Always wear your invisible crown

Confidence is an essential ingredient and a key character-istic of athletes[1] that can differentiate the successful from the unsuccessful.[2] In combining self-belief and positivity, confidence gives us a degree of certainty we can achieve our goals. It boosts our levels of resilience and mental toughness so we can fully focus on executing our physical, psychological and perceptual skills.[3] It is a lens through which we think and feel about everything that happens to us. The higher our confidence, the more rose tinted our glasses become.

Confidence levels influence how an athlete thinks, feels and behaves, impacting the choices they make and the goals they set. Low levels of confidence see them judge situations as outside of their capabilities, so they often avoid them. The higher their levels of confidence, the fewer situations they avoid so they set more challenging goals and commit more fully to them – ultimately improving performance.

High levels of confidence also help athletes stay calm and relaxed under pressure. Having a less cluttered mind leaves space to focus on what is needed to be successful, rather than on what is needed to avoid failure. It allows the athlete's cognitive processes to be more productive to increase effort and persistence[4] so athletes can overcome bigger obstacles. This isn't just in single competitions but over time as research shows that those who are confident tend to stay in sport longer and are less likely to drop out.[5]

Confidence also opens up a wider range of competition strategies to use[6] as once an athlete is striving to do well rather than aiming not to lose, their tactics change and become more positive. In team sports this would mean instead of playing defensively by trying not to miss a goal, efforts become focused on scoring. This mindset helps athletes to interpret nerves as excitement and challenge rather than negative, debilitating, anxiety which see us translate the competition as a threat which loses the athlete both concentration and focus.

Research supports all of these benefits and places a great value on the importance for anyone competing in a sport at any level to have high levels of confidence. 90% of Olympians say they have a very high level of self-confidence[7] and a meta-analysis of 48 studies clearly found a really distinct relationship between confidence and performance.[8]

Some research has suggested that confidence can act similarly to a placebo, with expectations influencing performance. When confidence has been manipulated (by providing false feedback to people so they think they are doing much better or worse than they actually are) the highly confident group outperform those with low confidence.[9] Similarly, research with weightlifters found that when the athletes were deliberately misled about how much weight they had lifted their confidence rose and they could lift increasingly heavier weights.[10] Further studies on weightlifters went even further. To boost their confidence, the athletes were told they were being given performance-enhancing drugs. This increased their confidence and consequently their performances improved. Once it was admitted they had actually been given a placebo their performance returned to previous levels.[11]

The holy grail of confidence for an athlete is robust confidence. This confidence is so strong that it will hold up in the face of significant challenges, setbacks and adversity. It is the confidence that keeps an athlete going when rationally they should have doubts. With it an athlete can feel invincible. But this robust confidence is quite unusual and many athletes find their levels of confidence can be quite fragile and take continuous nurturing. As a result, most athletes find their levels of confidence fluctuate over time, from fragile to optimal to occasionally over-confident. We will consider all three levels in this chapter.

Confidence can be found as both a state of being (coming from our current circumstances) and an inherent trait (deriving from our personality). Trait levels are more robust but even if they are naturally high they can still get knocked by a run of poor results. By contrast, confidence arising from current circumstances can change much more quickly as so many elements can impact it.

Confidence levels

To understand how confident an athlete is there are a number of questions to ask:

- When do you most often see your self-doubt arise?
- Are you ever afraid of certain elements of your sport?
- Do you truly expect to perform well or is there sometimes doubt?
- Is there a legitimate reason for any doubt?
- How do you react when things don't go the way you hoped?
- Does your confidence fluctuate during competition?
- Would you prefer your competition to be easy or tough to beat?

The answers to these questions[12] should give you an idea if an athlete is under-confident, has high and robust levels of confidence or is over-confident.

If an athlete is under-confident then self-doubt will impact their performance. They will struggle to close out matches or events, perform much better in practice than competition and will hesitate more often. They may freeze when trying to use previously automatic moves or focus on weaknesses rather than strengths. In the worst case their under-confidence will redirect the energy that should be going into their performance into fighting off anxiety, nerves and negative thoughts. It means they make safe or slow decisions which put them into a continual self-fulfilling prophecy of performing well below the level their physical ability dictates and never fulfilling their potential. Once an athlete doubts their ability to succeed they may start to withdraw their efforts as a way to protect their ego which becomes a catch-22 situation, increasing frustration and allowing even small setbacks to become a huge barrier to performance success.

There is an optimal point of confidence but this is slightly different for each athlete. It is where the athlete believes they can achieve their goals but still does everything they can to ensure it will happen. In this situation the athlete's body will do what it has trained to do and their Computer brain (from Chapter 1) will take over, letting the skills work automatically, preventing their Chimp from causing chaos. Having these high levels of confidence will not necessarily stop anxiety, but they can help athletes to manage it more productively and act as a bit of a buffer, lowering negative arousal levels, so they can self-regulate better and use mental tools to improve their preparation and performance.

While less common, it is possible to be over-confident. It can stunt the athlete's growth as they may become complacent and stop trying to improve or learn which will reduce their levels of mastery and long-term chances of success. It can limit success as those who are too sure they will do well may not put enough effort in to training or miss off essential elements of their preparation. This suggests a small amount of self-doubt can be beneficial, and even necessary, to keep up an athlete's desire to learn and improve and to ensure they stay hungry to perform well and prove themselves.

Sources of confidence

Research has identified multiple sources of confidence[13,14] and understanding exactly where an athlete derives their confidence from is valuable in developing their competition day confidence levels,[15] so 12 sources are highlighted here. Some come from the culture and organisation of the sport or the club the athlete trains in, some are internal, based on the athlete's own behaviours and personality traits and others, the most robust sources, stem from achievements already secured and skills already learnt.

Robust sources of confidence

The most robust sources come from having previous or current achievements to base their confidence upon – basically physical and mental evidence that they can do what they need to do. This evidence makes them more resilient and focused; despite any distractions or setbacks. There are two key sources of confidence here, mastery and preparation.

Mastery of previous performances or skills

These are not just official performances when competing (although those are great too) but skills or moves or speeds or heights an athlete has reached in training. All this evidence of what they have already achieved and mastered provides the strongest contributor to sport confidence. In fact, researchers have found that, in about half of all cases, past performance emerges as the most important reason someone is confident and mastery experiences are the most powerful tools for creating belief[16] and form a valuable foundation for other elements of confidence to be built on.[17] Knowledge that they have achieved the skill or required level before gives the athlete direct evidence that they can achieve the specific task they have set out to achieve. This becomes self-fulfilling so their confidence grows over time, allowing them to stretch their comfort zone and try things which are slightly more difficult. This source is so robust that even if an athlete has one bad competition or event they may be able to perceive that competition as an opportunity to learn or develop further personal insights so it doesn't diminish their confidence significantly.

Extensive preparation

The more preparation an athlete puts into a competition or challenge, the more confidence they will have when it comes to their performance. As obvious as this sounds, the more this is spelt out, the more focus the athlete can put into covering every element of their preparation. This extensive preparation needs to cover physical training, skills development and mental practice. It also needs to consider the logistics of the event so nothing is left to chance and a performance is not undermined by something basic like getting lost on the way to the venue, forgetting to pack the right shoes or being too late to warm up properly. Being fully physically, skilfully, logistically and mentally prepared will have a very positive focus on performance and provide a great source of confidence.

External sources of confidence

Less robust, but still valuable sources of confidence can come from the climate an athlete is training and competing in. These sources can be very powerful but how they are used may depend on personality or the context of the situation as they rarely fall under the athlete's control so can leave them vulnerable to a crisis of confidence if their circumstances change.

Vicarious experiences

As counter intuitive as it sounds, watching others perform successfully can actually help boost an athlete's own confidence, especially if they are athletes they feel some affinity to or similarity with. Others' successes and skills show what is possible and can give athletes the confidence to try things they may have been afraid to try before. As well as this, simply being involved with the success of others can bolster their confidence, especially if they believe that this other person closely matches their own qualities or abilities prompting the thought; 'If they can do it, so can I'.

Verbal persuasion

Others showing or telling us they have faith in us can massively increase our confidence. This has been shown through research in schools which found that when teachers are told certain students are gifted (even when they are not) the teachers give them much more focus, support and encouragement, meaning that by the end of the year the 'gifted' students are doing better than their peers and living up to their gifted title. Positive persuasion can also reduce the perceived effort an athlete is putting into something. Some athletes will find it much harder to train on their own and stay motivated and on task, compared to how motivated they become when they have a coach, personal trainer or even a friend alongside them.

Trust in advisors

If an athlete chooses to train with a coach then believing that they have the skills and experience to make the right decisions for them will bring them confidence. The athlete may have seen that expert work particularly well with others or have been inspired by their methods and really bought into their philosophy and ideas. Appreciating the way they work, and in particular the way they work with them, will help boost their confidence.

Environmental comfort

We gain a great amount of confidence from feeling comfortable and familiar in the environment we will be competing in. This can apply to both the physical environment, such as having already competed in the specific stadium or run on that course, or to the mental environment such as competing in a team of people the athlete knows and enjoys being with. While this is the ideal, some events will be on complex courses where there will not be any opportunity to practice or familiarise themselves ahead of competition. In these cases, the athlete can gain confidence from picking out key elements of a course (such as hills or altitude) or venue (lots of noise and wind) so they can practice these in advance and feel more in control on competition day.

Social support

Athletes having strong support from those around them will also find this to be a great source of confidence. Whether this is their family, friends, coach, clubmates or even workmates, knowing these people have confidence in them can transfer confidence over to the athlete. This needs to be handled carefully though to ensure the confidence doesn't get translated by the athlete as pressure or an expectation. When done well it can make the athlete feel much more comfortable in training and competition and help them to relax knowing others believe in them. This is a less robust source of confidence though because if the athlete moves away from their club, or has a change in family circumstances this source of confidence is lost immediately.

Internal sources of confidence

The final group of sources of confidence come from within the athlete.

Innate factors

This comes from the athlete feeling they have a natural ability in their sport. If they have grown up doing a specific sport or have regularly been told they have the body shape, skills or 'talent' for that challenge then it can give them a great amount of confidence every time they step into competition.

The athletes' view of their situation

This is when an athlete feels that things are going their way and that everything is going right. This is a fragile source as it can change so quickly, will depend on how optimistic or positive the athlete feels that day and can be influenced by things way outside of their sporting environment. If the athlete happens to feel that the situation is favourable to them that day then it can help boost their confidence but it changes so regularly that is not a safe source to rely upon.

Physiological states

If an athlete is able to associate certain physical feelings such as butterflies in their tummy or increased heart rate with excitement and readiness to take on a competition they will be better equipped for success. Athletes with low self-confidence will associate the feeling of butterflies in their tummy negatively and see it as anxiety. Those who are able to associate it with excitement and positive thoughts about preparing for a challenge (see challenge mindset in Chapter 1) can really get into the right headspace for competing and build their sporting confidence.

Physical self-presentation

It is estimated that between 50 and 70% of information given in any communication is non-verbal[18] so non-verbal behaviours including the look and style of athletes can influence our expectations of them and can even see people rank their potential performance abilities higher.[19] So how an athlete perceives that they appear to others can also give them a source of confidence. If they feel good about their body, weight, height and sporting attributes, then they will feel they are ready to compete. On top of this, some types of clothing, body language, or even how an athlete stands, can make them feel more confident. This source of confidence can be fragile as putting on or losing weight or mislaying a favourite piece of kit could change how the athlete feels into a more negative mindset. However, learning a few tricks such as how to stand confidently, or recognizing strengths in physical attributes, can certainly be beneficial.

Competitive advantage

Finally, when an athlete watches other athletes do poorly in a competition or knows that they have cracked before, this can help them feel they have a competitive advantage. Again, this is not robust as the athlete is focusing on others doing badly rather than on themselves doing well, but it is a valid source of confidence that some athletes use to help boost themselves.

Summary

Confidence isn't limited in supply. We all have the power within ourselves to grow it. There are lots of strategies that athletes can use, not only to increase the amount of confidence they have but also the number of sources from which they can get it. To help athletes build their confidence we need to develop an awareness of which sources they get their confidence from, build routines to help nurture the current sources, and find ways to add additional sources into the mix. Robust sources are most prized as they are more secure, enhance resilience and reduce an athlete's risk of having a crisis of confidence. If they can develop these robust sources, and a selection of others, the stronger their overall confidence will be and the greater their chances of performing well.

Key terms

- Competition strategies – the tactics an athlete uses in competition to improve their performance.
- Confidence – when we trust our abilities, qualities and judgement to achieve what we have set out to do.
- Cognitive processes – how we use our current knowledge to learn more and expand.
- Low confidence – when we do not believe we have the skills, fitness or techniques to perform well.
- Optimal point of confidence – when we personally feel we can perform in the way we want to while still preparing extensively.
- Over-confident – when we are so convinced we will perform well we don't prepare effectively.
- Robust confidence – confidence which gives us resilience to cope even when we perform poorly. This can come from knowing we have the skills and experience to do what is required and that we have prepared extensively.

Key messages to share with athletes about confidence

- Confidence differentiates the successful from the unsuccessful. It gives us a degree of certainty that we have what it takes to achieve our goals so we can focus on executing our physical, psychological and perceptual skills to the best of our ability.
- Having high levels of confidence benefits us by making us braver about taking on new challenges, increasing our commitment to those challenges, helping us stay relaxed, calm under pressure and persistent, have better competition strategies and help us feel more in control. Basically, confidence makes everything else in a competition easier.
- No one has unbreakable confidence. It needs to be built over time and topped up proactively.
- There are at least 12 sources of confidence. We develop our personal confidence from a variety of them.
- The strongest and most robust sources of confidence are mastery and preparation.
- Our confidence is fragile if it depends upon our performance relative to others. If we base our confidence on what we have learnt and can do well it becomes far more stable.

Strategies to help athletes grow their confidence

1 Goal setting (Strategy 2) will help an athlete know they have prepared fully.
2 Modelling (Strategy 3) to gain vicarious confidence.
3 Performance profiling (Strategy 4) means the athlete knows they will be focusing on the right elements.
4 Completing a skills sheet (Strategy 8) helps an athlete see they have worked hard on beneficial skills and techniques.
5 Completing a strengths audit (Strategy 9) reminds the athlete what they have to carry them through the challenge ahead.

6 Keeping and filling in a training diary (Strategy 10) will give an athlete evidence they have trained hard and worked on the skills they will need to use in competition.

7 Completing a confidence booster (Strategy 22) before every competition.

8 Creating a confidence jar (Strategy 23) will give the athlete a very visual reminder of what they have mastered previously.

9 Learning to use imagery (Strategy 25) well can be beneficial for confidence.

10 Overlearning skills (Strategy 27) helps an athlete feel really confident in a few key areas.

11 Acting confident (Strategy 31) is a way to kick start an athlete's confidence.

12 Developing and using a pre-performance routine (Strategy 37) helps an athlete feel in control and confident they have done all they can.

13 Creating a motivational mantra (Strategy 45) will help an athlete remember their motivation and goals throughout the competition.

14 Using verbal persuasion (Strategy 57) will help an athlete feel more confident.

15 Get a training partner (Strategy 64) for motivation and confidence development.

Notes

1 Vealey, R. S., & Chase, M. A. (2008). Self-confidence in sport. *Advances in Sport Psychology, 3*, 65–97.

2 Gould, D., Weiss, M., & Weinberg, R. (1981). Psychological characteristics of successful and non-successful big ten wrestlers. *Journal of Sport Psychology, 3*(1), 69–81.

3 Jones, G. (2002). What is this thing called mental toughness? An investigation of elite sport performers. *Journal of Applied Sport Psychology, 14*(3), 205–218.

4 Weinberg, R., Bruya, L., & Jackson, A. (1985). The effects of goal proximity and goal specificity on endurance performance. *Journal of Sport Psychology, 7*(3), 296–305.

5 Chase, M. A. (2001). Children's self-efficacy, motivational intentions, and attributions in physical education and sport. *Research Quarterly for Exercise and Sport, 72*(1), 47–54.

6 Vealey, R. S. (2001). Understanding and enhancing self-confidence in athletes. *Handbook of Sport Psychology, 2*, 550–565.

7 Gould, D., Greenleaf, C., Lauer, L., Chung, Y., & McCann, S. (1999). Lessons from Nagano. *Olympic Coach, 9*(3), 2–5.

8 Woodman, T. I. M., & Hardy, L. E. W. (2003). The relative impact of cognitive anxiety and self-confidence upon sport performance: A meta-analysis. *Journal of Sports Sciences, 21*(6), 443–457.

9 Nelson, L. R., & Furst, M. L. (1972). An objective study of the effects of expectation on competitive performance. *The Journal of Psychology, 81*(1), 69–72.

10 Wells, C. M., Collins, D., & Hale, B. D. (1993). The self-efficacy-performance link in maximum strength performance. *Journal of Sports Sciences, 11*(2), 167–175.

11 Maganaris, C. N., Collins, D., & Sharp, M. (2000). Expectancy effects and strength training: do steroids make a difference? *The Sport Psychologist, 14*(3), 272–278.

12 Adapted from the work of Loehr, J., Quinn, A., Groppel, J., & Melville, D. (1989). *Science of Coaching Tennis*. Champaign, IL: Human Kinetics.

13 Vealey, R. S., Garner-Holman, M., Hayashi, S. W., & Giacobbi, P. (1998). Sources of sport-confidence: Conceptualization and instrument development. *Journal of Sport and Exercise Psychology, 20*(1), 54–80.

14 Hays, K., Maynard, I., Thomas, O., & Bawden, M. (2007). Sources and types of confidence identified by world class sport performers. *Journal of Applied Sport Psychology, 19*(4), 434–456.

15 Kingston, K., Lane, A., & Thomas, O. (2010). A temporal examination of elite performers sources of sport-confidence. *The Sport Psychologist, 24*(3), 313–332.

16 Valiante, G., & Morris, D. B. (2013). The sources and maintenance of professional golfers' self-efficacy beliefs. *The Sport Psychologist, 27*(2), 130–142.

17 Feltz, D. L., & Reissinger, C. A. (1990). Effects of in-vivo emotive imagery and performance feedback on self-efficacy and muscular endurance. *Journal of Sport and Exercise Psychology, 12*, 132–143.

18 Burke, K. L. (2005). But coach doesn't understand: Dealing with team communication quagmires. In M. Anderson (Ed.), *Sport psychology in practice* (pp. 45–59). Champaign, IL: Human Kinetics.

19 Buscombe, R., Greenlees, I., Holder, T., Thelwell, R., & Rimmer, M. (2006). Expectancy effects in tennis: The impact of opponents' pre-match non-verbal behaviour on male tennis players. *Journal of Sports Sciences, 24*(12), 1265–1272.

3

Sustaining strong support systems

Athletes don't care what you know until they know you care

Standing in the middle of a sports field knowing there are hundreds of pairs of eyes on you is a very lonely place to be. If an athlete is ever going to feel under threat that time is now. Feeling safe in the knowledge that people around them have their back and like them however well they perform will reduce some of the threat and help them feel more like they are facing a challenge, not a punishment. Even novice athletes may have coaches, family, friends and other athletes supporting them. At the elite end we can add in physios, psychologists, strength and conditioning specialists, nutritionists, masseurs, doctors and team administrators. Some members of this support team can enhance their performance however others, completely unintentionally, may hinder it.

One way to ensure that those around the athlete help them to thrive is to create a climate of psychological safety. This is where team members believe their team (whether a formal team or those surrounding an individual athlete) provides a safe place to take risks. It means they can push themselves without fearing negative consequences towards their self-image, status or their sporting career.[1] They feel they can be candid and honest, more innovative with their strategies and can test ideas without feeling their sporting career will be cut short or they'll no longer get selected for a team because of it. It facilitates a more honest, challenging and goal driven environment. With this in place athletes should feel under less pressure to achieve specific outcomes and should be able to take bigger risks knowing it is safe to try. The focus will be on trying to do well rather than trying not to mess up, creating a high-performance climate where athletes feel secure to explore their role in their sport, push their boundaries and take risks to improve performance.

Creating a psychologically safe climate around an athlete requires coaches, family members, peers and wider supporters to promote open and honest communication, task-driven achievements, evaluation against where the athlete was previously, rather than against others and meeting their own goals, no-one else's. In short, a caring environment is inviting, safe, supportive and gives the athlete the feeling of being valued and respected. Much of the way to show this is through good communication.

The basics of good communication can usually be summarised as being direct, specific, clear and consistent, owning the message, stating what is required, explaining feelings, separating facts from opinion, having a focus on the most important thing and making sure body language reflects what is being said. When communication goes wrong and any of these elements have been omitted it can cause conflict, fall outs, a lack of confidence and poor performance. Often the channel used will be the culprit for the communication failure. If communication is face to face and the two people feel comfortable with each other then the message can be encoded positively and the recipient can ask for clarification about any ambiguity without fear. Email, text messaging or group messaging systems can give far more opportunity for ambiguity and less chance to clarify or soften the tone.

With great communication athletes can feel supported, safe and ok to fail because they will know it will be addressed in a respectful way. In giving athletes the space to fail, without judgement or fear of punishment they will fail regularly, but in a way that gives them valuable information on how to do it better next time. In this chapter we will look at the four key groups of people supporting athletes; coaches, family, peers and those online, and consider the communication techniques which could help all of them to build positive relationships with athletes.

Coaches

In sport there are many important relationships but it is the coach–athlete relationship which many see as especially crucial[2] as it is embedded as the foundations of what an athlete is doing day to day. Coaching is no longer just thought of as enhancing an athletes' physical, technical and strategic skills[3] but as something deeper which includes developing the individual's potential. In fact, especially when coaching young athletes, when in training or practice, coaches may be thought of as an athlete's primary care giver because as well as the teaching of skills and techniques they will often be providing security, safety and emotional support. The real challenge as a coach is to balance strategic thinking and logical development alongside empathy and emotional awareness while still being honest and open and having to share information or decisions an athlete may not want to hear.

This makes the relationship with the athlete crucial. It should be at the heart of all they do.[4] The relationship does not happen immediately though and it takes time and a proactive strategy to help it grow. It requires conversations, support, observations, time and effort invested. But the investment will pay off as the coach–athlete relationship has been found to impact the athlete's self-esteem,[5] physical and psychosocial development,[6] satisfaction,[7] motivation,[8] collective efficacy,[9] the way athletes evaluate their performance[10] and ultimately their performance.

Poor relationships will be characterised by a lack of closeness, commitment and complementarity.[11] Awful relationships will involve antagonism and exploitation[12] where the relationship is not just ineffective but actually harmful both in terms of a stressful, negative athlete experience[13] and regarding physical wellbeing like increased burnout.[14]

Positive coach–athlete relationships can enhance the athlete's performance, development[15] and their wellbeing[16] and have been found to reduce stress levels,[17] improve cognitive performance and lower levels of exhaustion.[18] There will be a focus on growth and development and a feeling of empathic understanding, mutual trust and respect, predictability about how each other might behave or communicate, knowledge of each other's strengths and a rapport between the two.[19]

The coaches who focus on positive, personal relationships with their athletes will help their athletes have success both in sport and outside of it, through shaping moral and ethical behaviours and developing an athlete's personal growth. So how to do this?

A good coach–athlete relationship can be recognised by the way thoughts, feelings and behaviours interact[20] using the concepts of closeness (the bond between coach and athlete characterised by mutual appreciation, trust and respect), commitment (both the athlete and coach being there for the long run) and complementarity (working in a way which is complementary and cooperative). In team sports it has been found that having high levels in each area will improve team cohesion,[21] motivation[22] and help individual members of the team feel surer about their role.[23]

However well the coach and athlete do get on, conflict is likely to arise at some point[24] so expecting this and having some preventative and responsive measures in place will be beneficial and ensure if the conflict appears around a high level competition the athlete is able to stay focused and give their mental bandwidth to the competition, not their disagreement.

A key focus to prevent conflict is around communication. Ten American football coaches who all received awards for their abilities to facilitate their athletes' personal development were interviewed and they all emphasised how important communication was.[25] Those with a policy of positivity, openness and assurance[26] and who proactively discuss any areas of disagreement get rewarded with a better relationship.

Athletes will have their own preferences about the way a coach communicates with them in terms of style, amount of information and prescription.[27] Frustration will usually occur when the coach speaks in so much shorthand they forget to explain what they are thinking or where their thinking has come from. The frustration will grow if a coach lacks the communication skills to share their expertise or shies away from difficult communications.

Athletes and coaches will never agree all of the time but any negative feedback will always be taken worse if communicated poorly. Difficult conversations will need to happen but by following some rules, some of the heat can be taken out of the sting. Most important is not to confront someone when either is angry. Then, rather than try to solve the athlete's problems, the coach should put the momentum onto the athlete. The most effective solutions will usually come from the athlete themselves but to get to them they need space and an open, welcoming environment to come up with them. A coach who shows they listen to their athletes, asks empathetic questions, summarises what they think the athlete is saying to them and then asks the athlete how they will work to address the issue will find it easier to broach difficult subjects.

This element is so important that athletes have been found to care more about how a coach will communicate with them than about what skills they may teach them.[28] Great communication by coaches grows shared knowledge and, in team sports, increases each member of the team's understanding about their own and shared goals, beliefs, values and opinions.[29] Regular catch ups and chatting during training can help build the trust between the coach and athlete which builds a better relationship.

Family

Sports can be all-consuming – with a huge amount of mental, physical and emotional preparation. Yet most athletes are only athletes for an hour or two a day. The rest of the time they are children or parents or family members. Their family will have a huge amount of power and influence over the way they processes their feelings about their sport. The power and influence is likely to be stronger the younger the athlete is. Whatever their age, the athlete will always be a person first and an athlete second, so they need their fundamental needs met before their sporting ones.

When a big competition is on the horizon an athlete may feel it is taking over their time, their thoughts and all their conversations. Support from their family in this period is vital. Whether it is knowing the dog has been walked, having a smiling face on the sidelines or feeling comforted during the dark moments of a competition, knowing that someone else has invested their time and cares about you can make a real difference.

Studies have found that the encouragement and support of friends and family is a key factor in building confidence in an athlete – confidence which can lead to success in competition. Researchers asked golfers about the social support systems they used and found during stressful matches those with strong social support systems improved their golf score by one shot per round.[30] Those without that system played worse. They found it was the social support which effectively 'buffered' the impact of stress on the golfers.

While really valuable as socialisers, role models and encouragers,[31] family can cause problems if they get too involved. They may take their role as a cheerleader too far, not being honest about the athlete's potential which can lead to disappointment later on. They may focus more on the competition aspect of sport and not enough on having fun or the lessons they are learning along the way. They may then miss the way everyone learns and develops at different speeds. They can also inadvertently put an emphasis on winning which creates an environment where the athlete's goals are ego orientated leading them towards social comparison and a continual emphasis on external rewards.[32] These environments can lead to disordered eating, over training, burnout and training when injured.

Instead it is important to remember and then remind the athlete that sporting failure is not personal failure. Focusing on encouraging positive sporting behaviours such as trying hard, supporting their team mates and being a good sport should be emphasised over competition outcomes. This helps separate competition results from an athlete's self-esteem.

A really important group of family members for junior athletes is parents. Parents are vital for the athlete's development process yet some are viewed by coaches, athletes and team staff as obstacles that children have to overcome to be successful. They may have really positive intentions but get sucked into unhealthy perspectives by falling foul of the rising pressure to win and putting expectations on their children. A study in the US found that 36% of tennis parents are seen by coaches as behaving in a way which actually hinders their child's development.[33] In the UK this has been recognised by the Lawn Tennis Association who now run parenting courses to help parents cope better with the pressures of having their child compete and to help them be better able to support their child.

When sports parenting does go wrong it can go really wrong. For junior athletes finding their sport mentioned constantly at home with competitors being discussed, lots of (often unasked for) feedback on performances given and a strong line that time and money has been spent on their sport means they feel under intensive pressure. Additionally, there may be a lack of time for social activities so there is little opportunity to escape these pressures. The athletes can start to get extra nervous when their parents watch and will then spend any stoppage time looking over to their parents for approval. Parents trying to coach their child from the sidelines may contradict what they are being told by their actual coach and some even go so far as to encourage children to be aggressive or fight with their competitors. It is not unheard of for parents to be asked to leave sporting venues for being too disruptive.

This type of intense environment has produced some very successful athletes; both golfer Tiger Woods and tennis player Andre Agassi have written about how they grew up like this, but they have also talked about how they didn't enjoy this intensity. Their fathers' goals became their goals and instead of being intrinsically motivated because they truly loved their sport, they had an extrinsic motivation to make their parents happy and 'pay back' their parents' investment. This is not the recipe for lifelong enjoyment of their sport. Sometimes it isn't even a recipe for instant gratification as Agassi wrote in his autobiography that when he won his first Grand Slam title, instead of a congratulations, his father responded with, 'You had no business losing that fourth set'.[34]

These overzealous parents push their children into seeing their sport as a chore and they either quit entirely or, worse, continue in it to keep their parents happy, causing themselves stress or burnout. Those who enjoyed and stayed confident in their sport felt their parents were involved, warm and supportive without being over-bearing.

What makes some parents behave so badly? Research suggests that parents feel tied to the success of their children; both in performance and behaviour.[35] Sport is very measurable, more so than many other parts of life, so it is very easy to feel they understand how their child is doing. Parents will also be spending time and money on their children's sport so want to feel their 'investment' is paying off. They feel that their child's success (or not) reflects upon them and start to over-identify with it. Their child's performance starts to become a measure of their own self-worth. Parents who used to compete themselves may be attempting to re-live their own past vicariously through their children. These parents are known in the US as having 'frustrated jock-syndrome'.[36] In many of these cases they fall in the 'reverse dependency trap',[37] struggling to separate out their own needs from those of their child's. They may well be the ones on the sidelines screaming 'advice' at coaches and abuse at referees.

A specific pressure comes when parents want to over-reach their children. The research on Talent Identification suggests that in most sports (excluding swimming and gymnastics where athletes become elite and retire while still very young) it is best for athletes not to specialise in their sport until around 13 or 14. Specialising too early is not only risky for a young child as it could cause long term repetitive injuries but also means they are less likely to succeed in sport at an elite level if that is their goal. Studies of the differences between elite and 'nearly elite' athletes found elites took up their sport later, didn't train so hard when younger and entered international competition two years later than near-elites.[38] Early specialisation also adds additional pressures onto young athletes and creates a sport-focused self-identity which may limit them as they get older. Speeding up their development is often due to the parent's ego of wanting to see their child get ahead of their peers and yet in doing so it means the child may miss out on trying sports they are actually better suited to and lose free time to a sport they are no longer motivated to do so they drop out of it before adulthood.

Peers

Support doesn't have to be within an athletes' current friends and family network. Identifying others with similar goals can provide a great safety net and lots of encouragement. Finding this 'tribe' is also one of the reasons many people take up a sport in the first place. Known as the 'affiliation motive' this is the opportunity sport gives us to hang out with our friends and to make new friends. Being in this peer group can help us feel accepted and psychologically safe when we compete. It can also enhance self-esteem, ensure we get help and guidance from others and provide emotional support.[39] It enhances wellbeing[40] and can have positive impact on behaviours including recovery from injury, coping with stress, burnout and performance.[41]

There are a number of types of support that peers can offer each other; listening (so someone feels like they have been heard without having to accept advice or judgement), emotional (feeling someone is on their side) and personal-assistance (where they are helping to make another's life easier). This positive impact may be because research has found that most of us enjoy training a lot more when we are with others and means we will have a friendly face to see at competitions. The enjoyment factor is really important as the more an athlete looks forward to a session, the more likely they are to turn up and to stick to their training.

For those competing in team sports, social support has been linked to increases in feelings of team cohesion and improved team climate. Occasionally though in a team there will be athletes who are 'loafing'. They have lost motivation and are putting in less effort than they could. In individual sports the only person who loses out in this situation is the athlete but in team sports it impacts their peers. Loafing has been identified in a number of sports[42] and can be down to a number of reasons including when an athlete feels no-one will recognise their contribution or their contribution feels too small to make a difference, whether they know their teammates and if they see their teammates as high in ability or feel dispensable compared to them.

To reduce loafing and encourage better peer relationships coaches can encourage the athletes towards joint goals, find ways of developing shared decision making or create opportunities for activities with various sized groups so there is space for everyone to shine and to support. Once someone in a team promotes social support, the enthusiasm and encouragement the athletes put in can be contagious and should encourage others to perform well.

For athletes in individual sports a really specific type of peer relationship is that of a training partner. It can sound counter intuitive for athletes who could be rivals to train together but if the right partnership is developed they can bring out the best in each other, spur each other on to better results and even increase an athlete's pain threshold.[43] The improvements can come from each trying to match the other on effort or outcome, wanting to impress their partner, copying better techniques from them or from simply being really inspired by them. Training partners relying on each other to turn up also increases their accountability.

Online support

Social support no longer comes just in person. Lots of athletes get their support online. Technology can be amazing for this. Some gadgets and trackers can generate a huge amount of data that athletes can use to analyse how they are performing. As well as the formal data, coaches and athletes are using technology to communicate quickly and effectively; sharing training plans or competition details over social media or setting up messaging groups of athletes to motivate each other or discuss training. Athletes in individual sports who often need to train alone can share data over technology, engage in debates on forums or check in with other athletes in messaging groups so they feel part of a community and benefit from enjoyable and supportive friendships.

The feedback athletes get from others on social media or the data they draw from technology can be helpful and motivating. Those who thrive from external validation of achievements, can find huge benefits from the feedback when it is positive, but having support online can also make athletes unhappy. Most sports technologies are built around gamification, a design feature which draws athletes back to the tool and increases their adherence to using it. This plugs into perfectly to the goal-driven nature of athletes. This gamification is very effective when the games or sessions are aligned with the athlete's own goals, but some find themselves drawn to deviate from their 'real life' goals and start to compete with others virtually through challenges which risk harming their performances in the real life competitions they actually care about. The data also brings with it a brutal honesty that can be harder to swallow. Coaches, peers and family members may sugar coat a poor performance highlighting any environmental, logistical or health issues which would have impacted the athlete. Data alone offers none of this context.

Bigger issues occur if they get injured as the constant reminders of other people doing their sport can prompt jealousy or despondency and leave them feeling very isolated. And if the athlete is prone to comparisons having so much data available can see them compare themselves to others or find it hard to switch off from notifications and reminders of other's training.

Summary

Athletes with strong support teams around them have reduced threat levels when they go into competition. To build strong support there needs to be positive and open communication and honest and trusting relationships between the athlete and those around them. When this communication and support is effective and focused on growth and development it enhances an athletes' physical, technical and strategic skills and provides safety and emotional support.

Key terms

- Closeness – the bond between coach and athlete characterised by mutual appreciation, trust and respect.
- Commitment – both the athlete and coach focusing on the same goals over a long period of time.

- Complementarity – working in a way which is complementary and cooperative.
- Ego goal orientation – a focus on social comparison and external rewards.
- Loafing – athletes reducing their effort levels when they don't feel their involvement will make a significant difference.
- Psychological safety – where an athlete feels able to take risks without fear of punishment.

Key messages to share with athletes around support systems

- The climate and environment around us has a big impact on our sporting experience. If we have strong support we will have reduced threat levels in competition.
- Support can come from coaches, family, friends, other athletes, physios, psychologists, nutritionists, masseurs, doctors and team administrators.
- Being a psychologically safe environment means athletes can stretch themselves and thrive.
- Great communication can make the support process much more positive.
- A good coach–athlete relationship has a big impact on performance; enhancing physical, technical and strategic skills and providing safety and emotional support.
- Family, a key support group for athletes, can be critical to an athlete's confidence levels. If they inadvertently focus on winning over process it can be harmful to performance and wellbeing.
- Peers can support each other to stick to their sport, make practices more enjoyable and can push achievement levels higher.
- Online support can be beneficial but needs to be considered carefully as there are risks if an athlete is very competitive, likes to compare themselves to others or gets injured.

Strategies to use support effectively for athletes

1 Modelling (Strategy 3) can help athletes see what is possible for athletes like them.
2 Getting into a pre-performance bubble (Strategy 40) helps athletes block out those who are unhelpful to their performance.
3 Becoming a self-expert (Strategy 52) helps the athlete remember what support they benefit from and enjoy.
4 All members of a support team can help an athlete through verbal persuasion (Strategy 57).
5 It is helpful for coaches to know an athlete's feedback preferences (Strategy 58).
6 All members of the support team, and the athlete, can benefit from learning how to have difficult conversations (Strategy 59).
7 An athlete can use payback points (Strategy 60) to give back to their supporters.
8 Completing a reality check (Strategy 61) will help an athlete stop themselves comparing themselves to others.
9 Support team identification (Strategy 62) is valuable to understand who an athlete could go to in a range of situations.
10 Having a technology strategy (Strategy 63) helps an athlete use online support effectively and safely.
11 Having a training partner (Strategy 64) can be beneficial.

Notes

1 Kahn, W. A. (1990). Psychological conditions of personal engagement and disengagement at work. *Academy of Management Journal, 33*(4), 692–724.
2 Jowett, S., & Cockerill, I. M. (2002). Incompatibility in the coach–athlete relationship. In I. M. Cockerill (Ed.), *Solutions in sport psychology* (pp.16–31). London: Thomson Learning.
3 Miller, P. S., & Kerr, G. A. (2002). Conceptualising excellence: Past, present, and future. *Journal of Applied Sport Psychology, 14,* 140–153.
4 Jowett, S. (2017). Coaching effectiveness: The coach-athlete relationship at its heart. *Current Opinion in Psychology, 16,* 154–158.

5 Jowett, S. (2003). When the 'honeymoon' is over: A case study of a coach-athlete dyad in crisis. *The Sport Psychologist, 17*(4), 444–460.

6 Davis, L., & Jowett, S. (2014). Coach–athlete attachment and the quality of the coach athlete relationship: Implications for athlete's well-being. *Journal of Sports Sciences, 32*(15), 1454–1464.

7 Jowett, S., & Ntoumanis, N. (2004). The coach–athlete relationship questionnaire (CART-Q): Development and initial validation. *Scandinavian Journal of Medicine & Science in Sports, 14*(4), 245–257.

8 Isoard-Gautheur, S., Trouilloud, D., Gustafsson, H., & Guillet-Descas, E. (2016). Associations between the perceived quality of the coach–athlete relationship and athlete burnout. *Psychology of Sport and Exercise, 22*, 210–217.

9 Hampson, R., & Jowett, S. (2014). Effects of coach leadership and coach–athlete relationship on collective efficacy. *Scandinavian Journal of Medicine & Science in Sports, 24*(2), 454–460.

10 Rhind, D. J., & Jowett, S. (2010). Initial evidence for the criterion-related and structural validity of the long versions of the coach–athlete relationship questionnaire. *European Journal of Sport Science, 10*(6), 359–370.

11 Jowett, S. (2003). When the 'honeymoon' is over: A case study of a coach-athlete dyad in crisis. *The Sport Psychologist, 17*(4), 444–460.

12 Brackenbridge, C. (2001). *Spoilsports: Understanding and preventing sexual exploitation in sport*. New York: Routledge.

13 Newsom, J. T., Rook, K. S., Nishishiba, M., Sorkin, D. H., & Mahan, T. L. (2005). Understanding the relative importance of positive and negative social exchanges: Examining specific domains and appraisals. *The Journals of Gerontology: Series B, 60*(6), 304–312.

14 Isoard-Gautheur, S., Trouilloud, D., Gustafsson, H., & Guillet-Descas, E. (2016). Associations between the perceived quality of the coach–athlete relationship and athlete burnout. *Psychology of Sport and Exercise, 22*, 210–217.

15 Bianco, T., & Eklund, R. C. (2001). Conceptual considerations for social support research in sport and exercise settings: The case of sport injury. *Journal of Sport & Exercise Psychology, 23*, 85–107.

16 Davis, L., Jowett, S., & Lafrenière, M.-A. (2013). An attachment theory perspective in the examination of relational processes associated with coach-athlete dyads. *Journal of Sport and Exercise Psychology, 35*(2), 156–167.

17 Nicholls, A. R., Levy, A. R., Jones, L., Meir, R., Radcliffe, J. N., & Perry, J. L. (2016). Committed relationships and enhanced threat levels: Perceptions of coach behaviour, the coach–athlete relationship, stress appraisals, and coping among athletes. *International Journal of Sports Science & Coaching, 11*(1), 16–26.

18 Davis, L., Appleby, R., Davis, P., Wetherell, M., & Gustafsson, H. (2018). The role of coach-athlete relationship quality in team sport athletes' psychophysiological exhaustion: implications for physical and cognitive performance. *Journal of Sports Sciences, 36*(17), 1985–1992.

19 Jowett, S., & Cockerill, I. M. (2003). Olympic medallists' perspective of the athlete–coach relationship. *Psychology of Sport and Exercise, 4*, 313–331.

20 Jowett, S., & Cockerill, I. M. (2002). Incompatibility in the coach–athlete relationship. In I. M. Cockerill (Ed.), *Solutions in sport psychology* (pp. 16–31). London: Thomson Learning.

21 Jowett, S., & Chaundy, V. (2004). An investigation into the impact of coach leadership and coach–athlete relationship on group cohesion. *Group Dynamics: Theory, Research and Practice, 8*, 302–311.

22 Olympiou, A., Jowett, S., & Duda, J. L. (2008). The psychological interface between the coach-created motivational climate and the coach-athlete relationship in team sports. *The Sport Psychologist, 22*(4), 423–438.

23 Olympiou, A., Jowett, S., & Duda, J. L. (2005, March). Psychological needs as mediators of social contexts and role ambiguity. Symposium on interpersonal relationships in sport and exercise. *Annual Conference of the British Psychological Society*, Manchester.

24 Greenleaf, C., Gould, D., & Dieffenbach, K. (2001). Factors influencing Olympic performance: Interviews with Atlanta and Nagano US Olympians. *Journal of Applied Sport Psychology, 13*, 154–184.

25 Gould, D., Collins, K., Lauer, L., & Chung, Y. (2007). Coaching life skills through football: A study of award winning high school coaches. *Journal of Applied Sport Psychology, 19*(1), 16–37.

26 Stafford, L., & Canary, D. J. (1991). Maintenance strategies and romantic relationship type, gender, and relational characteristics. *Journal of Social and Personal Relationships, 8*, 217–242.

27 Vargas-Tonsing, T. M., & Guan, J. (2007). Athletes' preferences for informational and emotional pre-game speech content. *International Journal of Sports Science & Coaching, 2*(2), 171–180.

28 Philippe, R. A., & Seiler, R. (2006). Closeness, co-orientation and complementarity in coach–athlete relationships: What male swimmers say about their male coaches. *Psychology of Sport and Exercise, 7*(2), 159–171.

29 Jowett, S. & Cockerill, I. M. (2003). Olympic medallists' perspective of the athlete–coach relationship. *Psychology of Sport and Exercise, 4*, 313–331.

30 Rees, T., & Freeman, P. (2009). Social support moderates the relationship between stressors and task performance through self-efficacy. *Journal of Social and Clinical Psychology, 28*(2), 244–263.

31 Fredricks, J. A., & Eccles, J. S. (2004). Parental influences on youth involvement in sports. In M. R. Weiss (Ed.), *Developmental sport and exercise psychology: A lifespan perspective* (pp. 145–164). Morgantown, WV, US: Fitness Information Technology.

32 Krane, V., Snow, J., & Greenleaf, C. A. (1997). Reaching for gold and the price of glory: A motivational case study of an elite gymnast. *The Sport Psychologist, 11*(1), 53–71.

33 Gould, D., Lauer, L., Rolo, C., Jannes, C., & Pennisi, N. (2006). Understanding the role parents play in tennis success: A national survey of junior tennis coaches. *British Journal of Sports Medicine, 40*(7), 632–636.

34 Agassi, A. (2010). *Open: An autobiography*. London: HarperCollins.

35 Coakley, J. (2006). The good father: Parental expectations and youth sports. *Leisure Studies, 25*(2), 153–163.

36 Smoll, F. L., & Smith, R. E. (2012). *Parenting young athletes: Developing champions in sports and life*. Lanham, MD: Rowman & Littlefield.

37 Smith, R. E., & Smoll, F. L. (2002). *Way to go, coach!: A scientifically-proven approach to youth sports coaching effectiveness*. California: Warde Publishers.

38 Moesch, K., Elbe, A. M., Hauge, M. L., & Wikman, J. M. (2011). Late specialization: The key to success in centimeters, grams, or seconds (cgs) sports. *Scandinavian Journal of Medicine Science Sports, 21*(6), 282–290.

39 Weiss, M. R., Smith, A. L., & Theeboom, M. (1996). 'That's what friends are for': Children's and teenagers' perceptions of peer relationships in the sport domain. *Journal of Sport and Exercise Psychology, 18*(4), 347–379.

40 Shumaker, S. A., & Brownell, A. (1984). Toward a theory of social support: Closing conceptual gaps. *Journal of Social Issues, 40*(4), 11–36.

41 Freeman, P., Rees, T., & Hardy, L. (2009). An intervention to increase social support and improve performance. *Journal of Applied Sport Psychology, 21*(2), 186–200.

42 Hanrahan, S., & Gallois, C. (1993). Social interactions. In R. N. Singer, H. Hausenblas & C. M. Janelle (Eds.), *Handbook of sport psychology* (pp. 623–646). New York: Macmillan.
43 Cohen, E. A., Ejsmond-Frey, R., Knight, N. & Dunbar, R. I. M. (2010). Rowers high: Behavioural synchrony is correlated with elevated pain thresholds. *Biology Letters, 6*, 106–108.

4

Improving concentration and focus

Where your focus goes, your energy flows

So many elements call for our attention when competing; other competitors, coaches, supporters, team mates, the venue, weather, music or announcements. Some of them are performance relevant, many are not. Concentration, our ability to apply deliberate mental effort on what is most important in each situation,[1] will help us focus on what is most relevant, shifting whenever necessary.[2] Our ability to concentrate comes from spotting relevant cues in the environment, being able to maintain focus for the full length of the competition, being aware of what is going on and being able to shift attention easily while showing mastery of our skills and techniques in competition.[3]

When trying to concentrate in a competition we are asking our brain to choose what is or isn't relevant for us to know about and then to focus on it while it blocks out unhelpful distractions. It isn't surprising that athletes struggle to maintain their concentration when humans naturally only focus for around five seconds at a time. When it comes to performing in sport we are asking a lot of our brains.

Despite the difficulties, mastering the ability to concentrate will pay huge dividends for athletes. Improved attentional control has been found to be a differentiating factor between the most successful athletes and those who don't do so well.[4] A study looking at the main mental and physical capacities that elite athletes feel are linked to high levels of performance identified eight key elements of which three were around concentration; being completely absorbed and in the moment, relaxed even when focusing and having a great amount of awareness of their bodies, and the environment around them.[5] Some call this optimal state of concentration 'flow'. Flow is a subject we will return to in Chapter 6. It happens only rarely but will be that occasion where the athlete feels everything has come together and they reach a high level of performance. A way to try to replicate this feeling of flow is to follow the principles of effective concentration; making a deliberate, intentional effort, only focusing on one thought at a time and focusing on actions which are specific and relevant.[6]

Dealing with distractions

Distractions when performing can make it impossible to focus effectively on the task at hand which can be critical in diminishing an athlete's performance. It means the athlete focuses on performance-irrelevant cues in their attentional field whether they are internal, external or outcome-based.

Internal distractions will include worries, negative or unhelpful thoughts, concerns or feeling fatigued. The running commentary in our heads can be very helpful at improving our concentration but, if it is mainly negative, studies have found the athletes perform poorly.[7] There are five of versions of this self-talk which can be unhelpful; worry (I'm going to lose), disengagement (I can't do this), fatigue (I'm too tired), irrelevant (I'm going to watch TV tonight) and ironic (I must not hit this ball in the water) which inevitably means you do exactly what you were trying to avoid.

External distractions are those which are in the environment around the athlete; usually visual (crowds, other competitors or scoreboards), auditory (supporters chanting, phones ringing or music being played over tannoy systems) or multi-sensory such as the weather. In some sports like archery, shooting or fencing these visual or auditory distractions can make a huge difference to the precision the athlete is able to achieve.

Outcome-based distractions involve thinking about past or future. Successful athletes will stay in the moment and focus on the specific tasks they need to complete – they are focusing on 'how' to perform well rather than the 'outcome' of performing well. The 'how' means they are less likely than others to get distracted by past events such as previous mistakes or losses[8] or future events such as imagining what will happen if they win their competition.

Any of these distractions can mean that an athlete's attentional focus will go to the wrong place and they have to spend time and energy trying to get back to where it should have been. Reducing distractions is the best strategy as every time an athlete's concentration is interrupted, and they have to switch focus, it comes at neurobiological cost, making them feel tired and mentally depleted. When an athlete gets into this state they start releasing cortisol, the stress hormone, which puts their body into a stress state, so they are unable to think clearly or make good decisions. If an athlete does get distracted though, it is important they know how to re-focus and practice doing so regularly.

Focusing strategies

Being able to concentrate is a skill just like any other element an athlete needs to learn. We constantly screen the information coming to us with the aim, when we are trying to concentrate for performance, of filtering out those elements which will distract. The screening process is tiring and slow though, so choosing how to concentrate in advance and putting the 'searchlight'[9] on the areas we need to can help an athlete focus only on what is important and do so with less mental effort.

Understanding there are dimensions of concentration based on width (narrow and focused on a specific thing through to broad and scanning the whole environment) and direction (internal thoughts in the athlete's head through to external cues from competitors)[10] can help athletes anticipate where their concentration needs to be. If their searchlight goes too wide they see more than is required to make a good decision. If their searchlight is in the wrong direction they get distracted. If their searchlight is too narrow they may miss important cues about the competition and what may be about to happen. Supporting an athlete into thinking about how they use this searchlight visually can help them incorporate it into their competition strategy. Talking about it in training, discussion where focus needs to be at each moment and planning with them in advance can highlight the tangible processes or actions athletes will need to follow so they can be clear on the elements they need to block out and the ones to focus on.

Some researchers have looked at eye movement patterns to understand where an athlete is putting their focus. They have found that expert athletes are far better at using something called 'quiet eye' where they are able to hold their focus for longer on the correct elements of the performance process.[11] Further, a study of sprint runners found those trained to use race plans with task-relevant cues to focus on ran faster than control groups.[12] So helping an athlete to keep attention on what is valuable at each moment will help them to improve performance.

Concentrating requires mental effort and energy and when we get tired there is far less available. As we will see in Chapter 7, our brain struggles to push our body once we have become mentally fatigued. It is not just the length of a competition that will impact on the risk of mental fatigue but what the athlete has been doing in the build-up. The fatigue will reduce the amount of available processing resources the athlete can access which means the athlete fails in whatever task they were attempting.[13] In long competitions, to minimise mental fatigue it is helpful for athletes to learn to switch their focus on when it's needed and off when it isn't. For example, a golf tournament round may last for four hours but the athlete actually needs to concentrate for less than ten minutes of that. Aiming to hold concentration for that entire time would be incredibly draining, and detrimental in the ten minutes or so where acute attention was actually required.

Focusing under pressure

When an athlete is calm, performing well and enjoying the competition they can switch pretty easily between attentional styles and use the most appropriate one for the state of play. But when they become stressed or anxious due to feeling like there is some type of threat their attention will change. As we learnt in Chapter 1, when under threat their body physiologically reacts with increased heart rate, sped-up breathing, release of adrenaline and cortisol and tighter muscles. This process also causes their attentional focus to change to one which is internal and narrow. An internal and narrow attentional focus means the athlete gives attention to the movement required instead of letting it happen automatically. This occurs because when we begin to learn a new skill we work on it very systematically until we feel comfortable with the feel of the movement and where our limbs need to be and when.

Skills actually work best when we don't think about them[14] so as an athlete gets more experienced and expert in using that skill they start to move it from conscious to automatic control. This gives them more bandwidth within their brain to read cues within the competition environment to change their type of attentional focus every few seconds.[15] When the athlete's focus moves to a narrow and internal one under threat they counter-productively start to focus on that previously automatic skill and this often causes mistakes to happen. They start to consciously process their moves,[16] an action often labelled 'choking'; where the athlete focuses so much on the mechanics of a movement they behave as if they are a novice.

Using the types of attentional focus

An athlete needs to use different types of attention based on the sport they do, the variant of it and their specific role (if in a team). Some of the differences will be in the length of time the sport takes place over, some in the amount of stop-start they have, others on whether they are alone when competing, against someone else or within a whole team.[17] The type and processes of concentration needed over the 100 metres on the track against seven other sprinters will be very different to an 80 minute rugby match with 29 other players and a referee on the pitch and different again to a three day golf tournament where you have just one other for company. The type of concentration required will also change regularly, particularly in team sports. The amount of time required to focus will be different too. Some sports like swimming are pretty continuous, sports like cricket have short breaks and some like heptathlon have lots of breaks. In these sports with breaks it can be difficult for an athlete to keep having to regain their concentration. But this can be a good strategy as trying to remain focused for the entire competition period will be too mentally draining.

Despite all the differences between sports and situational elements once the athlete understands the dimensions of attention and what they can be used for they can be much more reactive.

- Broad-external: This means the athlete focuses on the elements of the environment away from themselves; the wind direction, distance to go, ground beneath their feet, other competitors or supporters. It helps an athlete rapidly assess their situation.
- Broad-internal: This is when an athlete is thinking about previous times they have done this type of move, in these types of conditions and picking equipment to use. It is good for analysing and planning moves.
- Narrow-internal focus: Here an athlete monitors how they feel, breathes deeply, completes a pre-shot/move routine (if relevant) and imagines how they want the next moment to go. It is helpful to mentally rehearse next steps or to control emotional states.
- Narrow-external: Having a focus on exactly the thing they need to do, hit or kick a ball, move their body or equipment. It helps the athlete focus directly on an external cue (a ball, piece of equipment).

When our attention goes into the wrong axis for the part of the competition we are in we notice things which are unhelpful to our performance. On the start line of a 100 metre race we want a narrow-internal focus, readying ourselves for the next 10–20 seconds. We do not want a broad-external focus checking out how fit and healthy the other athletes on the start line look or the size of the crowds watching. On the other hand if an athlete is running down the rugby pitch with the ball trying to plot their next move to pass clearly to their team mate they want a broad-external focus to help them analyse every option for passing, not a narrow-internal one thinking about how hard they are running and whether they can maintain that pace.

As an athlete gets more skilled in their sport they begin to know intuitively what to pay attention to and how to move that attention flexibly depending on the state of play. Attentional skills can be learnt by novices[18] but some of the innate knowledge around search patterns, movement expectations, advance cues or predicting patterns comes from years and years competing and an athlete needs to feel 'expert' before they switch to unconscious processing and automatic control.

A key element of this process of being able to control their attention better is their level of situational awareness; their ability to scope out the competition they are against, the competition environment it is within and weighing up what they need to do and when, all while under time pressure often while being watched by other people. This is a skill which starts off being slow and clunky but as the athlete becomes more experienced in their sport this skill and the focus required become more automated allowing them to focus only on performance-relevant cues in their attentional field. As the athlete becomes even more of an expert they are able to develop a more complete attentional skill of being able to judge what is about to happen in a competition, before it has happened, so they can react quicker and perform better.

Dominant attentional styles

Most athletes have a dominant attentional style which they prefer. This will be the one where they are most comfortable and which they will fall back into automatically. Those with an internal focus style like to remain consistently focused on their sport – with a narrow vision so they don't get distracted. The athletes with an external focus style prefer to focus on their sport for specific periods of time and relax outside of those moments so they reduce their opportunities for negative or unhelpful thinking to take hold which will increase their nerves.

Helping an athlete understand their focus style, and to be able to explain to you where they prefer to be, will mean you can help them work out how to use it effectively in a competition. Reminding an externally-focused athlete to focus between points will simply push them towards anxiety. Trying to chat to an internally-focused athlete in a break will be just as negative.

Internally-focused athletes should avoid talking to others and think about just the performance they are trying to give at that moment. They should also aim to look carefully at what is going on in their area of play, rather than at crowds or other competitors. The goal is to reduce distraction opportunities. Externally-focused athletes need to focus carefully when they are actually performing but chat to other (externally-focused) people, letting their mind drift or looking around to see what else is going on when not specifically performing.

Summary

Concentration is our ability to apply deliberate mental effort and can make a huge difference in sport. We can think about it as a searchlight which moves along a width and direction axis to pick up on the thing which will help us perform best at that specific moment. As we get more skilled in our sport we will automatically know what to pay attention to and how to move that attention flexibly. We can speed up the process by learning concentration skills and practising but it is easier if we have the right conditions; feeling relaxed, undistracted and non-fatigued. With a much greater awareness of how attention and concentration works, and how it works for them, an athlete can improve their performance under pressure.

Key terms

- Attentional awareness – where we choose to focus.
- Attentional capacity – as an athlete becomes more proficient in their sports they are able to do many of their skills automatically so they are able to pay more attention to other cues.

- Attentional field – everything inside (thoughts, emotions, behaviours) and outside (sights, competitors, noise) that could be focused on.
- Choking – when an athlete feels under pressure and focuses attention in the wrong area.
- Concentration – focusing mental effort to give selective attention to a task.
- Focus – an athlete's ability to attend to the cues in their attentional field.
- Focus style – the athlete's preference for which type of cues they pay attention to.
- Performance-relevant cues – an athlete's technique, their tactics, the opponents, score, time left, people on the field of play.

Key messages for athletes to improve their concentration and focus

- Concentration is an athlete's ability to apply deliberate mental effort to what is most important in any given situation so they can focus on relevant cues to perform as required.
- Having high levels of concentration is a differentiating factor between the most successful and less successful athletes.
- Being able to concentrate effectively is a skill you can learn. Thinking about it as if it is a searchlight can be helpful.
- Athletes are vulnerable to three types of distraction; internal, external or outcome-based.
- Concentrating is harder when fatigued or feeling under threat (from feeling pressure, emotional or because the competition is important).
- There are four types of attention and they sit along width and direction axis. When our attention goes into the wrong axis for part of the competition it harms our performance.
- As we get more skilled in our sport we will automatically know what to pay attention to and how

to move that attention flexibly depending on the state of play. When we feel under threat though we may stop using these skills automatically and focus on the mechanics of the skill, thus behaving and performing like a novice.

Strategies to improve concentration and focus

1 Using control mapping (Strategy 1) to help an athlete understand where concentration should and shouldn't be in competition helps give guidance.
2 Post-competition analysis (Strategy 5) is a good opportunity for an athlete to understand how well they concentrated in their competition.
3 Attentional shift training (Strategy 13) is vital to get an athlete concentrating flexibly.
4 Using biofeedback (Strategy 15) will help an athlete concentrate on the task-relevant element they need.
5 Similarly, running an adversity session (Strategy 21) will help the athlete get used to coping and concentrating under pressure.
6 Having a clear competition strategy within a confidence booster (Strategy 22).
7 Using imagery (Strategy 25) helps practise maintaining focus in difficult situations.
8 Mental tapering (Strategy 26) is helpful to ensure an athlete has the brain bandwidth to flexibly change attention patterns.
9 Overlearning skills (Strategy 27) helps free an athlete's attention so they can perform more strategically.
10 Using simulation training (Strategy 28) will help an athlete practise coping with distractions and giving attention to the right things.
11 'What if' planning (Strategy 29) helps an athlete to prepare well to stop their fears occurring removing some of the threat and pressure.
12 Associative attentional strategies (Strategy 34) such as body checking will help an athlete focus on what is key in that moment.

13 Having a pre-performance routine (Strategy 37) means the athlete can do many of their warm up activities automatically without having to use energy and attention on them.

14 Having a respond, relax, refocusing plan (Strategy 41) for any time that concentration or focus is lost mid-competition.

15 Using a number of types of self-talk (Strategies 42–46) can be beneficial to focus and pay better attention to performance-enhancing elements rather than being detrimental.

16 Using metacognition (Strategy 50) to continually analyse where attention is focused helps to build awareness.

Notes

1 Moran, A. P. (2013). *Sport and exercise psychology: A critical introduction*. Abingdon: Routledge.

2 Perry, C. (2005). Concentration: focus under pressure. *Journal of Sport Psychology, 12*(5), 173–186.

3 Weinberg, R., & Gould, D. (2007). *Foundations of sport and exercise psychology* (4th Ed.). Champaign, IL: Human Kinetics.

4 Gould, D., Eklund, R. C., & Jackson, S. A. (1992). 1988 US Olympic wrestling excellence: II. Thoughts and affect occurring during competition. *The Sport Psychologist, 6*(4), 383–402.

5 Jackson, S. A., & Csikszentmihalyi, M. (1999). *Flow in sports*. Champaign: Human Kinetics.

6 Abernethy, B. (2001). Attention in sport. *The Sport Psychologist*, 12(5), 121–129.

7 Van Raalte, J. L., Brewer, B. W., Rivera, P. M., & Petitpas, A. J. (1994). The relationship between observable self-talk and competitive junior tennis players' match performances. *Journal of Sport and Exercise Psychology, 16*(4), 400–415.

8 Landers, D. M., Boutcher, S. H., & Wang, M. Q. (1986). A psychobiological study of archery performance. *Research Quarterly for Exercise and Sport, 57*(3), 236–244.

9 Perry, C. (2005). Concentration: Focus under pressure. *Journal of Sport Psychology, 12*(5), 173–186.

10 Nideffer, R. (1985). *Players' guide to mental training*. Champaign, IL: Human Kinetics.

11 Wilson, M. R., Wood, G., & Vine, S. J. (2009). Anxiety, attentional control, and performance impairment in penalty kicks. *Journal of Sport and Exercise Psychology, 31*(6), 761–775.

12 Mallett, C. J., & Hanrahan, S. J. (1997). Race modelling: An effective cognitive strategy for the 100m sprinter. *The Sport Psychologist, 11*, 72–85.

13 Wegner, D. M. (2002). Thought suppression and mental control. *The Sport Psychologist, 14*(3), 159–166.

14 Nieuwenhuys, A., Pijpers, J. R., Oudejans, R. R., & Bakker, F. C. (2008). The influence of anxiety on visual attention in climbing. *Journal of Sport and Exercise Psychology, 30*(2), 171–185.

15 Hemery, D. (1986). *The pursuit of sporting excellence: A study of sport's highest achievers*. London: Willow Books.

16 Gucciardi, D. F., & Dimmock, J. A. (2008). Choking under pressure in sensorimotor skills: Conscious processing or depleted attentional resources? *Psychology of Sport and Exercise, 9*(1), 45–59.

17 Burke, K. L. (1992). Understanding and enhancing concentration. *Sport Psychology Training Bulletin, 4*, 1–8.

18 Tenenbaum, G., Sar-El, T., & Bar-Eli, M. (2000). Anticipation of ball location in low and high-skill performers: a developmental perspective. *Psychology of Sport and Exercise, 1*(2), 117–128.

5

Developing emotional control

A head full of fears has no space for dreams

Competitive sport can elicit a huge number of emotions.[1] These quickly changing, energising forces drive our behaviours; sometimes helpfully, often less so. Ranging from mild to intense, how these emotions are elicited and how they impact an athlete can often depend upon their levels of emotional intelligence; the trait which helps them monitor and accurately reason with their emotions guiding how they think and act.[2]

Emotional intelligence has been found to positively impact sport performance[3] and this was shown in a study of 237 runners at the Verona Half Marathon where not only were those with higher emotional intelligence found to have better times[4] but their emotional intelligence was actually a better predictor of their race time than previous race experience or the number of miles they usually ran. It is assumed this is because these people with higher emotional intelligence are better able to manage the negative mid-race emotions that most runners will have once they start to tire.

Perhaps the emotional intelligence stops athletes interpreting so many situations as threats. Now we know how our Chimp can behave when we feel under threat, those with low levels of emotional intelligence may interpret the situation of not performing well as a threat to our ego or to our sense of self as an athlete and instead of a rational or logical reaction; 'I must try a new tactic' or 'I should focus on the action not the outcome', we have an immediate, irrational reaction; 'I am a loser' or 'I am not a real athlete'. This takes us away from the moment and pushes us into thinking about much bigger issues, ones which distract us from the needs of the sport. It can cause us to choke, miss balls or slow down. It certainly harms our performance.

As we learnt in Chapter 1, perceptions of pressure can be helpful, to amp up an athlete's body so they have the right activation levels to perform. But it can also become too much, prompting anxiety and making us emotionally fragile. An athlete with overly high activation levels may seem hyperactive, very nervous, quick to anger, shows frustration and makes poor decisions under pressure. They will often perform better in training than in competition.

Each athlete needs a different level of stress to hit their own optimal level of activation so becoming self-aware of where theirs is is a great first step. Then athletes need to become conscious of which part of their brain is in charge of their decisions at each moment. Having this understanding will help them become more aware of their emotions so they can understand and regulate how they feel during training and competition. If athletes can improve how they manage their emotions they will enjoy their sport more, can put it into a bigger context with more perspective and will improve their performances. Win-win.

A good question for athletes to ask themselves when they feel their emotions are out of control in a competition is: do I want to feel like this? If not, then it is likely their Chimp is in control. What they need to do next is to find ways to calm their Chimp and get back to concentrating on their sport. Within this chapter we will look first at what feeds an athlete's Chimp to make them anxious and then what we can do to calm it so their Human side can get back in charge and focused on competition. As the intensity of our emotions varies based on both the situation we are performing in and our own individual traits and preferences[5] we first need to identify the situations and personality traits in an athlete which feed their Chimp and its anxieties.

Causes of emotional control loss

There are numerous prompts, causes and reasons for athletes to lose emotional control but some come up time and time again. Some are external and outside their immediate control (although they can learn to block them out or respond differently to them), others are harder as they are internal expectations; often traits, deeply ingrained which require a vast amount of practice to develop coping mechanisms or reframing in order to handle the issues better.

External expectations

As an athlete, other people believing in you can give you self-confidence, banish anxiety and show that the hard work and dedication you have put in is acknowledged and recognised. This can help athletes soar. But when belief is shown in the wrong way or the athlete perceives it as a pressure it can also act as a burden, creating an expectation. And expectations take away the fun, create stress and give performance responsibilities. Excessively high expectations rarely result in great performances as they cause anxiety, fear of failure, overthinking, negative thinking and prompting athletes to either look too far forward (to the outcome of the competition) or too far back (ruminating on previous mistakes). They switch an athlete's aim from 'trying to win' to 'trying not to lose'.

Physically, the pressure can cause muscle tension, restricted breathing, poor coordination and the cortisol and adrenaline flooding an athlete's body from the amygdala seeing the situation as a threat can create a horrid sense of discomfort or nausea.

Expectations really set off our Chimp. Sometimes the expectations are our own (and we will look at these later on), but sometimes the problem is other people's expectations. Usually a coach, manager, parents, partner or team mates. At the highest levels of sport we also have fans and the media's expectations and some teams will have support staff who need the athletes to do well in order to keep their jobs. The athletes won't just perceive these pressures but be asked about them in press conferences, read about them in the papers or on social media and have it unhelpfully reiterated in team meetings. It isn't just distracting but makes the athlete feel under threat days before they have even arrived at a competition.

Often the expectations are entirely accidental. A reassuring phrase which sounds supportive like: 'I just know you will win' is very well intended but not only puts the focus on something the athlete cannot control (the outcome), it also gives the athlete no wiggle room; if they do win it was expected, if they don't win then they have failed twice over.

For this reason it is sometimes helpful for athletes to avoid people who will accidentally place expectations on them before a big competition. Some athletes call this going into the bubble and they will build in a technology strategy to switch off social media and avoid people who make them feel under pressure. If the athlete can't avoid those people (usually if they are close friends or family) explaining that they realise the sentiments are well intentioned, but they actually reduce the chance of them doing well, may help educate them out of it.

Other people's reputations can also cause expectations. A regular reflection after a competition is 'I should have won – she is ranked lower than me'. In these situations the athlete will never feel great because if they beat someone ranked lower they were expected to and if they lose they will feel doubly bad.

Specifically for children, as discussed in Chapter 3, they can feel a very specific pressure from their parents. The NCAA (the organisation surrounding sport in US colleges) found that only 1.6% of NCAA football players go onto compete professionally[6] yet 35% of the players report that their family expect them to play professionally.[7] So many are feeling an expectation that very few have any chance of achieving.

The first step is to help an athlete understand if an expectation is real. In challenging their perception the athlete may realise the expectation they are attributing to others is actually the expectation they are putting on themselves. And that is easier to work on. Some of the questions to ask an athlete about expectations of others are 'have they actually told you that?' 'Did they say that?'

It the athlete is using lots of 'I should', 'I must', 'I have to', this is another opportunity to question. Why must they? Who says? If they 'must practise' to improve because they want to progress this is great. If they 'must practise' because their parents have spent so much on lessons they feel they owe them or want to see them get value for money, then there is no ownership and simply expectation. Picking up on it every time they say 'I must' will help them become more self-aware and start to question these expectations for themselves. Pushing them to replace each 'I must or I should' with an active, positive process goal will make a difference, something they can control if they put in effort or the right behaviours. So instead of 'I must win' we ask them to break it down into what will it take to win? What it will take to win then becomes their goal. It helps them focus on the present and only on things they can do something about.

Where there are genuine external pressures to perform well though it can be thought of as socially prescribed perfectionism (the pressure from those around you to be perfect) which is worrying because athletes may find they are no longer working hard and investing in their sport for themselves but feel it is for others. They feel a huge lack of autonomy and any fun and enjoyment they used to feel in competing slips away. Not surprisingly, socially prescribed perfectionism has also been strongly linked with burnout.[8]

Internal expectations

Internal unhelpful expectations can come when athletes are so driven to achieve goals they create pressures to justify the efforts they have put in. 'If I don't do well I have wasted all my time' is one we regularly hear. Goals should not become expectations that weigh an athlete down. We should have a goal, work towards it and regularly evaluate it but turning them into 'I must' or 'I have to' suddenly makes it an additional stressor the athletes really don't need. In these cases our aim should be to help an athlete gain some perspective, this can often be to look how far they have come already or to help them see that they don't 'have to' do anything – they 'get to' do something. This takes it away from the idea they are sacrificing their time for their training and instead that they are investing their time and effort in something that excites them. It is a small semantic change but one which helps them feel more in control of their situation. Then, even if this one competition does not go to plan, everything they have invested is still inside them, banked, ready for the next time.

Perfectionism

Athletes are well aware of the need to focus hard, to prepare well and to practise regularly if they are to progress. But when they take these internal expectations to the extreme, putting in all the effort, making great results and yet are still not satisfied then they may well have traits of perfectionism. Thought of as an uncompromising pursuit of excellence,[9] perfectionism traits are found in a lot of high-performance athletes[10] which makes sense as they are often highly motivated, work hard and strive to be the best.[11] In fact, some regard perfectionism as an almost required psychological characteristic of Olympic champions[12] while others see it as a maladaptive characteristic which harms and hinders performance success.[13] In reality it is not as simple as either of these summaries imply as it is both multidimensional and multifaceted[14] with different elements; some of which can benefit athletes and others which harm them.

High internal expectations can be really beneficial in training or practice as they push athletes to focus on tiny elements of their skills and work on getting them exactly right. It is unhelpful in competition though where they need to react to the environment around them, play freely and focus on everything coming towards them, without needing to control it. Therefore, in training, perfectionism can be helpful but in competition it can feel like an unwanted imposition.

Perfectionism can create self-defeating outcomes and unhealthy patterns of behaviour in athletes[15] so they may also look at results in a very black and white manner: win or lose, rather than being able to take into account the bigger picture of progress made, new skills used, higher rankings secured or any mitigating circumstances. To be an exceptional athlete it will sometimes be necessary to take risks. Perfectionists struggle with this as their anxiety about making mistakes (and their belief that a mistake equals a personal flaw) prevents risk taking. If the athlete in competition is focused too much on their technique, is overanalysing their performance or holding back so they don't make mistakes, their ability to play with flow and full passion will be curtailed. One mistake will have a big impact on their competition motivation and they will struggle to see the big picture.

This not only causes upset but can become destructive (as they self-sabotage to give excuses for not achieving perfection) and can lead to anxiety[16] and anger.[17] It can also create additional mental fatigue, so the athlete is too tired to focus and do what is required. With this can often come burnout[18] where they find themselves emotionally and physically exhausted with a reduced sense of accomplishment.[19]

Stripping down perfectionism shows two different variants; perfectionistic concerns and personal standards.[20] Most perfectionists have both elements but some have just one or the other. There are scales and measures that can be used with athletes to identify which types they have. When an athlete[21] has personal standards perfectionism (sometimes known as perfectionistic strivings) it can be positive as it helps them to be conscientious, follow processes and tend to use mastery goals which have found to contribute well towards sport performance.[22]

The perfectionistic concerns element is more negative[23] as it focuses on mistakes, negative evaluation and discrepancy between expectations and performance. This leads to high levels of concern over mistakes, self-criticism, doubts about actions and worries about others judging performance.[24] It means athletes focus on avoiding making mistakes, something which is actually harmful to their performance.[25]

Unhelpful self-talk

Alongside external expectations and some athletes having perfectionistic tendencies, there are also internal traits or beliefs that can prompt anxieties and stress in competition causing emotions to run high. Managing each is part of the skill of being a successful athlete. One of these is having a head full of unhelpful self-talk.

Every thought an athlete has is them effectively talking to themselves, hearing thousands and thousands of thoughts each day. For some their head chatter is negatively charged and they talk down to themselves. This has a very unhelpful impact when it comes to competition as it is hard to stay confident or to concentrate when they continually hear a critical and self-demeaning voice.

When they have habitual unhelpful self-talk, with phrases like 'I am no good at it', 'I'll never be able to do it' and 'there's no point trying' the athlete increases their physical and cognitive anxiety,[26] negatively impacting their performance through a raised heart rate, inconsistent breathing, self-doubt and distraction. These thoughts don't just prevent the athlete from performing well but maintain a negative cycle of low self-esteem where they focus on weaknesses instead of strengths so come to expect failure, which becomes a self-fulfilling prophecy. To turn around this negative self-talk lots of work on reframing thoughts needs to take place to install more positive, but still authentic, phrases.

Low self-esteem

Another contributor to lack of emotional control comes from low self-esteem. Our self-esteem is our attitude towards ourselves and our self-perception. Self-esteem is different from confidence in that while confidence is about the athlete's belief in their ability to perform a specific task, self-esteem is more about the athlete, as a whole, all the time, so developing high self-esteem benefits us in many ways, just as low self-esteem will harm us in many ways. Like confidence though, self-esteem also impacts how we respond to stressors and low self-esteem can make an athlete feel under threat and unable to meet the demands of competition.

Fear of failure

Fear of failure is an encompassing term to cover many fears: of losing competitions, of negative social evaluation from others, of embarrassment, of letting others down, of putting in the effort but not getting the benefits, of not living up to other's expectations, of being rejected or of simply making mistakes. It can be a driving force for athletes to make them work really hard but there is also a down side. It may mean they avoid risky situations, stay safely in their comfort zone and perform cautiously. It is unhelpful because to be exceptional in sport it is necessary to fail and make mistakes that can be learnt from.

Fear of failure will often reflect whether an athlete has an extrinsic motivation for their sport and they are competing not because they love the sensation or feeling of their sport but to secure the recognition, outcomes or status boosts that come from performing well. Those who are more intrinsically motivated don't fear failure in the same way as, despite the pressures, competing is an opportunity to do something they love.

A way to think about fear of failure is to consider the theory of approach and avoidance motivation. The theory is based on our response to mental pleasure or pain. Some athletes will be driven towards the possibility of a pleasurable reward and others will be driven away from pain. The systems involved have been labelled the behavioural activation system (BAS) and the behavioural inhibition system (BIS).[27] Our BAS will engage when a pleasurable reward may be on the horizon and our BIS responds to indications that we may be due some pain; losing, criticism or status loss. If we are high on BAS we will be able to see the threats of pain more rationally (as our amygdala has not translated our fear as a threat) but if our BIS is high our amygdala is set off and we respond with fight, flight or freeze; all unhelpful outcomes.

Whether an athlete is being driven by BAS or BIS can change during the course of a competition. We may be doing well in a match and then realise that it has become ours to lose. The pain of losing then becomes stronger than the excitement of winning. Clearly then it is most helpful to have higher BAS levels, but with BIS levels not to be so low that they feel there is no challenge and become bored or complacent.

A way to help an athlete change their perception about their fear of failure can be through using optimism. It can be promoted through self-talk, imagery or by coaches consciously removing pressure for wins and promoting learning from activities showing the benefits of failure to create opportunities to learn and to grow.

Chimp soothing

These external and internal elements highlighted here can set off our feeling of threat and see us lose emotional control. A number of routes can be considered to help an athlete feel like they can take back some of that control.

Routines

One way some athletes try to control their emotions is through superstitions. Serena Williams is reported to tie her shoelaces a specific way, bounce the ball five times before her first serve and twice before her second and wear the same pair of socks during a winning streak. The footballer Ronaldo was said to always step onto the pitch with his right foot first. Michael Jordan always wore a pair of North Carolina practice shorts underneath his Chicago Bulls ones. Multi Olympic gold medal winning cyclist Laura Kenny once won a junior race wearing a wet sock and has ever since stepped on a wet towel before races.

While these superstitions are completely illogical (they usually arise after one great competition where we have attributed the result to something specific) they work because they help the athlete feel like things are under their control. When they do the superstitious behaviour they release adrenalin which triggers the feeling of readiness. And as they are task-specific they can help distract the athlete from anxiety or nerves, especially about the outcome of the performance so superstitions can work.

They help the athlete get into the right mindset to compete. Unfortunately, if the superstition involves a charm, or a specific piece of kit and that goes missing then all control feels lost and the athlete will become even more emotionally fraught. So, to gain the same level of control but in a more effective and safer manner, athletes should develop a pre-performance routine which will help them feel physically and mentally ready to perform.

Improving emotional intelligence

Using our knowledge that those with higher levels of emotional intelligence are better able to control their competition emotions it makes sense to develop strategies for athletes to build their emotional intelligence. Strong relationships have been found between emotional intelligence and psychological skills[28] and specific skills suggested include goal setting,[29] imagery and self-talk.[30] Other mental skills can be really helpful in an athlete proactively changing their physiology so activities like relaxation through deep breathing and muscle relaxation, can remove some of the physical symptoms the athlete experiences.

A focus on processes over outcomes

A key concern for athletes struggling with expectations is that they focus on results and not on the here and now. To cope better with expectations establishing mini process goals for individuals to focus on in competition can help them forget about the potential outcomes of competitions and more on actions they need to take mid-competition. The goals need to be specific and achievable within the time available. And it needs to have been designed by the athlete so they have full ownership, not imposed on the athlete by a coach or parent.

Self-awareness of BAS/BIS drive

Understanding their base drive, towards BAS or away from BIS, can help athletes who are struggling with anxiety to realise that they can focus on minimising their BIS level and increasing their BAS level. To do this they need to consciously focus on what they want to achieve and why that would be pleasurable. Part of this process can be to help athletes to set goals that see them master specific tasks or processes in sport[31] and to set these goals themselves so they feel they have full autonomy.[32]

Summary

Emotions can run very high in sport. While we each have personal responses based on the context, our personality traits and preferences and the internal and external expectations upon us, learning to control them by building our emotional intelligence and developing effective responses to the elements of our sport which trigger emotional responses can be an important lesson for athletes. When athletes build a better understanding of themselves and can identify the risk factors; such as whether they engage in habitual negative self-talk, show signs of perfectionism, have low self-esteem or suffer from fear of failure, then they can employ tactics to feel far more in control and less likely to become emotional.

Key terms

- Activation – how an athlete's body and brain responds to competition.
- Approach and avoidance motivation – a theory suggesting that we may have a preference to move towards a goal or a preference away from a threat and that this directs how we are motivated.
- Emotional intelligence – a trait which helps us monitor and reason with our emotions so we can think and act logically.
- Expectations – strong beliefs that something will happen.
- Negative self-talk – the head chatter of an athlete continually talking down to themselves.

- Perfectionism – an obsessive pursuit of exceptionally high standards.
- Perfectionistic concerns – focusing on mistakes, negative evaluation and discrepancy between expectations and performance.
- Perfectionistic strivings – high standards of performance.
- Self-esteem – an athlete's emotional evaluation of their own worth.
- Self-orientated perfectionism – striving and demanding absolute perfection from self.
- Self-sabotage – behaviours or actions athletes take which prevent them from reaching their stated goals.
- Socially prescribed perfectionism – pressure from those around an athlete for them to be perfect.
- Superstition – an irrational belief in what may bring us good or bad luck.

Key messages to share with athletes on emotional control

- Competitive sport can elicit a huge number of emotions and how we respond depends on our levels of emotional intelligence. Emotional intelligence can positively impact sport performance.
- The intensity of our emotions varies based on the situation we are performing in and our own individual traits and preferences.
- The situations where athletes most regularly struggle with emotional control are those when there is an external expectation upon the athlete which creates pressure and makes them feel under threat. Spending time questioning where our expectations comes from can highlight if there is a genuine expectation.
- The traits which make us less emotionally controlled in competition include a focus on habitual

negative self-talk, perfectionism, low self-esteem and fear of failure.

- The theory of approach and avoidance motivation identifies two systems within us; the behavioural activation system (BAS, it is alerted when a pleasurable reward may be on the horizon) and the behavioural inhibition system (BIS, when we feel pain is coming our way). When our BIS system is activated we feel under threat. To help reduce the feeling of threat ahead of and during competition we can use tactics to feel more in control.

Strategies to help athlete control their emotions for positive performance

1 Understanding what they can and can't control through control mapping (Strategy 1) helps put issues and frustrations into more perspective.

2 Goal setting (Strategy 2) led and completed by the athlete can help athletes focus on the right things mid-competition.

3 Learning from every competition through post-competition analysis (Strategy 5) and setback analysis (Strategy 7) will help athletes to gradually realise not every competition needs to be a win.

4 A strengths audit (Strategy 9) will help keep positive thoughts and skills front of mind when in a challenging emotional situation.

5 Adversity sessions (Strategy 12) can give athletes opportunities to develop mental skills and emotional control.

6 A brain drain (Strategy 16) helps to get worries and fears out of the athlete's head before competition.

7 Relaxation techniques such as progressive relaxation techniques (Strategy 19) for before a competition and colourful breathing (Strategy 18) for mid-competition can slow down activation.

8 If done positively with the athlete's ideal outcome in mind, imagery (Strategy 25) can re-wire the brain to give us evidence we have already achieved our goal previously.

9 Developing a 'what if' plan (Strategy 29) for all the elements they are worried will increase emotional control.

10 Developing a pre-performance routine (page Strategy 37) helps athletes feel more in control and physically and mentally ready to perform.

11 A mid competition routine (Strategy 38) can be valuable as a 'safety value' to help an athlete reset if their emotions get out of control.

12 Going into the bubble (Strategy 40) can help an athlete escape some of the pressures and expectations they feel have been placed upon them.

13 Reframing negative self-talk (Strategy 46) can help an athlete feel more in control and remove some of the emotional anxiety so they are better mentally ready to perform.

14 Using sensory management (Strategy 47) helps athletes reduce anxiety.

15 Mindfulness (Strategy 51) has been found to help increase an athlete's emotional intelligence.

16 Increased self-expert awareness (Strategy 52) of our motivations and drives will help us understand if we are driven towards a goal or away from failure.

17 Spending some time running a stressor identification (Strategy 54) gets athletes more aware of what is likely to trigger poor emotional control.

18 Creating a technology strategy (Strategy 63) to help reduce the feeling of expectations.

Notes

1 Botterill, C., & Brown, M. (2002). Emotion and perspective in sport. *International Journal of Sport Psychology, 33,* 38–60.

2 Salovey, P., & Mayer, J. D. (1990). Emotional intelligence. *Imagination, Cognition and Personality, 9*, 185–211.

3 Devonport, T. J. (2007). Emotional intelligence and the coping process amongst adolescent populations: A case study of student athletes. In A. M. Lane (Ed.), *Mood and human performance: Conceptual, measurement, and applied issues* (pp. 167–118). Hauppauge, NY: Nova Science.

4 Rubaltelli, E., Agnoli, S., & Leo, I. (2018) Emotional intelligence impact on half marathon finish times. *Personality and Individual differences, 128*, 107–112.

5 Botterill, C., & Brown, M. (2002). Emotion and perspective in sport. *International Journal of Sport Psychology, 33*, 38–60.

6 NCAA. (2018). Estimated probability of competing in professional athletics. Retrieved from www.ncaa.org/about/resources/research/estimated-probability-competing-professional-athletics (23/12/18)

7 Smith, J. (2017). Do parents place unrealistic expectations on their athletes. *USA Today*. Retrieved from https://usatodayhss.com/2017/do-parents-place-unrealistic-expectations-on-their-athletes

8 Appleton, P. R., Hall, H. K., & Hill, A. P. (2009). Relations between multidimensional perfectionism and burnout in junior-elite male athletes. *Psychology of Sport and Exercise, 10*(4), 457–465.

9 Thompson, J. M. (1995). Silencing the self: Depressive symptomatology and close relationships. *Psychology of Women Quarterly, 19*, 337–353.

10 Dunn, J. G., Dunn, J. C., & Syrotuik, D. G. (2002). Relationship between multidimensional perfectionism and goal orientations in sport. *Journal of Sport and Exercise Psychology, 24*(4), 376–395.

11 Stoeber, J., & Stoeber, F. S. (2009). Domains of perfectionism: Prevalence and relationships with perfectionism, gender, age, and satisfaction with life. *Personality and Individual Differences, 46*, 530–535.

12 Gould, D., Dieffenbach, K., & Moffett, A. (2002). Psychological characteristics and their development in Olympic champions. *Journal of Applied Sport Psychology, 14*(3), 172–204.

13 Flett, G. L., & Hewitt, P. L. (2005). The perils of perfectionism in sports and exercise. *Current Directions in Psychological Science, 14*(1), 14–18.

14 Enns, M. W., & Cox, B. J. (2002). The nature and assessment of perfectionism: A critical analysis. In G. L. Flett & P. L. Hewitt (Eds.), *Perfectionism: Theory, research, and treatment* (pp. 33–62). Washington, DC: American Psychological Association.

15 Flett, G. L., & Hewitt, P. L. (2005). The perils of perfectionism in sports and exercise. *Current Directions in Psychological Science, 14*(1), 14–18.

16 Frost, R. O., & Henderson, K. J. (1991). Perfectionism and reactions to athletic competition. *Journal of Sport and Exercise Psychology, 13*(4), 323–335.

17 Dunn, J. G., Gotwals, J. K., Dunn, J. C., & Syrotuik, D. G. (2006). Examining the relationship between perfectionism and trait anger in competitive sport. *International Journal of Sport and Exercise Psychology, 4*(1), 7–24.

18 Hill, A. P., Hall, H. K., Appleton, P. R., & Kozub, S. A. (2008). Perfectionism and burnout in junior elite soccer players: The mediating influence of unconditional self-acceptance. *Psychology of Sport and Exercise, 9*(5), 630–644.

19 Raedeke, T. D., & Smith, A. L. (2004). Coping resources and athlete burnout: An examination of stress mediated and moderation hypotheses. *Journal of Sport and Exercise Psychology, 26*(4), 525–541.

20 Flett, G. L., & Hewitt, P. L. (2005). The perils of perfectionism in sports and exercise. *Current Directions in Psychological Science, 14*(1), 14–18.

21 Blankstein, K. R., Dunkley, D. M., & Wilson, J. (2008). Evaluative concerns and personal standards perfectionism: Self-esteem as a mediator and moderator of relations with personal and academic needs and estimated GPA. *Current Psychology, 27*(1), 29–61.

22 Elliot, A. J., Cury, F., Fryer, J. W., & Huguet, P. (2006). Achievement goals, self-handicapping, and performance attainment: A mediational analysis. *Journal of Sport and Exercise Psychology, 28*(3), 344–361.

23 Stoeber, J., & Otto, K. (2006). Positive conceptions of perfectionism: Approaches, evidence, challenges. *Personality and Social Psychology Review, 10*(4), 295–319.

24 Frost, R. O., Marten, P., Lahart, C., & Rosenblate, R. (1990). The dimensions of perfectionism. *Cognitive Therapy and Research, 14*(5), 449–468.

25 Kaye, M. P., Conroy, D. E., & Fifer, A. M. (2008). Individual differences in incompetence avoidance. *Journal of Sport and Exercise Psychology, 30*(1), 110–132.

26 Hatzigeorgiadis, A., & Biddle, S. J. (2008). Negative self-talk during sport performance: Relationships with pre-competition anxiety and goal-performance discrepancies. *Journal of Sport Behavior, 31*(3), 237–253.

27 Gray, J. A. (1991). The neuropsychology of temperament. In Strelau, J. Angleitner, A. (eds.) *Explorations in temperament* (pp. 105–128). Boston, MA: Springer.

28 Lane, A. M., Thelwell, R., Lowther, J., & Devonport, T. (2009). Relationships between emotional intelligence and psychological skills among athletes. *Social Behaviour and Personality: An International Journal, 37*, 195–202.

29 Jones, M. V. (2003). Controlling emotions in sport. *The Sport Psychologist, 17*, 471–486.

30 Fletcher, D., & Hanton, S. (2001). The relationship between psychological skills usage and competitive anxiety responses. *Psychology of Sport and Exercise, 2*, 89–101.

31 Smith, R. E., Smoll, F. L., & Cumming, S. P. (2007). Effects of a motivational climate intervention for coaches on young athletes' sport performance anxiety. *Journal of Sport and Exercise Psychology, 29*(1), 39–59.

32 Smith, A., Ntoumanis, N., & Duda, J. (2007). Goal striving, goal attainment, and well-being: Adapting and testing the self-concordance model in sport. *Journal of Sport and Exercise Psychology, 29*(6), 763–782.

6

Becoming braver

The ship is safe in the harbour – but that is not what ships are for.

To achieve big we need to risk big. And risk is scary. Putting ourselves out there is daunting. Opening ourselves up to failure, to the judgement of others and to disappointment. What if we put lots of time, energy and effort into something and still fail? Not only will others think poorly of us, but we will think poorly of ourselves too; denting our self-identity and diminishing our self-esteem.

One (unhelpful but common) way athletes try to protect themselves from these risks is self-sabotage. To do well in competition every athlete knows it is essential to mentally and physically prepare yet they may well turn up late for training, not check out courses or venues or competitors in advance, eat or drink things they know are unhealthy, set too easy goals or talk negatively to themselves. All of these go against their best interests, diminish their confidence, create unfavourable circumstances and minimise their chances of success. But they also provide a neat excuse for the failure. Each small failure acts as an excuse to justify potentially failing at the big goal. Self-sabotage means while we fail a little on the small stuff we are protected from total failure because we have left the door open to trying again in the future. The athlete does enough to feel they are doing 'ok' but they are not risking everything to be very successful.

These self-sabotaging behaviours give athletes something that feels like a valid excuse. It protects them from others' judgement but also protects their own self-esteem if they don't do as they initially hoped. If an athlete still succeeds despite this behaviour it can enhance their confidence but they made everything much harder than it needed to be. If the athlete was able to succeed with their own hurdles in place how much better would they be able to do without the self-imposed barriers?

Procrastination is probably the most common form of self-sabotage. It wastes an athlete's (usually limited) time, makes the situation worse and lowers their chances of success. It means as well as still actually having to do the activity which they are procrastinating about they spend all the time when they are procrastinating in stressful anticipation of having to do it. Getting it out of the way means the weight is lifted and the amount of time an athlete is spending in anticipatory stress is reduced. But an athlete needs to be motivated enough, hold enough ownership of the required task and be in a safe place to feel confident to go for that. Putting some of these elements in place should help an athlete to feel braver so they can fulfil their potential.

Understanding the boundaries of the comfort zone

The opposite of being brave is staying comfortable. Comfort zones are lovely. They keep us safe. They physically protect us by stopping us tackling things beyond our current abilities and they psychologically protect us by keeping us out of stressful or anxiety-prompting situations. Unfortunately, these artificial mental boundaries also hold athletes back, slowing their development and preventing risk taking, both essential for improvement. We can all think of anecdotes when we have been forced into a difficult situation and we not only survived but often we had a realisation come with it that our limits are not where we thought they were. Taking this approach into sport can pay huge dividends to stop an athlete's fears limiting their success.

For an athlete to stretch their comfort zone they first need to identify what it looks like. Which areas they could they see themselves being able to stretch most comfortably?

What is it holding them back? Once they have established their current boundaries we can work with them to support them to stretch their boundaries little by little until they realise, reflecting back, that they have actually made a huge jump forwards.

Putting in place the fundamentals of motivation

A route to helping an athlete understand their motivation and current status within their comfort zone is to use Self-Determination Theory.[1] Self-Determination Theory has been labelled a meta-theory of motivation, emotion and personality[2] which really focuses on the quality of the motivation as well as the supporting factors that push an athlete to pursue their goals. It suggests that in order to be fully motivated to do something we need to have our natural tendencies supported in three areas: autonomy (being able to make our own decisions), competence (feeling confident we have the skills and abilities required for the challenge ahead) and relatedness (feeling connected, supported and comfortable with the people around us).[3] Only when all three needs are fully met will the athlete feel in a comfortable enough position to begin to stretch their comfort zone and start to take risks.

When the athlete feels unmotivated due to feeling incompetent, lonely or having stifled independence not only will they feel unable to push themselves but their wellbeing will be compromised and their development stunted. They may feel frustrated that their coach tells them what to do instead of discussing plans and collaborating. They may feel lonely if they don't have friends at training or are the only one in a group doing their specific event. They may feel incredibly nervous if they have a competition coming up that they don't feel ready or prepared for. These gaps will leave them feeling uncomfortable. Add onto this the need to stretch themselves out of the usual comfort zone boundaries and not only will they perform poorly but they won't even want to try. When these three areas are covered though they should start to feel so confident within their comfort zone they are happy to start stretching it.

Feeling safe

Another way to think about the importance of having an athlete feel secure and supported before they can expect to stretch themselves comes from the humanistic approach developed by the American Psychologist Abraham Maslow. Maslow suggested that we all have a hierarchy of needs (built up into a pyramid, with the most crucial needs at the bottom) and it is only when each layer of need is in place will we be able to benefit from the next layer.[4] The first four layers: physiological (our main physical requirements for survival; food, water, sleep and shelter), safety (physical, personal, emotional, financial and health), social belonging (friendships, family) and esteem (respect, sense of value, ego or status requirements) all need to be satisfied before we reach self-actualisation. This is the moment when some-one feels they have achieved their full potential; the desire, as Maslow puts it, to become the most that one can be. Today we realise these layers can flex regularly but that it is still necessary for many of the layers to be in place before we can reach the 'self-actualisation' level.

The first layer within Maslow's hierarchy pyramid is about physical safety. The second, third and fourth layers can all be considered elements to helping athletes feel psychologically safe. Full psychological safety comes when an athlete feels comfortable enough with a team (either a sporting team or the support team around them) to be authentic, vulnerable, express their opinions and take risks – all without fear of judgement or negative consequences.[5] The athlete in this environment will feel they can be accepted and respected whatever happens.

Opening the tap to a flow state

With the physical and psychological layers in place then Maslow argues that 'self-actualisation' is reachable. In sport, self-actualisation is often known as 'flow', to which a key element is having some level of intrinsic motivation for their sport. Intrinsic motivation comes when an athlete loves their sport; engaging in it for the satisfaction of developing their knowledge, achieving success or new skills and simply the physical sensation of participating. When an athlete is mainly driven by an extrinsic motivation, participating for some other purpose; a university scholarship, the medals they can win, the social recognition from those they admire, it will be much harder for them to reach flow and fully find themselves.

Alongside the intrinsic motivation, to get into a flow state it has been found that an athlete needs a great balance between the skills they already have and the challenge to learn more, to be able to get completely absorbed in what they are doing but still see very clear goals, to be able to totally concentrate on the action yet lose their self-consciousness and feel in control.[6] With these in place they should be able to feel that they are moving effortlessly, and with that comes a beautiful execution of their talent and training into performance. This is when it becomes much easier for an athlete to become braver. In fact, it gives them such confidence in what they do, they are likely to want to become braver.

The mindset and attribution for sporting bravery

What comes with having autonomy, competence, relatedness, psychological safety and the ability to get into a flow state is a higher likelihood of having a performance-approach mindset. This allows an athlete to play to win because they are thinking about the potential rewards of success. It differs from the performance-avoidance mindset where the aim is to avoid mistakes and evade danger. Athletes using a performance-approach mindset tend to perform above their expectations[7] and those using an avoidance-driven one struggle more in meeting their goals.[8] Athletes using an avoidance-driven approach are more worried about avoiding failure than achieving success and focus on the downsides of risk, behave cautiously and hold themselves back.

We can switch between approaches pretty quickly, and athletes regularly do so from starting a competition with a performance-approach and then, mid-way through when they assess they are doing well, start to think of the competition as theirs to lose, so switch to a performance-avoidance mindset in order to play very safely. This switch from performance-approach to performance-avoidant can be helpful right towards the end of a competition but often an athlete will switch too soon and it harms their performance.

The impact of an approach or avoidance mindset was interestingly displayed in a study of swimmers; swimming alone and in a relay team.[9] Those who were performance-approach focused swam faster in a relay because they were looking for the social approval of the others in the team. Those with a performance-avoidance approach swam faster alone as their goal in the relay was not to let others down, harming their performance. This highlights the importance of understanding whether an athlete is driven towards success or away from failure as it could not only have an impact on selection for types of events but, if it is understood better, then athletes prone to performance avoidance could have more safety measures put in place to help them focus more positively.

A further element directing the bravery of an athlete to take risks is based on how they attribute and explain their successes or failures.[10] There are many different explanations but they have been filtered down by psychologists into three specific dimensions.[11] The first dimension is how stable an explanation may be; does an athlete see themselves as having a strong talent and always working hard or do they attribute results to unstable things, such as only weaker competitors turning up that day? The second dimension covers the locus of causality; whether the athlete attributes the outcome to the effort they personally put in or whether there was an external factor, such as it being good weather which helped them do well. The final dimension is based around the locus of control, whether the athlete feels results are in their control or down to others.

How an athlete attributes their successes or failures has been found to impact how they expect a competition to go.[12] Stable factors will give an athlete an expectation of something similar happening again. An athlete who has an internal locus of causality and an internal locus of control may see their loss in a competition down to a lack of recent specific training because they didn't show up to practice. If they want to improve they will make the choice to turn up to training and focus on specific activities that will have a direct impact on their performance. An athlete who has an external locus of causality and an external locus of control may blame a poor result on their competitors having bought with them new, much stronger players. As there is little the athlete could do about this their only action may be to make weaker goals in future. Attributing something as outside of our control or influenced by others is a way of protecting our own ego and fragility if we don't do well – self-protection in the form of self-sabotage.

Summary

When we have fears we self-sabotage. We cannot get into the flow state, or into feeling confident enough to get brave and stretch our comfort zone while we are weighed down with these fears. These fears don't just give athletes low confidence, pre-competition anxiety, negativity, a preoccupation with results and high self-criticism but they often put the athlete's focus on not losing, rather than on what it will take to win. When they understand exactly what those fears are, have in place foundations of motivation (competence, autonomy and relatedness) and feel psychologically safe they will have the additional capacity and mental bandwidth to use a performance-approach mindset and attribute performances to changeable, internal factors which they can control. This state allows them to become braver to take the risks required for performance success.

Key terms

- Anticipatory stress – a sense of dread or fear that something will go wrong.
- Attribution theory – how athletes explain their successes or failures.
- Autonomy – being able to make our own decisions.
- Comfort zones – where things feel familiar and safe and the athlete feels in control of their situation. Has been described as being in an anxiety-neutral state.

- Competence – having and recognising that we have the skills and abilities required for the challenge we are facing.
- Extrinsic motivation – participating in sport for an external reason such as recognition or reward.
- Flow – being fully immersed, enjoying the moment and feeling in the zone.
- Hierarchy of needs – five layers of human need (physiological, safety, social belonging, esteem and self-actualisation) which are required to feel we have found ourselves in life.
- Humanistic approach – a psychological approach which considers the whole person and their uniqueness.
- Intrinsic motivation – comes when an athlete simply loves the process and sensation of doing their sport.
- Locus of causality – whether an athlete attributes the outcome of competition to internal or external factors.
- Locus of control – whether an athlete believes results are within their control or controlled by others.
- Performance-approach mindset – aiming to perform well.
- Performance-avoidance mindset – aiming to avoid mistakes.
- Procrastination – delaying or avoiding doing an activity even when doing so gives negative consequences.
- Psychological safety – when an athlete feels comfortable enough to be authentic, vulnerable, express their opinions and take risks without fear of judgement or negative consequences.
- Relatedness – feeling connected, supported and comfortable with the people around us.
- Self-actualisation – the moment when someone feels they have achieved their full potential.
- Self-Determination Theory – the idea that only when we have autonomy, relatedness and competence can we perform at our best.

- Self-esteem – how we perceive ourselves and the value judgement we assign to that.
- Self-identity – the way we describe and define ourselves.
- Self-sabotage – self-defeating behaviours (usually unconscious) which prevent us achieving our goals.

Key messages to share with athletes about being braver

- If we want to do well we have to leave our comfort zone. This can be really daunting so we need to understand our fears and then put in place some strategies to help us stretch its boundaries.
- We sometimes try to protect ourselves from failure through self-sabotage, especially using behaviours like procrastination.
- Self-Determination Theory suggests that in order to be fully motivated to do something we need to feel autonomous (able to make our own decisions), competent (confident we have the skills required) and related (connected to others around us). We need all three before we can feel confident stretching our comfort zone.
- Maslow's hierarchy of needs has five layers: physiological, safety, social belonging, esteem and self-actualisation. His theory says that each layer should be fulfilled before the next one is effective. The top layer, self-actualisation, he says, is what we are all aiming for in life. In sport this top layer is often referred to as 'flow'.
- To achieve flow (and the braveness which comes with it) we need all these layers in place as well as intrinsic motivation for our sport, a great balance between skills already established and the challenge to learn more, to get completely absorbed, have very clear goals and to feel in control.

- To become braver we also need a performance-approach mindset which helps us think about how we perform well rather than a performance-avoidance mindset where the aim is to avoid mistakes.
- We can also direct our bravery as an athlete more effectively by attributing our actions to stable, internal ones we have control of as we can then make appropriate changes.

Strategies to help athletes become braver

1 Control mapping (Strategy 1) helps an athlete explore their comfort zone boundaries.

2 To slowly stretch comfort zones, athletes need to be really clever with their goal setting (Strategy 2) to set really motivating and effective goals.

3 Athletes can use performance profiling (Strategy 4) to become clearer about what is needed for their ideal performance.

4 To help us overcome our self-sabotage we should follow the SCRIPT (Strategy 6).

5 A training diary (Strategy 10) is a useful tool for reflection to see where bravery has taken place.

6 'Try it Tuesday' (Strategy 11) helps athletes take brave steps without the pressure of performance.

7 Attribution retraining (Strategy 14) is vital to help an athlete take ownership (and longer-term responsibility) of their performances.

8 Taking part in familiarisation training (Strategy 24) is valuable so the athlete becomes used to elements of what is coming their way.

9 'What if' planning (Strategy 29) can take away some of the fear of the unknown.

10 Developing an alter ego (Strategy 32) is a great technique to get an athlete being brave (from someone else's shoes).

11 Breaking down a competition through chunking it up (Strategy 36) into smaller elements takes away some of the fears.

12 Using instructional self-talk (Strategy 42) to help an athlete follow brave instructions or a motivational mantra (Strategy 45) to boost confidence.

13 Following a process of value mapping (Strategy 48) helps athletes understand their values and motivations clearly so they can reach flow.

14 Athlete's knowing their why (Strategy 49) will help an athlete uncover their intrinsic motivations.

15 Through using metacognition (Strategy 50) and then becoming a self-expert (Strategy 52), the athlete they should consider where they are attributing success; stable versus unstable factors, locus of control and locus of causality.

16 Self-identity mapping (Strategy 53) allows athletes to understand better how they see themselves.

17 Thinking aloud (Strategy 55) can help an athlete become more aware of their thoughts and fears.

Notes

1 Deci, E. L., & Ryan, R. M. (2008). Self-determination theory: A macrotheory of human motivation, development, and health. *Canadian Psychology, 49*(3), 182.

2 Horn, T., & Smith, A. L. (2019). *Advances in sport and exercise psychology* (4th Ed.). Champaign, IL: Human Kinetics.

3 Deci, E. L., & Ryan, R. M. (2008). Self-determination theory: A macrotheory of human motivation, development, and health. *Canadian Psychology, 49*(3), 182.

4 Maslow, A., & Lewis, K. J. (1987). Maslow's hierarchy of needs. *Salenger Incorporated, 14*, 987.

5 Kahn, W. A. (1990). Psychological conditions of personal engagement and disengagement at work. *Academy of Management Journal, 33*(4), 692–724.

6 Jackson, S. A., & Csikszentmihalyi, M. (1999). *Flow in sports*. Champaign, IL: Human Kinetics.

7 Stoeber, J., Uphill, M. A., & Hotham, S. (2009) Predicting race performance in triathlon: The role of perfectionism, achievement goals, and personal goal setting. *Journal of Sport and Exercise Psychology, 31*(2), 211–245.

8 Elliot, A. J., Cury, F., Fryer, J. W., & Huguet, P. (2006). Achievement goals, self-handicapping and performance attainment: A mediational analysis. *Journal of Sport and Exercise Psychology, 28*(3), 344–361.

9   Sorrentino, R. M., & Sheppard, B. H. (1978). Effects of affiliation-related motives on swimmers in individual versus group competition: A field experiment. *Journal of Personality and Social Psychology, 36*(7), 704.

10 Heider, F. (1958). *The psychology of interpersonal relations.* New York: Wiley.

11 Weiner, B. (1988). An attributional theory of motivation and emotion. *Behaviourism, 16*(2), 167–173.

12 Biddle, S., Hanrahan, S. J., & Sellars, C. N. (2001). Attributions: Past, present, and future. In R. N. Singer, H. A. Hausenblas, & C. M. Janelle (Eds.) (2nd Ed., pp. 444–471). *Handbook of sport psychology.* New York: Wiley.

7

Pushing harder

Today's sweat is tomorrow's strength

We hear athletes in their post-competition interviews talking about how they gave it 110% or pushed well beyond their limits. While their linguistic realism is dubious, their intention is clear: 'I worked harder than I thought I could'. But what set that initial limit they felt they had gone beyond?

Traditionally, we thought of our physiological limits being forced upon us from within our body. The perception was that humans were machines with physiological limiters where exhaustion was caused by central and peripheral muscle fatigue[1] and our ability to perform came down to the amount of energy left in our muscles, the lactic we could handle, the rate at which our muscles fatigued, how much oxygen we could take in, the heat we could cope with and how many red blood cells we could transport around our bodies.

Modern testing has found that the situation is actually very different. We now know that even after we reach exhaustion an athlete's leg muscles are still capable of producing power[2] so there is still energy there. It is something else which has stopped us. The psychobiological model of endurance performance[3] suggests what stops us comes from effort-based decision making; so not our physiology but how motivated we are and how much effort we perceive we are putting in. When we want to stop is because our perception of effort, how our brain perceives how hard, heavy and strenuous a physical task is,[4] has gone too high and potential motivation (the highest effort we are willing to exert) has dipped too low. To perform better we must first increase our motivation and, once that is exhausted, engage in activities which make our efforts feel easier.

Increasing motivation

Motivation is the foundation of all sporting performances. It can be seen as our internal energy which determines how we behave and directs the ways we think and feel in setting the target and intensity of our effort. Without that initial desire all our other mental skills are redundant. If an athlete is properly motivated to improve in their sport and has a goal they are passionate about, then they will put whatever time and effort is required into their preparation and performances.

Motivation impacts everything that influences an athlete's sporting performance: physical conditioning, technical and tactical training, mental preparation, and general lifestyle including sleep, diet, school or work, and relationships. It is one of the only elements of performance that an athlete has complete control of. It can come from within the athlete based on their personality, goals or needs, from the situation in which they find themselves (the coach, the type of exercise, being in a team) or both.

When an athlete starts competing in their sport it is new and exciting. Their motivation will usually stay pretty strong as they continue to improve and have new experiences. Athletes will often see their performances improve with each competition, their skills develop and fitness increase. All of these are incredibly motivating and help the athlete stay engaged in their sport and working hard. As time goes on however, their performances will start to plateau. The low-level skills have all been mastered and the next set of skills are more nuanced and feel like they will take longer to reach. As the athlete starts to focus on competing rather than just completing, their mastery approach begins to get replaced with an outcome focus and as they begin to self-identify as an athlete and have incorporated training into their day to day life then not only does their sport take on more importance but they also feel pressure and expectations coming from their friends, family, club-mates and themselves to perform.

Not surprisingly the pressure and expectations that all of this causes can start to limit their love of their sport and reduce some of their keenness to perform. They may have developed an extrinsic motivation to perform, as they crave the congratulations or trophies they could win. With all this going on their intrinsic motivation (that which comes from the pure joy of doing their sport) reduces and they find it harder to push themselves to improve. An unmotivated athlete may well exhibit low energy, poor discipline, find themselves continually complaining, doing poorly in competition, becoming more unpredictable, missing or shortening training and making excuses for all of this. They will be unable to bring the commitment, effort and passion that is necessary to fulfil their athletic potential and when they face a dip in performance or a loss of confidence, they will not only find it difficult to push harder but to push at all. In the worst cases they may quit their sport.

As we learnt in Chapter 6, both intrinsic and extrinsic motivation are helpful as without desire or determination to improve in your sport everything else is wasted. Intrinsic motivation gives the athlete the knowledge they will enjoy what they are putting effort into and extrinsic motivation can give the athlete a visual and tangible goal to aim towards. Having both these in place will ensure the athlete is willing to put in the time, physical effort and mental preparation necessary to improve and achieve their goals even when confronted by fatigue, boredom, pain, or simply the desire to do something more enjoyable.

One of the most popular theories of motivation (Self-Determination Theory – discussed in Chapter 6) suggests that we each have three innate needs; competence (feeling we have the ability and have mastered the skills to achieve our goal), relatedness (being in an environment which supports and encourages us) and autonomy (seeing ourselves as in control of our choices). The theory proposes that when an athlete has these three needs met, they will have their highest levels of motivation so, working with an athlete to give them the skills and experiences to achieve their goals, creating an environment which supports and encourages them and developing an athlete-led philosophy should help to boost motivation levels and help the athlete push harder. However, our motivation is not limitless. If we are offered £1 million to set a new personal best or win a match that will be motivation enough. Doubling the reward will not double our motivation. So when we max out our motivation the next thing to do is to reduce our perception of effort.

Reducing perception of effort

Athletes fear that pushing hard will bring pain or injury. This is quite a legitimate perception – pushing ourselves really hard can hurt! If the effort levels are high the athlete may feel at risk so they then lower their effort levels. This high perception of effort then becomes a barrier to performance, particularly endurance performance, as we feel worse and stop sooner. Once an athlete understands this they can learn to recognise how much effort they are putting in and then adopt strategies to lower their perception of how high it is. There are a number of ways to do this but four specific routes we can consider here are to reduce mental fatigue, take caffeine, hold realistic expectations and simply to smile! We can consider each, one by one.

Reducing mental fatigue

We become mentally fatigued from extended periods of demanding cognitive activity.[5] In sporting environments mental fatigue has been found to impair gross-motor performance with cyclists reaching exhaustion sooner[6] and runners completing a 5k run slower[7] and fine-motor tasks such as arm pointing[8] and shooting decision accuracy[9] being diminished. A systematic review considering 11 studies on the impact of mental fatigue on sporting performance found the physiological variables that are usually linked to endurance performance (heart rate, maximal aerobic capacity, blood lactate, oxygen uptake, cardiac output) were not affected by mental fatigue but the speed was.[10] A further analysis of 29 studies found that mental fatigue also impairs decision making.[11]

Mental fatigue can impact any athlete, but it seems to have more of an impact the longer an athlete is competing in one go. Endurance athletes, who race for many hours and are often training long hours on top of a busy work or studying life, may see mental fatigue having a significant negative impact. This means while many athletes know to have a physical taper ahead of a big competition they would also benefit from a mental taper too.

Adding to this, another study saw 16 cyclists spend 90 minutes watching either a bland documentary or performing dull computer (Stroop task) tests and then tried to stick to a specific power output on a turbo.[12] They found that right from the start the cyclists who had done something mentally fatiguing had a higher perception of effort, it stayed higher and they reached exhaustion earlier. There was no significant difference in heart rate and it wasn't physically tiring but it had an immediate impact on the athlete's perception of effort. In fact, those on the computer programme gave up 15% quicker. This suggests athletes should not just taper but avoid mundane mental tasks before competition. Interestingly though a study has found that the impact of mental fatigue is felt more in amateur athletes than elites. A study comparing professional and amateur cyclists[13] found that while amateurs were impacted by mental fatigue, professionals were resistant to it, perhaps down to the hard physical training and demanding lifestyle they have. Perhaps the resilience that professional athletes have to develop in order to perform at the highest levels helps them to cope better with mental fatigue.

One explanation for the impact that perception of effort has on those of us not trained to manage it physically comes from researchers suggesting that mental fatigue comes from the accumulation of a brain chemical called adenosine.[14] They propose that sustained cognitive activity uses up glucose, especially in the areas of the brain which are associated with the mental processes around effort (the anterior cingulate cortex). This shortage, they say, could cause a rise in adenosine levels, which then blocks the release of neurotransmitters like dopamine. As a result, our perception of effort increases and our motivation decreases. We feel mentally fatigued.

Caffeine

One of the ways many researchers have suggested we reduce perception of effort is through using caffeine. There are a number of theories as to why it would help athletes and one again mentions adenosine, suggesting that caffeine blocks the action of adenosine as its molecular structure is similar so it can attach itself to the same receptors in the brain. This stops adenosine levels rising so our perception of effort doesn't rise. A further idea is that it works through the central nervous system, inhibiting certain neurotransmitters in the brain. Another suggests it speeds up our response times, something incredibly important when we are trying to focus when already fatigued within competition.

There is also a more recent view that perhaps it reduces the impact of mental fatigue. A study looked at how endurance cyclists coped with mental fatigue and their mood while taking caffeine (5mg per kilo of body weight). They found that, once a cyclist was mentally fatigued, taking caffeine improved their performance by around 14% and their mood also improved.[15]

The studies showing a decent effect of using caffeine in sport involve researchers giving much larger amounts of caffeine than are commonly found in energy drinks or coffee; about 6mg of caffeine per kilo of body weight.[16] For comparison a filter coffee contains about 120mg of caffeine and European Food Safety Authority guidelines suggest no more than 400mg a day.[17]

The latest research suggests that we individually respond to caffeine differently based on which version of a specific gene (the CYP1A2 gene) we have.[18] 95% of the caffeine we drink is metabolised by the CYP1A2 gene so a study used a spit test to identify which version of the CYP1A2 gene each participant had. Those with one version of the gene metabolised and broke down the caffeine quickly (something that is helpful for performance) and they were 6.8% faster in a time trail. Those with a different version metabolised it far slower and were 13.7% slower in the trial. So caffeine does seem to be very effective for those with the right version of the CYP1A2 gene who are using it at high levels.

Expecting the effort to feel hard

Studies using the psychological approach of Acceptance and Commitment Theory (ACT) have found that, if we learn to accept unpleasant feelings as something that must be endured as unavoidable, we can cope much better, and our perception of effort reduces. A study worked with non-exercisers and, using the ACT process, reduced the perceived effort they were putting in to exercise by 55% and increased their time to exhaustion by 15%.[19] They learnt to 'brace themselves' for the discomfort by expecting it and so when it did their perception of effort reduced.

The aim is not to make something so scary in advance that the real thing feels simple (because if we do that no-one will show up) but we do want to build an attitude that it is supposed to be difficult so that the expectations are laid and when it is do-able athletes feel better able to cope and feel their perception of effort is lower. This theory suggests that the more an athlete tries to control and resist difficult moments, the worse they will feel, so an athlete accepting uncertainty in this way should ultimately cope and perform better.

Subliminal smiles

Finally, an interesting area of research has looked at ways to reduce perception of effort by using non-conscious visual cues, specifically smiling. It is so simple and so easy to do yet research is starting to find it has some great benefits, especially in endurance sports. It is based on two pieces of research finding that smiling in competition can reduce an athlete's perception of effort, increase their positive thoughts and increase their running economy.

An experiment used individuals on bikes doing time to exhaustion tests and found that those who were subliminally primed with happy faces were able to cycle 12% longer than those who saw grumpy faces and the perception of effort level they reported was lower.[20]

A further study found that runners who purposely smiled when struggling found their running economy improved. They also found that perceived effort was higher during frowning than smiling.[21] This, they suggested, was down to the idea that it relaxes your emotional state so reduces your perception of effort, giving the athlete a greater difference in speed.

There is also a theory around the benefits of smiling at your rivals. A psychological concept called 'interpersonal complementarity' suggests we naturally follow the social cues around us. Someone smiles, we smile back. Someone puts out their hand to shake it and we do the same. A Stanford psychologist used this to his advantage when he realised he was in a difficult situation with a potential mugger barging into him aggressively. He fought an aggressive reaction back and instead pretended to know the guy, was overly friendly and completely caught him off guard, giving him time to escape safely. An athlete won't be mugged on the field of play but may well come up against raw aggression or sledging from competitors so smiling at them could put them completely off their guard, while having the added benefit of reducing perception of effort and thus helping the athlete perform better.

Summary

Researchers no longer believe that we are solely limited in performance by physiological fatigue. Instead we can work from the idea that our limits come from effort-based decision making. In this case, in order to push themselves harder, athletes need to increase their motivation. They can do this once they feel competent in their sport, connected to those around them and autonomous, secure they are making their own decisions. With these in place they can pick goals which make them excited and fairly confident they would be able to achieve them. Once their motivation is all maxed out their next step is to reduce their perception of effort. There are lots of techniques used to do this and more are being identified all the time but four to try immediately could be minimizing mental fatigue, taking caffeine, expecting their efforts to feel hard and smiling.

Key terms

- External motivation – where an athlete competes because they like the accolades from others when they do well, the prize money or trophies they win at competitions or the way others treat them for being in that sport.
- Intrinsic motivation – where an athlete finds their need to take part in their sport is self-determined and driven by the enjoyment and sensation they get from doing it.
- Mental fatigue – a psychobiological state caused by extended periods of demanding cognitive activity.
- Motivation – an athlete's ability to initiate and persist at a task.
- Perception of effort – how our brain perceives how hard, heavy or strenuous a physical task is.
- Potential motivation – the highest effort someone will exert to succeed in a task.
- Self-determination theory – the idea that we need to feel competent, related and autonomous in order to have a high level of motivation.

Key messages to share with athletes about how to push harder

- Traditionally it was thought we were limited in performance by physiological fatigue but the psychobiological model of endurance performance says our limits come from effort-based decision making. To push ourselves harder we need to increase our motivation or reduce our perception of effort.
- Self-determination theory says if we have three key needs met; competence, relatedness and autonomy, an athlete will have high levels of motivation.
- There are a number of techniques used to reduce our perception of effort including minimising mental fatigue, taking caffeine, expecting our efforts to feel hard and smiling.

Strategies to help an athlete push harder

1 Knowing what your goal is through goal setting (Strategy 2) helps an athlete push through negative thoughts or pain.

2 Using a training diary (Strategy 10) can be good to remind an athlete of their motivations.

3 Brain endurance training (Strategy 17) helps athletes to get used to mental fatigue.

4 Completing a confidence booster (Strategy 22) ahead of competition helps remind an athlete of their goal and motivation for competing.

5 Imagery (Strategy 25) is a wonderful way to boost motivation for competition and prepare yourself for the pressures you will be facing in competition.

6 Mental tapering (Strategy 26) is really important to reduce mental fatigue ahead of competition.

7 The process of smiling (Strategy 30) has been found by researchers to make us run more efficiently thus reducing our perception of effort.

8 Boosting motivation by amping up (Strategy 33) particularly through listening to motivational music can be beneficial.

9 To reduce perception of effort some athletes will take a dissociative attentional strategy (Strategy 35).

10 The process of chunking (Strategy 36) can help athletes feel less overwhelmed by how much required effort is ahead of them.

11 Choosing how to use pain interpretation (Strategy 39) will help the athlete feel like they are putting in less effort than they may otherwise feel.

12 Talking to ourselves positively through self-talk (Strategies 42–46) can boost our motivation and reduce our perception of effort.

13 Athlete's knowing their why (Strategy 49) reminds them continually of their motivation to keep pushing.

14 Having a training partner (Strategy 64) can make training sessions feel easier and go by faster.

Notes

1 Amann, M., & Dempsey, J. A. (2008). Locomotor muscle fatigue modifies central motor drive in healthy humans and imposes a limitation to exercise performance. *Journal of Physiology, 586,* 161–173.

2 Marcora, S. M., & Staiano, W. (2010). The limit to exercise tolerance in humans: Mind over muscle? *European Journal of Applied Physiology, 109,* 763–770.

3 Marcora, S. M., & Staiano, W. (2010). The limit to exercise tolerance in humans: Mind over muscle? *European Journal of Applied Physiology, 109,* 763–770.

4 Marcora, S. (2010). Effort. perception of. In E. B. Goldstein (Ed.), *Encyclopaedia of perception* (pp. 380–383). Thousand Oaks, CA: SAGE Publications Inc.

5 Boksem, M. A., & Tops, M. (2008). Mental fatigue: Costs and benefits. *Brain Research Reviews, 59*(1), 125–139.

6 Marcora, S. M., Staiano, W., & Manning, V. (2009). Mental fatigue impairs physical performance in humans. *Journal of Applied Physiology, 106,* 857–864.

7 Pageaux, B., Lepers, R., Dietz, K. C., & Marcora, S. M. (2014). Response inhibition impairs subsequent self-paced endurance performance. *European Journal of Applied Physiology, 114,* 1095–1105.

8 Rozand, V., Lebon, F., Stapley, P. J., Papaxanthis, C., & Lepers, R. (2016). A prolonged motor imagery session alter imagined and actual movement durations: Potential implications for neurorehabilitation. *Behavioral Brain Research, 297,* 67–75.

9 Head, J., Tenan, M. S., Tweedell, A, J., LaFiandra, M. E., Morelli, F., Wilson, K. M., Ortega, S. V., & Helton, W. S. (2017). Prior mental fatigue impairs marksmanship decision performance. *Frontiers in Physiology,* 8, 680.

10 Van Cutsem, J., Marcora, S., De Pauw, K., Bailey, S., Meeusen, R., & Roelands, B. (2017). The effects of mental fatigue on physical performance: A systematic review. *Sports Medicine, 47*(8), 1569–1588.

11 Pageaux, B., & Lepers, R. (2018). Chapter 16 – The effects of mental fatigue on sport-related performance. In S. Marcora & M. Sarkar (Eds.), *Sport and the brain: The science of preparing, enduring and winning, Part C,* 240, 2–370.

12 Marcora, S. M., Staiano, W., & Manning, V. (2009). Mental fatigue impairs physical performance in humans. *Journal of Applied Physiology, 106,* 857–864.

13 Martin, M., Staiano, W., Menaspà, P., Hennessey, T., Marcora, S., Keegan, R., Thompson, K. G., Martin, D., Halson, S., & Rattray, B. (2016). Superior inhibitory control and resistance to mental fatigue in professional road cyclists. *PLoS One*, 11(7), e0159907.

14 Martin, K., Meeusen, R., Thompson, K. G., Keegan, R., & Rattray, B. (2018). Mental fatigue impairs endurance performance: A physiological explanation. *Sports Medicine, 48*, 2041–2051.

15 Azevedo, R., Silva-Cavalcante, M. D., Gualano, B., Lima-Silva, A. E., & Bertuzzi, R. (2016). Effects of caffeine ingestion on endurance performance in mentally fatigued individuals. *European Journal of Applied Physiology, 116*(11–12), 2293–2303.

16 Ribeiro, B. G., Morales, A. P., Sampaio-Jorge, F., de Souza Tinoco, F., de Matos, A. A., & Leite, T. C. (2017). Acute effects of caffeine intake on athletic performance: A systematic review and meta-analysis. *Revista Chilena de Nutrición, 44* (3), 283–291.

17 EFSA Panel on Dietetic Products, Nutrition and Allergies (NDA). (2015). Scientific opinion on the safety of caffeine. *EFSA Journal, 13*(5), 4102.

18 Guest, N., Corey, P., Vescovi, J., & El-Sohemy, A. (2018). Caffeine, CYP1A2 genotype, and endurance performance in athletes. *Medicine and Science in Sports and Exercise, 50*(8), 1570–1578.

19 Ivanova, E., Jensen, D., Cassoff, J., Gu, F., & Knäuper, B. (2015). Acceptance and commitment therapy improves exercise tolerance in sedentary women. *Medicine & Science in Sports & Exercise, 47*(6), 1251–1258.

20 Blanchfield, A., Hardy, J., & Marcora, S. (2014). Non-conscious visual cues related to affect and action alter perception of effort and endurance performance. *Frontiers in Human Neuroscience, 8*, 967.

21 Brick, N. E., McElhinney, M. J., & Metcalfe, R. S. (2018). The effects of facial expression and relaxation cues on movement economy, physiological, and perceptual responses during running. *Psychology of Sport and Exercise, 34*, 20–28.

8

Learning from competition

You either win or you learn

No-one enjoys losing – but no-one can win everything. So we either sulk about it or we see it as an opportunity to learn. For those of us able to do this it means that far from fearing the barriers or problems we encounter, we see them as lessons which will make us much better equipped and prepared for our next event. It is a long-term perspective that can help us develop into great athletes who have the resilience to stay in our sport even when we hit tough times.

The reality though is that many athletes guiltily beat themselves up when they make a mistake or a competition doesn't go to plan. Some block off the memory and move on straight away. Others over-analyse the mistakes they made and ignore any of the positive elements achieved. Those who get a good balance of the analysis while still looking forward are the ones who will be appreciating their successes, learning from their mistakes and benefiting from improvements from each one.

This 'win or learn' approach would benefit all athletes. Whether they are training to get a new personal best or move up the rankings; whether they want to improve their skills or just feel more comfortable, there are some great lessons athletes can learn from themselves through reflection. The approach helps athletes see that every competition doesn't have to be an 'outcome success' but a stage on their journey to be a better athlete. Whether they feel the competition has gone well or disastrously, if they can take a lesson away from that competition then it was worth their time in doing it. This growth mindset ensures the focus is less on winning and more on the performance and process of competing.[1]

This approach will help an athlete replace 'I can't' when they try a new skill, or distance or technique with a more helpful; 'I can't yet'. When used in education this mindset been found to increase resilience,[2] persistence[3] and improve performance.[4] For athletes it will help them to strive to achieve a little more and for them to continually grow as an athlete. It really helps them focus on the process goals, the skills they need to learn and the attitude they will benefit from taking instead of being driven by results. It creates a mastery climate, something shown to drive great performance. Their sport then feels more controllable and competition less of a judgement. This should then improve their wellbeing and attitude towards competition.

It is important though that the athlete does not focus on their mistakes or try to learn mid-competition. During a competition it is important for the athlete to focus on the now. Not previous or potential mistakes; just what do they need to do at this moment to perform well. After the competition, once the athlete has calmed, then it is the time to acknowledge any mistakes, consider what went wrong, think through what is required to fix each issue and then put in place a plan to fix it. Alongside this it is important to help the athletes identify their reactions to each mistake so they can ensure their response at the time doesn't hinder their overall performance.

Post-competition analysis

Studying the coping mechanisms of successful athletes highlights that using a process approach (based on an interaction between an athlete's self-beliefs, goals and values and their external environment[5]) can be really beneficial for the athlete. It helps them to reflect in a helpful, process-driven manner which focuses on improved performance,[6] lower levels of anxiety[7] and more pleasant sporting experiences.[8]

Studies into how athletes cope when they make mistakes found 36 coping responses to failure or mistakes and placed them into five categories; problem-focused, emotion-focused, appraisal-focused, avoidance-focused and failing in coping.[9] While different situations often demand different skills and different coping strategies, using a problem-focused approach when analysing a competition was by far the most popular and effective[10] as it involves targeting strengths and weaknesses and learning from previous mistakes and failures by analysing what has happened and aiming to alter the stressful situation through seeking new information, planning and setting goals and being assertive over the things they can control. It has been found to have a positive impact on the athlete[11] and is particularly effective for those elements over which an athlete has some control.[12]

Emotion-focused coping looks at the emotional distress that comes from the mistake or issue[13] and can be effective when the athlete has little or no control.[14] Other coping mechanisms are used but seem to be more maladaptive (such as simply avoiding the distressing situation) and are likely to see an athlete have reduced levels of performance,[15] unable to pursue careers in professional sport[16] or drop out of sport completely.[17]

A problem-focused approach can be developed through post-competition analysis. It is helpful to have input from a coach or other support members for this but the analysis will have the biggest impact if the athlete completes this themselves as, once they have acknowledged the issues, they will be better inclined to deal with them if they feel they 'own' the required actions. Coaches can support athletes with their analysis of physical mistakes by not giving the answer as to what was wrong but instead allowing them an active involvement in identifying it, improving empowerment and increasing motivation.

Analysing their competition through the same format and process each time means that there will always be practical, logistical, mental and strategic lessons they can take from any competition which they can use to improve and become more self-aware. Studies have found that knowledge of results will influence retrospective recall[18] so it is important to help an athlete think about both the positive and negative elements of a competition. The reflection and analysis process isn't just for mistakes but to also highlight elements which work well and should be continued. In fact, it is vital to consider what did work well as this can be built into an athlete developing a greater understanding of their strengths and add to their confidence through their mastery experiences.

Once the athlete has completed their analysis it becomes a great base for a conversation on what went well and what needs to change. It can help the coach and athlete improve training plans and actionable process goals can be woven in, leaving the athlete feeling more positive. Attribution (Chapter 6) becomes important here so mistakes or failures are not attributed to a lack of ability as that will only develop a really fixed, negative mindset. Each element must have something proactive that can be attempted and can improve with effort and motivation.

Long term, having a stack of sheets, all analysing competitions the same way will help identify long-term trends, actions which are never actioned or technique failures which require some specific tuition.

Expectation scrutiny

One of the really valuable things an athlete can learn from their post-competition analysis is how to manage expectations better, especially the expectations coming from others. This is hard to prepare for in advance of competition but using a recent competition to look back over and consider where expectations fitted in will give the athlete a very recent and realistic framework to use to see how helpful (or more usually unhelpful) those expectations were and whether they harmed or hindered their emotional control.

Athletes will often thrive when they have, and feel, the support of their friends and family. As we saw in Chapter 2 this can be a good source of confidence for the athlete as they can see others believe in them, reducing anxiety and showing them that their hard work and dedication has been acknowledged and recognised. However, when someone phrases their confidence in the athlete without thinking through the repercussions (such as saying 'I know you will do well') then that support can feel like an expectation and the athlete feels they 'must do well'. Then, as Chapter 5 highlighted, the expectations take away the fun, create stress, even stop the athlete being able to perform skills properly. They give the athlete additional performance responsibilities they never asked for.

Once the competition is over it can be helpful to talk to the athlete to understand where they felt expectations came from. This provides an opportunity to assess whether the expectations were real (or just perceived) and whether they focused on behviours or performance outcomes. This acts as a valuable reality check.

Post-competition blues

For big one-off endurance challenges, local derby matches or championship competitions where the date has been in the athlete's diary for months and they have focused intently on it, the days after the event, whether it went brilliantly well or was an unmitigated disaster, are important. In theory, the athlete should be able to relax and to treat themselves, to rest and recover to build-up for the next season. Often however, in a way that may feel illogical, when they have focused on a specific date for so long, and been buried in their training and preparation, it can actually feel like a big comedown afterwards. It has been labelled the 'post-competition blues'. Those who didn't meet their goals will have the comedown and could be berating themselves for not succeeding in their aim. Those who achieved what they wanted may feel a big void left by the competition having passed and feel quite deflated. Helping an athlete expect this void and plan for this period can help them to adjust better to their change in focus.

Once an athlete has completed their post-competition analysis, understood the impact of any external expectations and dealt with any post-competition blues they should focus on two important, and enjoyable tasks; celebrating their success and ensuring they give something back to those who helped and supported them.

Celebrating success

A great way to help beat off the post-competition blues is to celebrate the successes the athlete did have. Even if their 'big' event went poorly, spending some time analysing their whole season or the period building up to the competition will offer some elements of success they could want to celebrate. It can help them relax, see what they learnt from the process and has a really important role in ensuring they maintain their love of their sport. It helps them reflect on what has gone well and how to continue doing that, rather than getting caught up in our negativity bias of focusing on what went wrong.[19] Focusing on the good helps them build a positive memory bank of evidence that reminds them they can achieve their goals if they put the time and effort in. This helps when it comes to goal setting in the future, increases their motivation to work hard and improves their confidence levels.

Celebrating also helps the athlete feel more grateful for what they have been able to do. The Broaden and Build Theory of positive emotion describes how a group of positive emotions (joy, interest, contentment and love) can extend our thought–action repertoire[20] to create a broadened mindset. This positive mindset can build an athlete's psychological resources as opposed to the narrowed mindset resulting from the way we respond to potential threats (as discussed in Chapters 1 and 4). The positive psychological resources (such as new skills or supportive relationships) can develop into long-term reserves which can be drawn upon, improving resilience and increasing an athlete's wellbeing.[21]

One of the routes to developing these positive emotions is by expressing gratitude. Studies have found proactively using gratitude can increase an athlete's wellbeing and decrease psychological distress and athlete burnout.[22] When combined with the right coaching support researchers have found that gratitude can really help athletes perceive difficult situations or experiences in a more positive way and confront challenges instead of avoiding them,[23] making an athlete performance-approach rather than performance-avoidant motivated. Celebrating also helps create an enhanced sense of inclusiveness and distinctiveness and helps build camaraderie among team members and gives the athlete a chance to thank those who've been supportive. So, spending the time thinking about what they enjoyed, valued and feel privileged for is a helpful way for an athlete to feel happier both mentally and physically and to ward off the post-competition blues.

Giving back

Finally, the nature of training seriously for a big competition, challenge or event can make even the most considerate athlete quite selfish as to be successful they need to be single-minded and driven. They may feel they need to block out others so they can focus, spend time training without disruption and may get more tired, hungry and nervous than usual.

To ensure long-term harmony for the athlete it can be helpful to have them think of intense training periods as blocks of time when they openly focus on their goals, and the times around those training periods as their opportunity to give back to others. The way they do this will be personal to them but many will choose to give their family some focus. These will be the people who most often lose out on the athlete's time if they have been training hard. Giving them full attention for a while will boost family harmony and the athlete's wellbeing. Other opportunities may include helping others in their sport who need some support, teaching others skills or techniques that they have, campaigning for new facilities or opportunities in their sport or running sessions to introduce newer people into their sport.

Summary

Taking a win or learn approach to competition helps us to see each performance as part the sporting journey and means we can always find something of benefit, so no competition is ever judged to be a waste of time. By using a framework to analyse each competition and identifying actions to take, athletes can increase their self-awareness, make better decisions in future and become more aware on the importance of focusing on processes and growth rather than outcomes.

Key terms

- Broaden and Build Theory – the idea that positive emotions don't just make us happier but help us develop psychological growth and improved wellbeing.
- Growth mindset – where an athlete believes they can improve through hard work and effort.
- Negative bias – the way negative information influences our evaluations in a stronger way than positive information.
- Post-competition analysis – detailed analysis driven by the athlete of what went well, didn't go well, should continue, should change and an action plan.
- Post-competition blues – a period of low mood and deflation after a big event.
- Win or learn approach – finding a silver-lining in every competition by proactively seeing what can be improved for next time.

Key messages to share with athletes about learning from competition

- We can learn far more from the competitions that go wrong than the ones we win so the 'win or learn' approach helps us see each competition as part of our journey to be a better athlete.
- Using competitions as learning experiences helps us focus on process goals over outcomes.
- Completing a post-competition analysis gives us a framework to structure learnings; improving self-awareness, decision making and future performances.
- After a big competition or challenge is it not unusual to get post-competition blues. Having a proactive plan with some activities in place for the days after a competition can prevent this.

- Athletes should celebrate their successes to maintain their love of their sport and boost their memories of doing well in their sport. They can also give back to those who have supported them.

Techniques to try to improve learning ability

1 Their post-competition analysis can help feed future performance profiles (Strategy 4).
2 A few days after a big event or competition it is important to work on a post-competition analysis (Strategy 5). For a specific setback outside of competition then setback analysis (Strategy 7) is valuable.
3 The post-competition analysis can be done within a training diary (Strategy 10) to help give long term continuity.
4 During less intense periods athletes can have time and space to do a 'try it Tuesday' (Strategy 11) to try out more innovative ideas.
5 Adversity sessions (Strategy 12) can be designed for an athlete based on what comes out of their post-competition analysis.
6 Attribution retraining (Strategy 14) can help an athlete see more of their mistakes as under their own control.
7 Thought stopping (Strategy 43) is helping to stop focusing on previous mistakes during a competition.
8 The increased self-awareness that comes with a post-competition analysis can help the athlete become more of a self-expert (Strategy 52).
9 The period after competition is a good opportunity for the athlete to earn some payback points (Strategy 60).
10 The process of analysis will help the athlete with their reality checking (Strategy 61).

Notes

1 Groppel, J. L., Loehr, J. E., Melville, D. S., & Quinn, A. M. (1989). *The science of coaching*. Champaign, IL: Leisure Press.

2 Yeager, D. S., & Dweck, C. S. (2012). Mindsets that promote resilience: When students believe that personal characteristics can be developed. *Educational Psychologist, 47*(4), 302–314.

3 Mueller, C. M., & Dweck, C. S. (1998). Praise for intelligence can undermine children's motivation and performance. *Journal of Personality and Social Psychology, 75*(1), 33.

4 Dweck, C. S. (2008). *Mindset: The new psychology of success.* New York: Random House Digital, Inc.

5 Lazarus, R. S. (1999). *Stress and emotion: A new synthesis.* New York: Springer.

6 Pensgaard, A. M., & Duda, J. L. (2003). Sydney 2000: The interplay between emotions, coping, and the performance of Olympic-level athletes. *The Sport Psychologist, 17*, 253–267.

7 Campen, C., & Roberts, D. C. (2001). Coping strategies of runners: Perceived effectiveness and match to pre-competitive anxiety. *Journal of Sport Behavior, 24*, 144–161.

8 Ntoumanis, N., & Biddle, S. J. H. (1998). The relationship of coping and its perceived effectiveness to positive and negative affect in sport. *Personality and Individual Differences, 24*, 773–778.

9 Poczwardowski, A., & Conroy, D. E. (2002). Coping responses to failure and success among elite athletes and performing artists. *Journal of Applied Sport Psychology, 14* (4), 313–329.

10 Poczwardowski, A., & Conroy, D. E. (2002). Coping responses to failure and success among elite athletes and performing artists. *Journal of Applied Sport Psychology, 14* (4), 313–329.

11 Ntoumanis, N., & Biddle, S. J. H. (1998). The relationship of coping and its perceived effectiveness to positive and negative affect in sport. *Personality and Individual Differences, 24*, 773–778.

12 Anshel, M. H., & Kaissidis, A. N. (1997). Coping style and situational appraisals as predictors of coping strategies following stressful events in sport as a function of gender and skill level. *British Journal of Psychology, 88*, 263–276.

13 Lazarus, R. S., & Folkman, S. (1984). *Stress, appraisal and coping.* New York: Springer.

14 Folkman, S. (1991). Coping across the life span: Theoretical issues. In E. M. Cummings, A. L. Greene, & K. H. Karraker (Eds.), *Life-span developmental psychology: Perspectives on stress and coping* (pp. 3–19). Hillsdale, NJ: Erlbaum.

15 Lazarus, R. S. (2000). How emotions influence performance in competitive sports. *The Sport Psychologist, 14*, 229–252.

16 Holt, N. L., & Dunn, J. G. H. (2004a). Grounded theory of the psychosocial competencies and environmental conditions associated with soccer success. *Journal of Applied Sport Psychology, 16*, 199–219.

17 Klint, K. A., & Weiss, M. R. (1986). Dropping in and dropping out: Participation motives of current and former youth athletes. *Canadian Journal of Applied Sport Sciences, 11*, 106–114.

18 Brewer, B. W., Van Raalte, J. L., Linder, D. E., & Van Raalte, N. S. (1991). Peak performance and the perils of retrospective introspection. *Journal of Sport and Exercise Psychology, 8*, 227–238.

19 Ito, T. A., Larsen, J. T., Smith, N. K., & Cacioppo, J. T. (1998). Negative information weighs more heavily on the brain: The negativity bias in evaluative categorizations. *Journal of Personality and Social Psychology, 75*(4), 887.

20 Fredrickson, B. L. (2004). The broaden-and-build theory of positive emotions. *Philosophical Transactions of the Royal Society B: Biological Sciences, 359*(1449), 1367.

21 Fredrickson, B. L. (2004). The broaden-and-build theory of positive emotions. *Philosophical Transactions of the Royal Society B: Biological Sciences, 359*(1449), 1367.

22 Gabana, N. T., Steinfeldt, J., Wong, Y. J., Chung, Y. B., & Svetina, D. (2018). Attitude of gratitude: Exploring the implementation of a gratitude intervention with college athletes. *Journal of Applied Sport Psychology*, 1–12.

23 Chen, L. H., & Wu, C. (2016). When does dispositional gratitude help athletes move away from experiential avoidance? The moderating role of perceived autonomy support from coaches. *Journal of Applied Sport Psychology, 28*(3), 338–349.

Coping with setbacks and injury

We can't always control the situation – but we can control our response to it.

We can set exciting and realistic goals, have put in place the mental and physical training and processes to achieve them, followed them consistently, created routines and strategies to get ourselves to the starting whistle in our absolute best form. But, even with brilliant planning and our best intentions, life can get in the way and sometimes stuff happens that simply disrupts our ability to perform in the way we want to.

Setbacks

Setbacks for athletes are inevitable. Sometimes they may be visible to everyone (such as a crash in a bike race) or very public (being dropped from a team), other times they are handled behind the scenes (such as family or medical issues). The setback can feel catastrophic and the athlete struggles to see a way past it, yet they are rarely as serious as feared and can often be a valuable part of the process of growing and improving as an athlete.

Helping an athlete manage their mindset to cope with these disruptions is vital. As we learnt in Chapter 1, if we help athletes going into competitions use mastery-orientated thinking then, as they go through competition, they will be able to think more about the processes they are following and engaging with rather than being driven by outcomes. This becomes really helpful when they come up against a setback as the outcome further out of reach becomes less of an issue. Some process goals they had set may become harder to follow with a setback (such as an injury or less time to train) but there will still be some which the athlete can stick to (such as good quality diet or imagery practice) so they can still have a focus on improvement.

As well as the process goals, an athlete with a positive mindset can cope better with disruptions or setbacks when they expect them. If they expect things to occasionally knock them off-course they are much easier to deal with. Often it is the unanticipated nature of something which causes the indignation or feeling of unfairness which comes with a setback. So, when an athlete writes realistic goals with potential setbacks in mind it makes it easier to cope if a setback does come. A training plan allowing for the occasional missed session, perhaps split into must do and nice to do sessions gives athletes a way to maintain some training without feeling too much under pressure in difficult periods. This means when a disruption or setback arises, be it illness, or a big work project or a holiday, the athlete has a little wiggle room and doesn't feel like they have failed if they have to tweak their plans.

An injury will almost always be a setback but because it is so common and has been studied extensively it is a setback we can approach very specifically. Where an injury is so extensive that it will be career ending time may need to be spent working with a psychologist to help the athlete come to terms with the dramatic change in lifestyle and life focus they will have to deal with.

Injury

To create an ideal athlete the correct muscle strength, skeletal structure, tendon elasticity, heart and lung size and precisely the right interaction between anatomical, biochemical and physiological systems are needed. The chance of this occurring is lower than 1 in 20 million.[1] Adding in environmental elements such as overtraining, equipment interaction and poor playing conditions and psychological factors such as personality traits, stressors and coping resources, means it is highly likely that an athlete will, at some point, become injured.

Getting injured is really tough for athletes as injuries don't just cause them pain and stop them physically training but they can also initiate an array of negative emotions such as devastation, feeling cheated, restlessness and isolation[2] and can negatively impact the long-term psychological wellbeing and life satisfaction of the athlete.[3] On top of all this, some athletes will develop a pervading and debilitating fear of re-injury.[4] Elite athletes may fear the potential financial penalty too as they only have a limited amount of time to make a money from their sport.[5] In the worst cases athletes will drop out of their sport to prevent further injuries.[6]

An area where many athletes will struggle is around their mental health. Many amateur athletes use sport as a coping mechanism for stress as it provides a physical release of any pent-up frustration, some head space to calm down and some thinking space to put everything into perspective. It has been found to be the equivalent of medication or psychological therapies as an effective tool to reduce depressive symptoms in those diagnosed with depression.[7] Therefore, when an athlete is injured and not able to be active they don't just lose one of their favourite things to do but also lose this valuable coping mechanism that they have come to depend upon.

How an athlete responds to their injury can be impacted by up to 55 different factors[8] including their belief system, attitudes towards change, coping strategies, self-identity and personality traits. Those likely to struggle include athletes with a weak and narrow social support network,[9] who are ego- rather than task-orientated,[10] who have low levels of optimism, hardiness and self-esteem[11] and are more introverted.[12]

For athletes who do become injured, it has been shown that those who use the situation to learn about their injury and its cause will be better able to understand where weaknesses may be in their own bodies so they can build up strength for the future to prevent further injuries. Additionally, if an athlete has not been living a balanced lifestyle before an injury or has placed their sporting life above all other elements to the detriment of their overall wellbeing, stress-related growth can actually be a positive outcome from the situation, especially if they use it re-ignite their passion and give them higher motivation to compete again in future.[13] This means that while an injury is never welcomed, if it is approached with the right mindset, it doesn't have to be devastating. Researchers have found that those who are able to stay confident and keep their anxiety low increased their likelihood of a speedy and successful recovery from injury.[14]

There are a number of strategies to help athletes improve their rehabilitation behaviour and gain a positive rather than a negative consequence of injury[15] and these can be incorporated into five steps for athletes to follow when dealing with an injury. Proactively following these steps should help them cope better with the challenges they will face to get back to good health.

Anger

Being upset over an injury is perfectly ok. It is not irrational or weak. It does not make the athlete fragile. They will be grieving for what they think they will be missing; their training, the exercise, their social life and any competitions. Giving the athlete a few days to do this will get these emotions to the surface and out of their system. Then they will be in a better place to get focused on getting healthy again.

Part of the anger may well be the uncertainty the athlete is feeling. Not knowing what to expect but knowing that things will change. Change is hard for any of us to deal with as humans, and when we depend on our sport to keep us mentally, physically and socially healthy it is disconcerting to know things will be different for a while. When we don't know how different because we don't have a specific diagnosis or a timeline for recovery an athlete may feel frustrated as well as angry. So, the next step is for them to get the information they need to put some concrete plans in place.

Information gathering

Athletes can only make their decisions based on the information they have. But they can make better decisions and have more options when they have more information to pick from. This process of finding out more about an injury is known as instrumental coping and has been found to improve adherence to rehabilitation and give more positive long-term consequences.[16]

As well as learning about their injury, spending some time to reflect on their injury and the circumstances surrounding it can help them understand what may have caused it. Some will be simple (such as an impact injury caused in a crash or fall), other causes, particularly overuse injuries, will be harder to identify. Once the athlete is better informed then they can focus on rehabbing from it in the immediate instance and learn what additional work they should be doing long term to strengthen any weak areas to reduce the risk of the injury happening again.

Finding experts to help

The third step (though this can be completed alongside and as part of information gathering) is for the athlete to identify and approach experts to help them. Depending on the injury they may consider a physio, osteopath, sports massage therapist, specialist sports doctor or GP but it needs to be someone they trust and respect so they are more likely to follow their advice. They also need an expert who is clear and concise with what is required (both in time spent on rehabilitation exercises and how to do them properly) as studies have found the greater the athlete's self-efficacy in their ability to perform the rehabilitation exercises, the stronger their beliefs were in the treatment efficacy, the greater their compliance and the more positive they were about long-term recovery.[17] So, having experts who can clearly promote the benefits of rehabilitation to athletes should mean the athlete recovers more successfully.

Goal-set recovery

The athletes who recover best are those who take their recovery as seriously as they do their training. Just as athletes create specific goals and training plans for their sport they should do the same for coming back from injury so step four is to goal set for injury. A goal-setting intervention in injured athletes found that those using goals adhered better to their rehab programme[18] and a review of 11 studies (covering 983 injured athletes) found those who focused on positive psychological responses, such as having goals for their rehabilitation from injury, had a higher return to sport rate, returned to their sport quicker than athletes who didn't and had the highest chance of returning to pre-injury participation levels.[19] The process helps the athlete feel positive that they are doing something productive and when they feel down they can clearly see the right elements are in place to get them back to full health and fitness. Prompting and then supporting with this goal setting is where coaches, mentors and sport psychologists can be really beneficial in the recovery process. Importantly though the goals have to be driven by the athletes themselves as those who believe they have personal control over their health outcomes will adhere more to a medical regime[20] and those who consider recovery rate to be controllable have a greater adherence to rehabilitation.[21]

The process goals that have been set will be really important here. They may involve seeing a physio every week until recovered, completing strengthening exercises for 30 minutes each day or spending some time while off sport coaching others to maintain knowledge and social engagement. These process goals help the athlete stick to the elements of their recovery like their physio exercises (the percentage of those who do not do exercises set by their physio has been estimated to be as high as 70%)[22] and ticking them off regularly helps them feel more positive as they get the dopamine buzz which comes from hitting small individual goals (the progress principle).

Fill the injury gap

When athletes are unable to train or compete through injury they will have more time to spare. While physio or rehabilitation exercises will take up some time it is likely there will still be some time gaps, and there will definitely be a gap mentally where they have less of the sport they love to fill their mind. Three routes can be considered to help fill the injury gap: expanding the athlete's self-identity, helping them to stay social and learning mental skills which will benefit them once they get back to sport.

The time without training or practice sessions can be seen as an opportunity for the athlete to expand their self-identity so they have more strings to their bow. If they are able to acknowledge and 'feel' all their different self-identities it is easier to switch when the sports part of their life is less accessible for a while. Identities to discuss with an athlete may be around family (son or daughter, mother or father, brother or sister), work (professional, mentor, boss, co-worker, expert), social life (friend, volunteer) or another hobby. This raised awareness of their other identities can remove a little bit of the sting when they are unable to train or compete for a while.

Despite focusing on building other self-identities, they will still feel like an athlete and much of their social engagement is likely to be within their sport, especially if they have been competing for a while. Social interaction is really important when injured as it can act as a bit of a buffer for the emotional trauma of injury. If an athlete loves their sport often some of their passion for it is driven by the friends they have made in it. Studies have found the more social support an athlete has, the lower the initial depressive symptoms[23] and that regular monitoring of this makes a big difference to how an athlete responds.[24] In fact, a study identifying the coping strategies of injured athletes found 81% of them valued the support of others during their rehab process.[25] As staying involved with their club and remaining engaged socially helps athletes recover quicker they may benefit from teaching or mentoring novice athletes within the club. This will give the social element they crave but also help them to maintain their skills and keep them front of mind as they really embed them by teaching them.

When an athlete is physically unable to practice or train they can use their spare time to learn new skills or techniques which will help their sports performance in the long term. Trying new sports like swimming, joining a yoga or pilates course or booking in some strength and conditioning sessions could be really valuable. They can also spend the time practising the mental skills that can get forgotten when they are focused on their physical training. Skills such as imagery, breathing techniques and self-talk can all help build an athlete's confidence and give them an advantage when they get back to competition. Learning these psychological skills can help athletes deal with what initially seems like a negative situation, see it in a more positive light and can help the athlete recover mentally and emotionally. The athlete will then become a more focused, flexible, and resilient athlete and competent in skills that will help them when back to full fitness and speed up the recovery process.[26]

A particular benefit of spending the time off training learning mental skills is that there often comes with recovery from injury a fear of reinjury.[27] Many of the suggested mental skills have been found to reduce the likelihood of injury which should offer the athlete some reassurance. Mental skills interventions which have been found to be effective in reducing injuries include attentional control, imagery, team building and developing better ways to communicate.[28] Studies specifically looking at mental skills development found that using associative attentional strategies reduced overuse injuries in marathon runners[29] and imagery usage reduced injuries by 52% in swimmers and 33% in football players.[30] Incorporating some of these mental skills into the schedule of injured athletes will be beneficial for their future performances and help to reduce their risk of, and fear of, reinjury.

Assessing pain

No coach or supporter wants to see an athlete in pain, yet they will want to see them safely progress, and sometimes that requires discomfort. One of the most difficult things for athletes (especially those returning from injury) to do is assess whether they are feeling discomfort due to the efforts they are putting in or pain due to the previous or a new injury. Until we purposefully think about this subject in our heads we will usually see everything as pain (which is why pain interpretation – Strategy 39 – can be helpful) yet when more educated about it we can start to become more highly attuned for anything not feeling exactly as it should be.

Using biofeedback (Strategy 15) and a training diary (Strategy 10) can be a helpful route for athletes to learn much more about how their body feels before, during and after training. What feels normal for them and what is unusual and should be investigated? Training diaries (if used well) are particularly helpful for spotting patterns and seeing what is causing discomfort (but quickly subsides and never turns into an injury) and what may actually be painful and potentially harmful. Over time this means we should stop reading so much into every twinge and niggle within our body and read our bodies much better so we know when it is safe to push harder and reinterpret the pain as information and when to stop and rest.

Technological impact on the injured

Where those hindered by setback or injury may really start to struggle is where they are very social or using lots of technology in their sport. While they know rationally that training while ill or injured could be harmful to them and their long-term aspirations it can be frustrating when they see others training, over social media, fitness trackers or in their club. They may find themselves comparing what they are doing (or not doing if completely side-lined with injury) and comparing. They may know nothing of others' circumstances or training history but will compare and become jealous or ignore medical guidelines about rest and recovery. If they realise they are in danger of burnout by training seriously on top of work or family commitments and see quotes telling us we must toughen up or read stories of people who are 'doing it all' it can be difficult for the athlete to know if they are being lazy or sensible. Athletes with pessimistic tendencies may find themselves berating themselves for being lazy – even when their mind and body needs the rest so a technology strategy can be helpful to help the athlete use it for good, not harm.

Summary

Injury and setbacks are the bane of every athlete's life. At the track, in sports halls and beside every pitch and court setbacks and injury are an all too common conversation. They see dreams dampened and fitness fall. Learning to read their own bodies and developing a true understanding of whether they are in genuine pain or expected discomfort is an important part of injury prevention. If the injury does hit them though, following the five stages of recovery, bringing in mental skills education and developing a technology strategy ensures that athletes can get back up and competing without too much wasted time or miserable moments.

Key terms

- Coping strategies – techniques, tactics and strategies used by athletes to help them deal with difficult situations.
- Mastery-orientated thinking – having a focus on learning and improving skills.
- Personality traits – our behavioural or emotional characteristics.
- Progress principle – breaking down tasks into small chunks so we feel pleasure every time we achieve one of them.
- Self-identity – the way we think of ourselves. We can have many self-identities.
- Stress-related growth – where someone develops as a response to stressors they have encountered and overcome.

Key messages for athletes facing a setback or injury

- Even with brilliant planning and great intentions we can suffer from setbacks and injuries. They can often feel catastrophic but they are rarely as serious as we initially fear and can often be a valuable part of the process of growing and improving as an athlete.
- Using mastery-orientated thinking will help us cope better with a setback as can expecting, preparing and planning for setbacks.
- A very specific and well-researched type of setback is an injury. It is highly likely that we will, at some point, become injured. Injuries cause pain, stop us training and competing, prompt an array of negative emotions, negatively impact our long-term psychological wellbeing and life satisfaction and can prompt a fear of reinjury.
- There are a large number of factors that will impact how we respond to an injury and these include our belief system, if we have a threat or challenge mindset, our attitude towards change, the coping strategies we use, our self-identity, personality traits and support network.
- There are five steps we can take to help us approach our injury to speed up recovery and secure stress-related growth; anger, information gathering, finding experts, goal setting and filling the space.
- While recovering we can consider how we use technology and social media so it provides benefit and not additional stress or pressure and practice reading our bodies more so we can distinguish between pain and discomfort.

Strategies for setbacks or injury

1 If an athlete is facing a setback then completing a setback analysis (Strategy 7) can help them learn from the issue they are facing.

2 It is really helpful for an athlete to do a technology strategy (Strategy 63) when they get injured so they understand if they are likely to feel pressure online.

3 A key part of the recovery process is goal setting (Strategy 2) to keep an athlete motivated.

4 Athletes can use the time out from their sport to learn some key mental skills such as imagery (Strategy 25), breathing techniques (Strategies 18–20) and self-talk (Strategies 42–46).

5 If the athlete is struggling then spending some time learning mindfulness (Strategy 51) and thought labelling (Strategy 56) can help them understand themselves better.

6 Using biofeedback (Strategy 15) means over time the athlete learns to read their own body better.

7 For those situations where the athlete is in discomfort they can learn to use pain interpretation (Strategy 39).

8 Athletes could use the time away from sport to become more of a self-expert (Strategy 52) in their training and performance preferences, strengths and weaknesses.

9 Injuries are more likely when we are stressed so running a stressor identification (Strategy 54) will help filter out stressors the athlete can control.

10 For the athlete to become less reliant on their sport to feel like themselves it can be helpful for them to use self-identity mapping (Strategy 53).

11 Knowing your why (Strategy 49) can be helpful to keep an athlete motivated while out injured or confronting their setback.

Notes

1 Puthucheary, Z., Skipworth, J. R. A., Rawal, J., Loosemore, M., Someren, K. V., & Montgomery, H. E. (2011). Genetic influences in sport and physical performance. *Sports Medicine, 41*(10), 845–860.

2 Evans, L., Hardy, L., Mitchell, I., & Rees, T. (2008). The development of a measure of psychological responses to injury. *Journal of Sport Rehabilitation, 17*(1), 21–38.

3   Kleiber, D. A., & Brock, S. C. (1992). The effect of career-ending injuries on the subsequent well being of elite college athletes. *Sociology of Sports Journal, 9*, 70–75.

4   Christakou, A., Zervas, Y., Stavrou, N. A., & Psychountaki, M. (2011). Development and validation of the Causes of Re-Injury Worry Questionnaire. *Psychological Health Medicine, 16*(1), 94–114.

5   Connor, J. (2009). The athlete as widget: How exploitation explains elite sport. *Sport in Society, 12*(10), 1369–1378.

6   Webborn, N. (2012). Lifetime injury prevention: The sport profile model. *British Journal of Sports Medicine, 46*(3), 193–198.

7   Blumenthal, J. A., Smith, P. J., & Hoffman, B. M. (2012). Is exercise a viable treatment for depression? *ACSM's Health & Fitness Journal, 16*(4), 14.

8   Wiese-Bjornstal, D. M., Smith, A. M., Shaffer, S. M., & Morrey, M. A. (1998). An integrated model of the response to sport injury: Psychological and sociological dynamics. *Journal of Applied Sport Psychology, 10*(1), 46–69.

9   Andersen, M. B., & Williams, J. M. (1988). A model of stress and athletic injury: Prediction and prevention. *Journal of Sport & Exercise Psychology, 10*, 294–306.

10 Duda, J. L., Smart, A. E., & Tappe, M. K. (1989). Predictors of adherence in the rehabilitation of athletic injuries: An application of personal investment theory. *Journal of Sport and Exercise Psychology, 11*, 367–381.

11 Ford, I. W., Eklund, R. C., & Gordon, S. (2000). An examination of psychosocial variables moderating the relationship between life stress and injury time-loss among athletes of a high standard. *Journal of Sports Sciences, 18*, 301–312.

12 Newth, S., & DeLongis, A. (2004). Individual differences, mood, and coping with chronic pain in rheumatoid arthritis: A daily process analysis. *Psychology & Health, 19*(3), 283–305.

13 Podlog, L., & Eklund, R. C. (2007). The psychosocial aspects of a return to sport following serious injury: A review of the literature from a self-determination perspective. *Psychology of Sport and Exercise, 8*, 535–566.

14 Forsdyke, D., Smith, A., Jones, M., and Gledhill, A. (2016). Psychosocial factors associated with outcomes of sports injury rehabilitation in competitive athletes: A mixed studies systematic review. *British Journal of Sports Medicine, 50*, 537–544.

15 Levy, A. R., Polman, R. C. J., Clough, P. J., & McNaughton, L. (2006). Adherence to sport injury rehabilitation programmes: A conceptual review. *Research in Sports Medicine 14*(2), 149–163.

16 Udry, E. (1997). Coping and social support among injured athletes following surgery. *Journal of Sport & Exercise Psychology, 19*, 71–90.

17 Taylor, A. H., & May, S. (1996). Threat and coping appraisal as determinants of compliance to sports injury rehabilitation: An application of protection motivation theory. *Journal of Sports Sciences, 14*, 471–482.

18 Evans, L., & Hardy, L. (2002). Injury rehabilitation: A goal-setting intervention study. *Research Quarterly for Exercise and Sport, 73*(3), 310–319.

19 Ardern, C. L., Taylor, N. F., Feller, J. A., & Webster, K. E. (2013). A systematic review of the psychological factors associated with returning to sport following injury. *British Journal of Sports Medicine, 47*(17), 1120–1126.

20 Stanton, A. L. (1987). Determinants of adherence to medical regimens by hypertensive patients. *Journal of Behavioural Medicine, 10*, 377–395.

21 Laubach, W. J., Brewer, B. W., van Raalte, J. L., & Petitpas, A. J. (1996). Attributions for recovery and adherence to sport injury rehabilitation. *Australian Journal of Science and Medicine in Sport, 28*(1), 30–34.

22 Sluijs, E. M., Kok, G. J., & van der Zee, J. (1993). Correlates of exercise compliance in physical therapy. *Physical Therapy, 73*(11), 771–782.

23 Manuel, J. C., Shilt, J. S., Curl, W. W., Smith, J, A., Durant, R. H., Lester, L., & Sinal, S. H., (2002). Coping with sports injuries: An examination of the adolescent athletes. *Journal of Adolescent Health, 31*(5), 391–393.

24 Hartwig, T. B., Naughton, G., & Searl, J. (2009). Load, stress, and recovery in adolescent rugby union players during a competitive season. *Journal of Sports Sciences, 27*(10), 1087–1096.

25 Gould, D., Bridges, D., Udry, E., & Beck, L. (1997). Coping with season-ending injuries. *The Sport sychologist, 11*(4), 379–399.

26 Bloom, G. A., Horton, A. S., McCrory, P., & Johnston, K. M. (2004). Sport psychology and concussion: New impacts to explore. *British Journal of Sports Medicine, 38*(5), 519–522.

27 Morrey, M. A., Stuart, M. J., Smith, A. M., & Wiese-Bjornstal, D. M. (1999). A longitudinal examination of athletes' emotional and cognitive responses to anterior cruciate ligament injury. *Clinical Journal of Sport Medicine: Official Journal of the Canadian Academy of Sport Medicine, 9*(2), 63–69.

28 May, J. R., & Brown, L. (1989). Delivery of psychological service to the U.S. Alpine ski team prior to and during the olympics in calgary. *The Sport Psychologist, 3*, 320–329.

29 Schomer, H. H. (1990). A cognitive strategy training program for marathon runners: Ten case studies. *South African Journal of Research in Sport, Physical Education and Recreation, 13*, 47–78.

30 Davis, J. O. (1991). Sport injuries and stress management. An opportunity for research. *The Sport Psychologist, 5*, 175–182.

10

Strategies to set and achieve goals

Strategy 1 – control mapping

Competition outcomes are not controllable. Even the best athletes in the world can have a bad day, or an injury, or have to battle conditions they had no idea to expect. Worrying about these uncontrollable elements simply wastes an athlete's energy, energy they could be putting into something which they can control and give them much more value for effort in their sport.

Control mapping helps athletes to identify all the areas that impact their performance when they compete and helps them understand which areas they can and can't influence so they can focus on just the areas which will make a difference. With this approach they take responsibility for the things they can control and influence and stop wasting effort and attention on elements they can't.

Control mapping can be helpful when athletes are approaching competition, are facing a setback or before they start working on their goals for the season. It helps them focus process goals on areas which will have the most impact and where they can make the most difference so they take more ownership, move away from worrying about things they can't control to instead develop task-focused actions which they can influence and impact.

How to do it

An effective way for an athlete to complete a control mapping exercise is to do it alongside them. This means you can give them some prompts and ensure they have thought about every relevant element. No worksheet is needed. Just a sheet of paper and perhaps a schedule of their usual competition day. Draw two vertical lines down the paper to split it into three even sections and title each section:

1. Can control
2. Can influence (through others or by their own behaviours)
3. Can't control.

The areas to prompt them about are:

- Personal stressors – the individual worries the athlete has. This can be considered through 'what if' planning (Strategy 29).
- Performance environment – surface, venue facilities, equipment, weather, food and drink available.
- Logistics – travel, support, costs, warm up.
- Opposition – the attitude, effort levels and behaviours of others (parents, supports, spectators, coaches, competitors, officials or referees) and the goal the athlete has sent themselves.
- Self – attitude, skills, effort levels, thoughts, feelings and behaviours.
- Results.

Common uncontrollables will be the crowd, the venue, the opposition, the referee, the court/pitch/competition surface, whether friends or family have come along and watch and the result.

Common controllables will be elements like tactics, skills, abilities, movement, warm up, behaviours to themselves and others.

Completing control mapping at least a few weeks before a competition gives athletes a chance to work on some of the elements they can influence so they feel as prepared as possible by the time they get to their competition. Once an athlete has mapped this out they can invest their time and efforts extensively on what they can control and a little on what they can influence.

This activity is suitable for younger athletes too and it is valuable to help them focus on the things which are most important. With younger athletes though they will sometimes need to rely upon others (parents or coaches) for travel, logistics and information so these may become areas they can influence but not yet control.

Strategy 2 – goal setting

Study after study shows that setting clear, specific, realistic and timely goals which come completely within an athlete's control can increase their motivation, commitment, concentration and confidence, reduce negative anxiety and improve their performance. Goal setting helps athletes to maintain their motivations, to focus on processes over outcome, reduce the need for comparisons with other athletes and will give athletes confidence that they have prepared as best they can. It is about turning an athlete's intentions into actions and is a key foundation to set the tone, direction and structure for everything else the athlete works on. At its simplest it is the athlete deciding on what they want to achieve and working backwards to create a plan to make it happen so their motivation is boosted by giving direct attention and energy into achieving their overall goal.[1]

Goal setting helps the athlete consider every element required for them to succeed. This will often include planning their physical training, practising mental strategies, understanding the logistics, strength and conditioning and nutrition. It allows the athlete to see clearly the skills, improvements and achievement required to succeed and is designed to give an athlete continual confidence boosts. For it to work well there are well-researched structures to follow and lots of frameworks to put in place to maximise the chances of success.

Key is being strict about having only one outcome goal. Having multiple goals can risk an athlete achieving none of them as their focus becomes split and sometimes achieving both goals is just not possible. One which regularly comes up is that the athlete wants to achieve a new personal best and to enjoy their sport more. They may see enjoyment from being able to spend time with their friends at training and joking about during sessions. This is not conducive to consistent improvement and achieving better performances. Both are valid goals but can rarely be achieved at the same time. Once the outcome goal is chosen the focus moves onto performance elements[2] and then specific action goals.[3]

Goal setting can be used really effectively for injured athletes – it can be a key tool in their recovery and it has been found that those using it adhere to their rehabilitation better[4] and return to their sport quicker than athletes who don't.[5] It can help them feel they are doing something productive to get back to health and fitness and will help them identify useful actions or tasks to replace the time they would usually be training. The only difference will be that an injured athlete's outcome goal will focus on recovery instead of performance. It could also make sense for an athlete to complete their recovery goal setting with their physio to ensure their rehab is planned in an effective way and any timings or deadlines match the timeline for recovery that the physio has in their head.

How to do it

1   The first step for the athlete is setting their outcome goal.
    An outcome goal needs to be:

    • Stretching – enough to make them really focus and work hard.
    • Realistic – so they don't feel out of their depth and that it is not worth trying.
    • Exciting – something they really want to achieve and feel is worth the investment.
    • Controllable – so achievable despite others.
    • Positive – because we are more likely to stick to goals if they are things we can proactively do rather than try to avoid.

Outcome goals don't always need to be a score, a result, a ranking or a personal best. There are a number of other, often more intrinsic goals which can inspire athletes such as environment goals (to compete in new places), fulfilment goals (using their sport as a way of helping others) and development goals (focusing on long term skill mastery). Once this outcome goal is established everything else can flow.

2   Performance goals come next. Performance goals provide the staging posts so the athlete can see whether they are on track towards their outcome goal. These are often specific times, distances, skills or scores the athlete will need to be hitting if they are to achieve their outcome goal and will be a mixture of short- and medium-term elements which helps the athlete stay motivated. Key here is keeping the goals very specific and measurable so the athlete is unable to wriggle out of them and make excuses. And again these goals need to be positive, setting out what the athlete needs to accomplish rather than what should be avoided.

3   Process goals give us the building blocks of the pyramid. Process goals sit directly below performance goals and are the behaviours, actions, strategies and tactics that an athlete will need in place if they are to achieve each performance. These are all actions the athlete should be able to control (with the right support and work ethic) and can be incorporated into their training and preparation. Following them should facilitate regular progression and allow momentum to build up as they are gradually ticked off.

4   Once the athlete has their goals they can maximise their effectiveness by making sure they fit the SMARTER guidelines:

- Specific – so they set a very purposeful direction and target.
- Meaningful – so when training gets tough or they hit a slump their 'why' (Strategy 49) will get them focused.

- Accountable – having other people know their goals will help them stay on track.
- Recorded – goals should be written down and visible so they stay front of mind.
- Timed – setting a deadline focuses the mind and prevents drifting.
- Evaluate – keeping track of goals gives the athlete a boost if they are doing well but also gives an opportunity to make changes if a setback arises.
- Realistic – goals only work if they are not too much of a stretch so time spent checking the processes suggested can actually fit into the time an athlete has available will prevent upset or despondency later on.

No adaptation of this strategy is required for younger athletes but they may need a lot more guidance to write their goals – specifically their outcome and performance goals as they may have become used to coaches or teachers telling them what they are aiming for and are unused to being able to decide this independently. To keep them focused on their goals throughout the season it can be helpful to help them celebrate their 'mini-successes' so they can see how they are moving towards their larger performance and outcome goals.

Strategy 3 – modelling

Seeing others try hard and succeed can motivate us and build our confidence.[6] As an athlete, this vicarious confidence comes when we notice people similar to ourselves succeeding so we believe if we apply the same framework we could achieve similar success. A great example of this is Roger Bannister breaking the four-minute mile. For years it had been stated that this was not possible and yet as soon as Bannister showed it was possible others quickly followed. In the year following his record more than 12 other runners managed to break the same 'impossible' barrier.[7] We all have our own barriers but if we can find someone who has already achieved what we would like to do and model their behaviour it can help us overcome our barriers, enhance our self-confidence and be more persistent.[8]

How to do it

Have a conversation with your athlete about who in their sport they admire and what they admire about them. Try to get into characteristics, mindsets and strategies rather than elements based on talent or success. Ways to help them include:

- If the person the athlete chooses to model is well known then they can study them from afar by reading interviews or autobiographies or watching YouTube clips or post competition reflections. Pull out what within their behaviours and attitudes they admire and would like to emulate.
- If the athlete is likely to get disillusioned by someone who is way out of their league, then instead suggest they identify someone who is quite like them. The athlete picked needs to be fairly like them but doing a little better. Ask the athlete to identify what it is they admire about that person. Encourage comments around their work ethic or tenacity rather than success or talent.
- If the athlete struggles to find someone they really admire in their own sport they can look to other sports. Borrowing ideas and inspiration from other sports can be really enlightening.

Once the athlete has picked the person they wish to model ask them to write down five elements they could learn from them. Pick one as a goal for the next few weeks and ask the athlete to focus on trying to develop that skill, attitude or behaviour and build it into their training and competition processes and strategies. Once that has been incorporated, pick another element. During the process, ask the athlete to consider the flaws of their role model too. This will help the athlete realise when they make mistakes that everyone else, even those we aspire to be like, does too.

Strategy 4 – performance profiling

Performance profiling helps an athlete to really understand the barriers and obstacles that stand between them and their goals.[9] It helps take their goal and turn it into an actionable, focused plan which is entirely tailored to them and their own understanding of themselves as an athlete. It is a really good way to flesh out overall goals for a year or season and helps the athlete break it down very specifically into the actions they can take which will make the biggest difference to their performance.

It is helpful to complete this strategy alongside the athlete's goal setting as it can really strengthen each process, bring the goal to life and show how much work will be required. The process is valuable for understanding the reality of what they want and whether they realistically have the time, energy or discipline to bridge those gaps. As they head towards their goal they have something to reflect against and when they get to competition day it gives athletes confidence they have completed the right training.

It is important that a sport psychologist or coach doesn't create this for an athlete. We can prompt or offer ideas, but this profile is most effective when it has been written directly by the athlete and they feel ownership of it. However, completing this process together is helpful as it ensures the coach and athlete are communicating effectively and are on the same page[10] and any discrepancies offer an easy conversation starter as to the areas you each believe are critical to success.

How to do it

There are various ways to create and complete a performance profile and different sport psychologists have their own versions. To create one which can be used alongside goal setting (Strategy 2) the athlete should be considering a goal which is about four to six months away. This means there is enough time to work on it but it is not too far away to be daunting or demoralising.

1   With the goal agreed ask the athlete about the characteristics of a person that has already achieved that goal. Think about the characteristics in terms of:

  • Lifestyle and support
  • Technical and tactical skills

- Physical preparation and fitness
- Logistical planning
- Psychological behaviours and tactics.

Prompt them to come up with at least three for each area giving you 15 characteristics.

2   With these characteristics in place ask them to rate the importance (I) of each characteristic on a scale of zero (not at all important) to 10 (extremely important). This helps them prioritise what will make the most difference to them achieving their goal.

3   Ask them to look at where they are right now (R) for that characteristic, again out of ten.

4   Work out their discrepancy score; I x (10 − R). For example, if a tennis player felt that someone who had achieved their goal had a strong second serve and rated this 7 in importance (I) and that currently their second serve was weak enough to be considered a 4 (R) we would get a score of 7 x (10−4) = 42. This does not tell us anything in itself but balanced against the other 14 scores will tell us if working on a strong second serve will make a big difference to the tennis player's performance success.

5   The scores can be placed in a bar chart to help the athlete clearly see the areas which will have the biggest impact on their improvement. The higher the score the more emphasis they should place on developing that characteristic as this is where the biggest difference to their performance can come from.

6   High scoring areas can be immediately addressed by developing them into specific process goals and building the processes into activities that can go into their training plan.

If the discrepancy scores are high across the board it may be the goal is too much of a stretch right now and needs to be considered a longer-term one. Then the athlete needs to go back to the drawing board with finding a new outcome goal which is still exciting and stretching but more achievable in the near future.

Asking the athlete to re-rate themselves every couple of months will help them see which areas they are improving in and means they can refocus their efforts on the areas that now have the biggest discrepancies.

To make this strategy engaging for younger athletes we can ask them to draw themselves in the middle of the paper. Around their head they list the psychological behaviours and the logistical planning that needs to be taken into account. Around their arms they write the lifestyle and support elements, by their legs the physical preparation and fitness and at their feet the technical and tactical skills. If they struggle to come up with these they will sometimes respond well to being asked to think about a popular player in their sport who has achieved what they want to achieve or someone in their club that they look up to.

Strategy 5 – post-competition analysis

No athlete wins every competition. Even world champions and Olympic gold medallists have off days when it just doesn't happen for them. Instead of a poor competition eating away at an athlete's confidence and filling their heads with negative thoughts, some well-structured post-race analysis can turn a failed competition into a unique opportunity to learn, improve and become a better athlete. Making this a formal learning process can help athletes see there has been a benefit of taking part, and that there are proactive things they can do differently next time, even if it feels raw and emotional at the time.

Research has found the analysis process can constitute an effective coping mechanism which can improve an athlete's future performances.[11] It also helps the athlete develop a more tactical understanding of the way they compete and the way they cope (or don't cope) under pressure. It pushes them into considering their strengths and limitations and makes these more visible. Finally, it will help them to learn which competition tactics and strategies work best for them.

Using both an immediate appraisal of the events but also adding in a reflective appraisal gives a chance for full analysis. This means ideally the analysis is started the evening after the competition but then completed a few days later when it will be considerably less impacted by emotion.[12]

How to do it

We can follow the 'Effective, Ineffective, Continue, Change and Action (EICCA)' process to ensure that following any competition, whether it has gone well or not, there will be practical, logistical, mental and strategic lessons the athlete can take to improve and become more self-aware. We ask them to focus on effective and ineffective rather than good and bad as this helps the athlete focus on only their own actions, thoughts and behaviours rather than things outside of their control or influence.

We ask the athlete to draw a big cross on a sheet of paper so they have four boxes:

1   In the top left the athlete writes all the things which went well and worked **effectively** for them in both competition and the build-up.
2   The top right is for all the actions and behaviours which were **ineffective** and didn't go to plan.
3   Ideally we are looking to see the same number of points in both the effective box and ineffective box – this helps reduce some of the negative bias we may have after a particularly poor competition.
4   If the athletes struggle they can be prompted across the following areas: physical fitness and conditioning, skills used, tactical nous, preparation, logistical, equipment, nutrition, mental approach and focus, strategy used.
5   The bottom left hand box is for the things the athlete will **continue** doing in the future.
6   The bottom right is for those elements they will **change** in future. If they struggle with this some prompt questions to ask may be what they learnt from the situation or if it did happen again in competition how would they like to respond.
7   These two bottom boxes become the athlete's **action** plan which they can incorporate into their training, logistics, race strategy planning and mental skills development. This minimises the chances of similar things going wrong again and helps the athlete feel more positive and proactive. If they feel comfortable doing so an athlete should share their analysis with

their coach, mentor or psychologist so the actions can be incorporated into their training plan.

It can be helpful for the athlete to keep all the EICCA sheets they create as over time they can looking back over them to gather useful information of what is regularly being ineffective and whether longer-term more significant changes may need to be made.

Strategy 6 – SCRIPT

Self-sabotage was something we learnt all about in Chapter 6. It allows athletes to give a valid sounding excuse for any failings made on small elements of their sport so they have a full justification for any large failings, thus protecting their ego and self-identity. SCRIPT is a strategy to help them identify when they may be employing self-sabotage methods and to work on strategies to overcome them.

The process is to help an athlete think about the excuses they make most often, look at each excuse, help them analyse if it is rational or irrational and, if irrational, prompt them to counter it with a plan for the next time they find themselves making the same excuse. This is a worthwhile exercise to follow every few months to help keep athletes focused and on track. It is also very helpful to do if you spot specific self-sabotaging behaviours in athletes. Some common ones are turning up to training late or not at all, not being in the right shape for training or having some kind of drama when they get to competition.

How to do it

The process for the athlete to follow has the acronym, SCRIPT: **spot** the behaviour, **capture** the trigger point, investigate your **reason** for doing it, identify the goal you actually want to achieve, **prepare** a plan for when you hit the trigger, **tackle** the behaviour.

1   The first step is **spotting** the behaviour. What does the athlete do in training, competition and their outside life

that impacts negatively on their sport performance? Some common behaviours include:

- Procrastination over training
- Not preparing properly for competition
- Eating poor nutrition or not sleeping enough
- Turning up but not fully committing to a training session.

2   Next the job is to **capture** the trigger point. The point at which the athlete chooses to follow a self-sabotaging behaviour. Is there anything specific about that point; is it tiredness, hunger, feeling negative, following a bad day or training session?

3   When the trigger point is established you can investigate their **reason** for doing it. If one of their worries is that they will quit when things get tough they could look at their effort barriers. They could think about times when they have quit in the past. How did it make them feel? How uncomfortable were they at the time and how uncomfortable does the memory make them now? What reason did they give others for quitting? And was that the true reason? Asking all these questions helps illuminate the true reason.

4   Once we know the behaviour, the trigger point and their reason they can start to **identify** the goal they actually want to achieve. This is often a good opportunity to take the athlete back to their goal setting (Strategy 2). It may be their goals are not getting them excited or enthusiastic enough to want to make the sacrifices required or are so daunting the athlete feels they need a get-out clause. Resetting goals which genuinely excite the athlete but without scaring them will make them want to self-sabotage less.

5   The next step is to prepare a **plan** for when the athlete next hits that trigger so they can interrupt the ingrained pattern and replace it with a more proactive solution. For example, many athletes procrastinate when they worry a session is too hard for them or may go badly.

6   Once they have **spotted** the behaviour (procrastinating), **captured** the trigger point (having changed into sports

kit but before going out the door) and identified the **reason** (fear of failure) they can **identify** why they were doing the session in the first place. It may be a key session to build mental toughness or an important session to practice a new skills. With the goal identified they can **prepare** a plan to **tackle** the behaviour with something specific which may help trigger a more helpful action.

Strategy 7 – setback analysis

Many successful athletes, when they reflect back, say they learnt far more from failing at something than they ever did at winning. And every athlete has setbacks. They may not always be obvious to those watching but they are really common.

Studies outside of sport have found that alongside the negative impact, a setback can sometimes propel someone to a higher level of functioning[13] with the processes the athlete uses to deal with the setback helping them develop a wider and more mature perspective and find better coping mechanisms.[14] This is often called stress-related growth.[15] For the athlete this stress-related growth can see changes in their relationships with others, their sense of self and their life philosophy.[16] So, while the setback, usually poor results, injury, getting dropped from a team or seeing other athletes progress past them, can feel overwhelming and even catastrophic at the time, it can actually be a really important part of the athlete's journey. It can give the athlete perspective on their sport, perhaps find better ways of doing things and refresh their motivation. So, if they learn to deal with them effectively they can come back a stronger, more focused athlete.

A study has found that those athletes who are able to develop stress-related growth have high levels of hardiness and that these athletes specifically used two coping mechanisms; emotional support and positive reframing.[17] A setback analysis is one way in which this positive reframing can take place. Going through a setback analysis process allows athletes to proactively reframe the setback as a learning experience, providing them with feedback and showing what is not currently working well so changes can be made. From these elements a new goal can be set and within this an action plan created to overcome the setback. This focuses the athlete on being able to see the setback as a learning opportunity to help hone their route to success rather than a failure.

How to do it

An athlete will often need a little time to grieve their setback; to rant about the unfairness, the changes in their season it may cause or to mourn the results they felt they deserved. Giving a day for this is fine as it will help dissipate the anger and emotion and should give the space needed so the athlete is not only being open to new experiences but actually welcomes them.

Once working on the analysis the key is for the athlete to separate themselves from the emotion of the setback. If they struggle with this suggest they think about the setback as happening to a friend or club-mate so they have a little head space to look at the issue more rationally while being kinder to themselves.

The athlete should then take stock of which elements of that setback they are in control of. Some elements will be entirely out of their control (terrain, weather, some mechanicals, spectators, crashes, impact injuries) but even these should be considered as we may have some influence on them and making changes such as wearing shoes that match the terrain, being alert when spectators are close by or practising in different weather conditions would all make a more positive outcome next time.

Once the elements they neither control nor influence are filtered out the athlete can focus on where they do have control in order to move forward. If they are able to break the setback down into a number of potential causes or contributing factors then the more elements of their sporting preparations, practice and competition there will be that can be improved and the more effective their action plan will be to ensure they come back stronger.

Over time, once the athlete has overcome the setback further reflection can be beneficial to ask what they learnt from it. How do they now frame that setback? Asking them what part of the reflection, analysis and action plan process worked well for them and how they will do things differently in the future as a result of their setback will help confirm to them the setback had a long term-benefit, hopefully improving their reaction to the next one.

Strategy 8 – skills sheet

One of our most robust sources of confidence comes from the knowledge that we have the skills required in our sport, we have mastered them and we can employ them when necessary. It helps the athlete feel more competent as well as confident so very deliberately learning skills will not only help them physically but also mentally. A skills sheet helps the athlete to track and maintain the knowledge.

The process of creating a skills sheet helps an athlete to proactively identify the skills they will need to have mastered to achieve their goal and then directs them to regularly practice them so they have the best chance at doing well. Once it is complete the athlete will have a great piece of visual evidence to show themselves when they get nervous to remind them of all the skills they have mastered and should help them feel more confident about using it in competition. This stops the worries that they will be embarrassed or inadequate compared to other athletes.

How to do it

A skills sheet is a good activity to use after an athlete has completed their goal setting (Strategy 2) and performance profiling (4) as both these activities will highlight all the skills that will be required to get them competition ready. This should see the athlete identify around ten skills. These may well be technical and physical skills but could also be mental skills or tactics.

Once they have listed them and you both agree these will be the skills that, once mastered, can help the athlete make the next step up in performance, then they should be listed on a sheet of paper with five empty boxes next to each skill. Every time the athlete demonstrates one of their listed skills in competition or masters it in training they write the date in one of the boxes. Once they have completed the sheet they will have around 50 pieces of evidence in front of them that they have the skills they need to help them feel really confident, and competent when they head into competition.

Strategy 9 – strengths audit

A strengths audit is a list of all those elements which make an athlete feel confident they can achieve their goals. Proactively identifying strengths is helpful because memories are not always reliable and often the memories we pull forward reflect the mentality of how we feeling at that moment. So, after a dreadful training session when an athlete just couldn't seem to master what they wanted they are likely to focus and reflect upon the ten other difficult training sessions they have had this year, rather than the 50 great ones.

We are also prone to a number of cognitive biases, such as confirmation bias where we are more likely to notice things which support what we already believe[18] or negativity bias where we focus more on negative information than positive.[19] Countering these by promoting positive elements, reminders and memories can help us overcome these biases to stop downplaying everything good and seeing it through this negative lens.

Conducting a strengths audit should help an athlete to boost their confidence, even if they don't believe they have a natural talent for their sport, as they should be able to still see some elements which help them perform well in it. It helps them focus on themselves, and their skills and abilities, not on those of their competitors. A further benefit is once as athlete has audited their strengths they can build these into their competition strategy (Strategy 21) so they are focusing on where they are strong and maximising their chances of success.

How to do it

It is helpful to work on a strengths audit twice in a season; right at the beginning when designing the training plan and then a few weeks before big competitions to maximise confidence and develop the most effective competition strategies.

No equipment or templates are needed to develop an athlete's strengths audit. The athlete can write their strengths in their training diary or on the notes section of their phone. Some athletes prefer to see things visually so put their strengths on their wall or on pieces of paper they keep together in a jar. It is important for this the athlete puts aside their humility and fear they may be judged as arrogant. They need to be honest as to the areas where they shine. They should look for at least two strengths for each element:

- Fitness
- Strategy
- Skills
- Tactics
- Mindset
- Support.

To begin with, going through their training diary (Strategy 10) is helpful as it can quickly illustrate where strengths are. If they struggle to find sporting strengths then help them explore other areas of their lives which may highlight transferable strengths. For example, doing well in exams can transfer to show they have strengths around preparation, focus and diligence towards achieving a goal.

If they still struggle to identify their own strengths (and many athletes, especially if they are in a bad period within their training will find this hard) they can talk to other people about where they see their strengths coming from. It could be a coach, parents, friends or club-mates. These people in their support network will often see the strengths the athlete has even when they cannot see them in themselves. Knowing the strengths they have are strong enough to be recognised by others should mean they can be confidence boosting for the athlete to remember in the build-up to and during competition.

If the athlete is elite and has one strength come up over and over again the athlete may start to shape this as their super strength. The super-strengths approach focuses on positive traits and experiences, strengths and optimal functioning[20] to identify a specific area where they can get a world-leading edge.[21] This strength may well be fairly unique to them and in an area of their sport that they know they can always rely upon. It may be that they have a really strong start, a great sprint finish or that they very rarely foul a jump. Or it could be high resilience to bounce back from setbacks or being able to block out pressure in big competition. Knowing they have one element in their performance which makes them stand out can be a great confidence booster and help them feel less intimidated by competitors. This doesn't mean in their training they stop working on any of their weaker areas, but it does give them a confidence boost when they need it and allows their self-comparison with other competitors to become less fraught.

When the strengths audit is complete suggest the athlete keeps a copy of it in their kit bag or in their wallet so whenever they feel nervous they can look through it and remember the positive elements of their performance, rather than the elements they are fearing.

Strategy 10 – training diary

Robust confidence can come from knowing you have the skills required to excel in your sport and that you have got lots of evidence of having used them before. Athletes can train extensively to make sure they have both the skills and experience but if they don't remind themselves of this regularly they can struggle to turn that knowledge into the confidence boost that it should. Therefore, key to remembering what they have achieved; both outcomes (such as wins, scores or new personal best times) and the skills and strategies they have mastered, is to keep a training dairy.

Ideally in this diary athletes would log their physical training, fitness sessions, physical or mental skills they are working on, any niggles or injuries they are feeling, the types of training they enjoy and how they are emotionally engaging with their training. Filling this in every day will mean that when they come to competition or to take on a challenge they will have a huge amount of information at their fingertips to help them prepare effectively. It could be tempting to not write anything on rest days but they should be considered as the time the body catches up with the training or practice that has been done by mending and building in preparation for more efforts to come. Reflections on rest days may well differ in nature from other training days and will help the athlete understand the importance of regular scheduled rest days but also help them reflect on how they feel, think and behave when they are less active.

When done well the training diary becomes a physical record of what the athlete is doing, how they are doing it and why they are doing it. If used strategically it can:

- Help athletes to track their process, performance and outcome goals (Strategy 2).
- Give the athlete the space to reflect to become more self-aware and more of a self-expert (Strategy 52).
- Logging strengths (Strategy 9) and noting weaknesses.
- Help the athlete and coach to spot patterns of behaviour, injury and illness and adapt their training if required.
- Become the basis for the athlete's confidence booster (Strategy 22).
- Help them process feelings and fears around injury or illness better.

Their training diary will really come into its own a few days before a big competition. If the athlete has conscientiously been writing in depth about their achievements and efforts they will be able to look back and see how they've managed difficult situations in their sport in the past. They will find sessions they didn't think they could do, and did. They will be able to see the efforts they put into their goals and find evidence of the strengths they have developed. All of these are helpful to cementing their confidence when their nerves begin to kick in.

How to do it

Online training diaries are great for convenience, but many restrict athletes from adding in that extra information so a paper diary, with lots of space is best. A paper diary means as well as keeping track of what their body is doing, the athlete can also keep track of what is going on in their head. An additional benefit of training diaries was identified in a study using MRI machines where they found that writing things down physically (rather than typing them into a computer) helps the athlete learn from it far better as they are better processing what they have learnt, hopefully speeding up acquisition of any new skill.[22]

To make completion of the training diary a habit it is suggested it is completed at the same time each day, either after training, early in the morning or in bed at night.

If an athlete struggles to write without instructions the key areas they could consider covering may be:

- My goal for today's session was ... and I ...
- Physically I did ...
- My fitness levels seem ...
- The skill I mastered best was ...
- What I did well in this session ...
- Any niggles or cramps?
- The negative thoughts I had were ...
- What I have gained by doing this session?
- How do I feel?
- How tired am I?
- Is there anything in my life right now causing me mental fatigue?

Beyond this, some longer-term reflections would be valuable to be written every month or so. Some suggestions could be:

- The obstacles I am currently facing are ...
- The three strengths I have that I value the most are ...
- When I achieve my outcome goal I will feel ...
- What could I change in my environment to help me succeed would be ...

- I feel strongest when ...
- I am held back when ...
- My sporting hero is ... . I admire them because ... .
- In my training/competing in the last few weeks I am proudest of ... .
- When it gets hard I need to remember ...
- What makes me feel strong?
- My most effective strength is ...

The process shouldn't be onerous and often the answers may just be single word but running through these questions should help the athlete to reflect really well, keep track of any issues, and will give them some great evidence to use when they get to competition day and need to remind themselves of all the great training they did to prepare.

For younger athletes a diary without lines can be even better as some like to draw how they are feeling or doodle their thoughts. This is an easier process for them and has the benefit that drawing has been found to be an effective way to make memories.[23]

Strategy 11 – 'try it Tuesday'

New approaches keep us motivated, help us to learn new skills, improve overall body fitness, give us a mental break from the pressure of our core sport and make training more interesting. Athletes can feel comfortable with what they know but proactively trying something different can not only be beneficial towards their main sport but also help to reignite their passion about sport in general. 'Try it Tuesday' prompts an athlete to consider doing something different. It may be a different type of training, a new skill, a different sport with cross-over benefits, or even a different type of recovery. Some athletes will be trying new things anyway but giving space to do this within training plans ensures it fits into an overall plan while giving the athlete a taste of something new.

It is suggested this approach is taken when an athlete is either finding it tough to choose their outcome goal because they are feeling less passionate about their sport or when they are finding their training quite stale.

How to do it

The athlete and coach need to work together to agree the activity. There may well be more buy-in if the athlete gets to choose it but the coach will usually have more idea what will be most beneficial to complement their sport.

The activity chosen can be based upon the athlete's fitness, their sport, any clearly related sports, their attitude to trying different things, their flexibility or strength, your own approach and philosophy and their current levels of motivation. As an example, for a runner, the list of 'try it Tuesday' activities could be:

- A different event in the same sport; trail running, treadmill, orienteering, cross country or a track session.
- A different type of recovery; a group stretching session, wearing compression gear or a yoga class. It will take their mind off some of the monotony of their day to day training, strengthen their legs and improve their running motivation.
- A different sport; swimming as cross training, pilates for strength; cycling to turn legs without being weightbearing or ballet to improve core.

If there is anything the athlete really enjoys within their Try it Tuesday and it seems like it could be beneficial to their long term performance then it can be incorporated; widening the athlete's repertoire and helping you tailor a programme they really enjoy.

Notes

1 Locke, E. A., & Latham, G. P. (1990). *A theory of goal setting & task performance.* Englewood Cliffs, NJ: Prentice-Hall, Inc.
2 Jackson, S. A., & Roberts, G. C. (1992). Positive performance states of athletes: Toward a conceptual understanding of peak performance. *The Sport Psychologist, 6*(2), 156–171.
3 Kingston, K. M., & Hardy, L. (1997). Effects of different types of goals on processes that support performance. *The Sport Psychologist, 11*(3), 277–293.
4 Evans, L., & Hardy, L. (2002). Injury rehabilitation: A goal-setting intervention study. *Research Quarterly for Exercise and Sport, 73*(3), 310–319.

5 Ardern, C. L., Taylor, N. F., Feller, J. A., & Webster, K. E. (2013). A systematic review of the psychological factors associated with returning to sport following injury. *British Journal of Sports Medicine, 47*(17), 1120–1126.

6 Vealey, R. S., Garner-Holman, M., Hayashi, S. W., & Giacobbi, P. (1998). Sources of sport-confidence: Conceptualization and instrument development. *Journal of Sport and Exercise psychology, 20*(1), 54–80.

7 Bannister, R. (1955). *The four-minute mile*. New York: Dodd, Mead.

8 Corbin, C. B., Laurie, D. R., Gruger, C., & Smiley, B. (1984). Vicarious success experience as a factor influencing self-confidence, attitudes, and physical activity of adult women. *Journal of Teaching in Physical Education, 4*(1), 17–23.

9 Butler, R. J., & Hardy, L. (1992). The performance profile: Theory and application. *The Sport Psychologist, 6*(3), 253–264.

10 Dale, G. A., & Wrisberg, C. A. (1996). The use of a performance profiling strategy in a team setting: Getting the athletes and coach on the 'same page'. *The Sport Psychologist, 10*(3), 261–277.

11 Pensgaard, A. M., & Duda, J. L. (2003). Sydney 2000: The interplay between emotions, coping, and the performance of olympic-level athletes. *The Sport Psychologist, 17*(3), 253–267.

12 Vallerand, R. J. (1987). Antecedents of self-related affects in sport: Preliminary evidence on the intuitive-reflective appraisal model. *Journal of Sport Psychology, 9*, 161–182.

13 Calhoun, L. G., & Tedeschi, R. G. (2006). *The handbook of posttraumatic growth: Research and practice*. Mahwah, NJ: Lawrence Erlbaum Associates.

14 Park, C. L., & Fenster, J. R. (2004). Stress-related growth: Predictors of occurrence and correlates with psychological adjustment. *Journal of Social and Clinical Psychology, 23*(2), 195–215.

15 Park, C. L., Cohen, L. H., & Murch, R. (1996). Assessment and prediction of stress related growth. *Journal of Personality, 64*, 71–105.

16 Calhoun, L. G., & Tedeschi, R. G. (1999). *Facilitating posttraumatic growth: A clinician's guide*. New York, NY: Routledge.

17 Salim, J., Wadey, R., & Diss, C. (2015). Examining the relationship between hardiness and perceived stress-related growth in a sport injury context. *Psychology of Sport and Exercise, 19*, 10–17.

18 Oswald, M. E., & Grosjean, S. (2004). Confirmation bias. In R. Pohl (Ed .), *Cognitive illusions: A handbook on fallacies and biases in thinking, judgement and memory* (pp. 79–96). Hove: Psychology Press.

19 Vaish, A., Grossmann, T., & Woodward, A. (2008). Not all emotions are created equal: The negativity bias in social-emotional development. *Psychological Bulletin, 134*(3), 383.

20 Duckworth, A. L., Steen, T. A., & Seligman, M. E. P. (2005). Positive psychology in clinical practice. *Annual Review of Clinical Psychology, 1*, 629–651.

21 Ludlam, K. E., Butt, J., Bawden, M., Lindsay, P., & Maynard, I. W. (2016). A strengths-based consultancy approach in elite sport: Exploring super-strengths. *Journal of Applied Sport Psychology, 28*(2), 216–233.

22 James, K. H. (2012, January 23). How printing practice affects letter perception: An educational cognitive neuroscience perspective. *Presented at Handwriting in the 21st Century? An Educational Summit*, Washington, DC.

23 Fernandes, M. A., Wammes, J. D., & Meade, M. E. (2018). The surprisingly powerful influence of drawing on memory. *Current Directions in Psychological Science, 27*(5), 302–308.

11

Strategies for preparing for competition

Strategy 12 – adversity sessions

When something feels like a significant stressor to an athlete and causes them anxiety their natural instinct is often to avoid it. In sport this may mean they won't take part in certain types of events or competitions or they shy away from difficult moves or strategies. The more the athlete avoids these stressors the more they are forming a habit, taking them away from achieving their overall goals and ambitions.

Adversity sessions take athletes out of their comfort zones in training or practice so that when they turn up to a competition it will feel less intimidating. Sometimes known as stress inoculation training or exposure therapy, they help athletes slowly stretch their comfort zones so they can develop new skills, build confidence and reduce pre-competition anxiety – it gives them the confidence to take part in elements of their sport they had previously shied away from. While it is not possible to prepare for every eventuality in competition, these types of sessions should help an athlete to develop mental toughness and prove to themselves they are more resilient than they may have thought. Athletes who demonstrate resilience to adversity are those more likely to reach specific goals[1] secure long-term benefits[2] and think on their feet.

Gradually exposing themselves to fearful situations until they feel they have mastered it will give them enough confidence to tackle the next step. If they do this often enough they may be surprised just how much bigger their comfort zone has become. Adversity sessions help athletes recognise that although they will feel pain and discomfort for a little while in competition, they have felt similar in the past and survived. This exposure means the athletes feel slightly uncomfortable while doing them, but doing it more and more gives reassurance they are better able to cope. In small doses they get evidence that the stressor no longer causes them the terrible outcome they had imagined so they become less anxious and better able to deal with it.

How to do it

Adversity sessions can be designed by a coach or the athlete can design the session themselves to test an area they feel weak in.

To match as closely as possible the environment the athlete is going to be putting themselves in, these sessions can be designed after completing a 'what if' planning session (Strategy 29). Work with the athlete to look through their 'what if' plan and pick out a few areas which can be supported through adversity training. If they struggle with this, another route is to look at their goal setting and discuss what is holding them back from achieving it right now.

To begin break down the fear which is to be targeted into tiny steps and design ways for the athlete to meet that fear within a controlled environment. They start with the least stressful version of the activity so they feel supported and can see the process is gentle and less intimidating than they were expecting. If a fear is performing in a new venue then perhaps setting up a session for a whole squad to train together in a different venue than they are used to; safe because they are with friends but a little scary as it is a new place. If performing in front of others is a fear then a session may be designed where each athlete has to show a skill to each other; still safe because only to one other person but starting to stretch their comfort zone. Adding adversity sessions into an athlete's training can help them confront each fear gradually and make competition days less daunting.

Using this process will gradually expose an athlete to small amounts of stress so they become able to cope with increasing amounts of it. If they struggle at any stage they can drop down a level and build up again. It means athletes learn skills for dealing with different stressors so they become more attuned to how they are feeling and can become quicker to understand which mental skills will work for them in each situation. Over time this means the athletes develop learned resourcefulness.

Calling the sessions something positive can help the athlete prepare well so it seems more like an exciting challenge rather than a threat. Anything that can be measured is helpful so the athlete can see how well they are doing, something which will boost their confidence. Celebrating successes in these sessions helps to highlight the benefits of putting in the required effort and bravery for these type of sessions in future.

If they struggle in the sessions then motivational mantras (Strategy 45) can be used such as 'there will be an end to this', 'I'll feel really good about this when I've finished' or 'this will make competition feel a lot easier.'

Strategy 13 – attentional shift training

Paying attention to appropriate cues is vital for sporting performance. It has been estimated that in soccer a player makes between eight and ten tactical decisions each minute[3] so at least 720 decisions in a match. The slower the athlete is in noticing where they should be paying attention or what they should be doing, the lower their ability to perform effectively.

Three key components of attention have been identified; direction of attention (either internal or external), the breadth of that focus (broad or narrow) and how well the athlete is able to shift the focus of their attention.[4] In competition an athlete will need to be able to draw upon the right attentional style at the right time to ensure their most effective performance. They each have benefits for different times in a competition. For example, in rugby, a player would use a broad-internal focus to scan the field to find the right teammate for their strategy, run as far as they can, shift focus to narrow-external to spot their team-mate, shift to narrow-internal to throw the ball, then shift attention back to broad-external to scan the field for where they should go next.

When an athlete understands where their attention naturally lies they can become more aware of where they are focused at any time. This is particularly important when we are under pressure[5] as this is when we tend to think less logically and make decisions based on threat rather than logic. Understanding the dimension in which we feel most comfortable also helps us to manipulate it better when required so we are able to rapidly change the attentional channel we are using so we can pick the one which will be most effective.

How to do it

The process of understanding how well athletes are able to switch attention can either be run through a survey[6] or through watching videos of athletes competing and talking through where they would have felt their attention was at each moment.

Once areas of comfort with attention have been identified, practice using all types of attention can take place. This will start with some education about the four types of attention and when they may need to use each one. They can do this anywhere but doing it somewhere like an office or study room is helpful as it will show whether the understanding is strong enough to translate into other elements. An example in an office may be:

- Narrow-external: Counting how many different colours they can see in the paintings on the wall.
- Broad-external: Going outside the office door and listening out for all the sounds going on and naming them all.
- Broad-internal: Making a mental tactical plan for their next race.
- Narrow-internal: Naming all the managers of their favourite football club since they became a fan.

Once the athlete understands each type of focus you can get them discussing them in a sport-specific way. This can be done through watching videos of competitions in their sport; prompting them to talk through where they would ideally want to have their attention at each moment. You can break it down into five or ten second periods. This really helps understanding of each dimension of attentional focus as they are continually describing it so it becomes easier to do when under pressure in a competition environment. It should also highlight any areas of attentional focus that the athlete struggles with. Finally, you can take the training into the sporting environment and use the terminology as the athlete is training to help them become more attuned to where focus should be at each moment.

Strategy 14 – attribution retraining

Attributions (explanations for the causes of events) help athletes make sense of their competitions. Sometimes these attributions are adaptive and help the athlete develop mastery in their sport,[7] improve their self-efficacy[8] or boost their motivation.[9] Sometimes the attributions are maladaptive and athletes struggle cognitively, emotionally or behaviourally.

To prevent these negative outcomes a number of studies have tested attribution retraining to help athletes manipulate dysfunctional attributions so they can develop more functional and beneficial explanations for their sporting outcomes.[10] Studies have found the training to be very effective, not just at improving performance[11] but also for confidence[12] and increasing motivation.[13]

When trying to find more helpful attributions for failure in a competition, athletes can consider elements like lack of effort or poor strategy but these must be a true genuine reason, otherwise the athlete may work harder or change strategy and still not improve and will become incredibly unmotivated.

How to do it

The most popular version of attribution retraining involves using information (educating and developing an athlete's self-awareness about how they attribute) and giving consensus feedback (explaining how others have also struggled and how they overcame similar issues) so that athletes can follow a similar route. Ideally, we want to work on the retraining around elements which are changeable (such as effort or strategy) and within their control to do something about. The training does not need to be extensive or take long, some set it up to only last 20 minutes.[14]

1   To begin, we can **educate** athletes about the different dimensions (covered in Chapter 6) asking them to identify where they feel they sit within each dimension, identifying the habitually unhelpful intuitive attributions.

2   With the education element complete you can help the athlete **understand** more by reflecting on their intuitive thinking. Spending lots of time on the controllability elements will help the athlete be more constructive in what they come up with. It will also help them drop the pressure on themselves over elements they genuinely have no control over.

3   Using the direct rating method[15] athletes state their **reasons** for their performance outcome and map those onto the attribution dimensions. It should show if any adaptations are maladaptive by identifying if something is unstable through a discussion on whether the same explanation can be given for a number of poor results. Then, using control mapping (Strategy 1) an athlete can determine what within their competition is within their control, what they can influence and what they can't change.

4   Next, we offer **consensus information** which explain how others may approach the same task – usually that they similarly found it hard but over time they persevered, found new strategies to use, and started to find it easier and were now able to do it much better. Helping the athlete focus different strategies or processes they could have used in that situation helps them to attribute their lack of success to not having found the right strategy, rather than being poor at the strategy.

5   Discussions can then take place on what could have been done **differently**. The process helps athletes feel more in control as they see they have the opportunity to choose an appropriate strategy.

6   Long term, key messages can be built in practice discussions so that athletes learn to attribute any failure to changeable and controllable elements.

Strategy 15 – biofeedback

While the aim of the athlete is to control their sporting movements in competition other key elements of their physiology will also impact their performance, involuntarily controlled by their nervous system such as heart rate, skin temperature and blood pressure. It is hard to regulate these levels when we don't have very accurate ways of knowing what they are so we try to gain more control of these involuntary functions, using biofeedback. Biofeedback is a tool to self-regulate physiological responses with the idea that by becoming more aware of what is going on inside their body, the athlete can learn to consciously control it better until the control becomes automatic.

Biofeedback uses an athlete's sensations to help them focus and improve their attentional control. It often uses electronic devices (usually watching a screen or listening to a noise) to amplify specific body functions so athletes can get some psychosomatic feedback[16] to help them modify their behaviour or actions until they match their personal optimal zone of performance.[17] These bodily sensations can give us objective feedback, unhindered by cognitive attributions or bias.

The process attunes the athlete to their body so they are better able to recognise helpful and unhelpful behaviours. Over time the athlete begins to do some of the training without the equipment, so they no longer depend on the feedback but do maintain that awareness of physiological changes. It has been used to increase running economy in long distance runners,[18] improve basketball free throw scores,[19] overall performance[20] and is regularly used to reduce anxiety[21] by helping the athlete to relax and reduce their arousal levels.

Due to the technology requirements biofeedback has previously required a laboratory but there are now far more portable devices so it can be used much more easily with athletes, especially as a way to test and enhance the effectiveness of mental skills strategy training,[22] where it has been found to result in better performances.[23]

There are a number of versions of biofeedback utilising different technologies such as electrodes attached to skin or with finger sensors. The technology is becoming more transportable but many versions do need to be used in a lab so require significant time from the athlete. One tool used regularly is Heart Rate Variability (HRV). Developing high HRV has been found to have health benefits,[24] helps athletes to regulate competitive stress and mood[25] and improves performance.[26] It is a measure of the interplay between the sympathetic and parasympathetic influences on our heart rate and a high HRV shows we have a flexible automatic nervous system that responds well to internal and external stimuli and gives us fast reactions. Another popular test is for skin temperature. Skin temperature can be measured with a biodot, a small disc that changes colour depending on the temperature of the athlete's skin. Watching the dot colour change as an athlete tenses and relaxes will help them to learn to eventually do it without the dot. Neurofeedback is also being used to measures brainwaves which is helpful for athletes to learn to improve their concentration levels and focus for longer.

How to do it

Biofeedback which can be run without technology is particularly helpful for athletes suffering with over-arousal or anxiety. Under stress our heart rate speeds up, muscles tighten, blood pressure rises, we sweat and our breathing quickens. Seeing these stress responses visually helps us respond to them to try to improve them, and we get immediate feedback. We can do this through:

- Deep slow breathing (Strategy 20) to slow our heart rate levels or counting our breaths per minute with the aim of slowing them down and reducing our arousal level.

- Progressive muscle relaxation (Strategy 19) is a really helpful biofeedback method to help athletes learn to identify the differences in muscle tension from tight through to relaxed muscles. When muscles are too tight they can get injured and learning to recognise the increase in tension and to relax them on demand will give an athlete a fuller range of movement for their sporting performance.
- Meditation or mindfulness (Strategy 51) can also be helpful for giving an athlete the space to become more aware of the feelings in their body. When an athlete has learnt meditative skills they will have a more developed awareness of their physical and psychological cues so can learn to respond to them on competition day when equipment is not able to be used.

Strategy 16 – brain drain

When athletes are really anxious and feel like they don't have the resources required to deal with the stressors they are facing they have to spend so much mental energy and space focused on trying to find a suitable coping mechanism that they are unable to focus fully on the sporting elements they really need to.

A tactic which can be used by any athlete is to write down all their anxieties and worries before a competition. Making this part of an athlete's warm up process before a competition can get the negative thoughts and fears out of their head before they start. This has a number of benefits. Firstly, it frees up working memory so that athletes can focus on just the physical tasks in front of them. Secondly, seeing the stressor written down can sometimes highlight that it is actually not as bad as their brain was building it up to be. Thirdly, with a list in front of them they can proactively consider if anything can actually be done to deal with each stressor.

This strategy is backed up by researchers who set up anxiety-inducing conditions before a maths exam and asked half the students to sit and wait before the exam, and the other half to complete a creative writing piece about their anxieties for ten minutes. The students who just sat and waited dropped their scores on the exam by 12%. The students who wrote down their fears improved their results by 5%.[27] Therefore, even when there is nothing that can be done beforehand, scribbling down and acknowledging any worries, anxieties or stressors they have been ruminating over should mean that athletes feel comfortable these thoughts are captured for later giving them the space to focus on what needs to be done at just this moment.

How to do it

The athlete can use a sheet of paper or their training diary for this activity. We ask them to write down anything they are worried about ahead of their competition. Be clear it does not have to be shared so no-one else need know what they write. If they struggle to write freely perhaps suggest bullet points or some themes to use (such as equipment, competitors, outcome, skills, other people's opinions, environment).

The athlete should only use about ten minutes for this activity and it can be good to do as part of their pre-performance routine – before their physical warm up. If they have time they can consider if there is anything they can do to mitigate anything which they wrote down but even without extra time it will be worth reiterating that simply the process of writing it down could help them perform better.

Strategy 17 – brain endurance training

In Chapter 7 we learnt that the limits of our sporting performance come from how motivated the athlete is and how much effort they feel they need to expend. Change the perception of effort being put in and you change the performance levels of the athlete. Lots of elements impact our perception of effort; some are physical like dehydration, heart rate or fitness but some are psychological like motivation or mental fatigue. And mental fatigue is key as the negative impact of mental fatigue can be as large as the impact of muscle fatigue on an athlete's performance.[28] If we can control mental fatigue then we should be able to push harder to perform better.

This means to improve performance an athlete can either avoid anything mentally tiring in the build up to a competition, or learn to use it extensively so they become more resilient to it. Brain Endurance Training (BET) aims to train the brain to adapt to become more fatigue resistant so that pushing harder feels easier. Purposeful mental fatigue then behaves as a training stimulus.

Early testing has been incredibly positive. A study put 35 athletes up against each other with half completing 12 weeks of physical training (indoor cycling three times a week) and half completing 12 weeks of exactly the same physical training but also adding BET.[29] The BET involved doing a mentally fatiguing computer task at the same time as cycling. VO^2max testing showed similar improvements in both groups yet while those who just did physical training improved their time to exhaustion by 42%, those who did the BET programme improved their time to exhaustion by 126%.

How to do it

Brain Endurance Training programmes are run as intensive 60–90 minute sessions, five days a week. It takes time for an athlete to build their tolerance to be able to complete 90 minutes though, so start in five minute blocks.

The training involves completing very dull cognitive tasks on a computer; often tasks such as clicking on arrows or doing number games. They are incredibly boring, but they are supposed to be since the boringness is what creates the mental fatigue so making them more tolerable would be pointless. These tasks can be found online – you can for search the classic cognitive neuroscience tasks such as Stroop, Flanker and Attention Network Tasks. Try for five minutes to begin with and then build up as the athlete's mental endurance improves. Then get them into physical training straight afterwards.

Strategy 18 – colourful breathing

We all breathe, all day, every day. About 12–18 breaths a minute in fact. Yet few of us learn how to breathe well and how to use it effectively as a tactic to control our body. Vitally for athletes, breathing strategies help control our levels of activation and can be particularly valuable to lower the activation or arousal levels in an athlete who is overly anxious. They help athletes relax, to feel free of physical or mental tension, and to be calm; both in the midst of competition and day to day when pressures in life and sport get on top of us.

Breathing is a particularly important element in competition because everything our body does physiologically feeds back into our brain, giving it signals as to how we are feeling. Our brain then responds to those signals. If we are taking shorter sharper breaths we are signalling to our brain that we are panicking, that we are in difficulty. This stresses our body, makes us tighten up, puts us on alert and gets our heart beating much faster. Our brain's reaction to this is to slow down the body, usually the opposite of what we want when performing in most sports. Focusing on breathing to keep it working effectively will help athletes control it, rather that it controlling them.

Colourful breathing helps athletes control their heart rate and slow down their breathing level to only five breaths a minute. It helps them take oxygen deeper into their lungs and gain better posture. It is a great strategy when time is short and an athlete needs to quickly regain composure and reduce their arousal level. Each round only takes 12 seconds so in some sports it can actually be used during competition. As the athlete focuses on the colours and the process of breathing it takes their mind off from the pressure of competition and gives them a short break from everything going on around them.

How to do it

Ask the athlete to pick two colours they like or that matter to them (sometimes their team colours). Here we will use blue and red. The script we would read to the athletes would be:

1   Start with thinking about your breath as being held gently just behind your belly button.
2   Draw air in through your nose for a count of four – as you do this think of the air going in as hot red.
3   Hold the air behind your belly button for a count of two.
4   Breathe out through your mouth for a count of six – as you do this think of the air leaving their body as cool blue to build a calmer feeling.

They can repeat this until they feel calmer.

Strategy 19 – progressive muscle relaxation

Progressive Muscle Relaxation (PMR) has a triple purpose. It helps athletes to relax and reduce their anxiety levels,[30] improves pain tolerance[31] and it works as a biofeedback mechanism, helping an athlete increase their awareness of how their body feels in different states of tension, thus improving efficiency and effectiveness in using the right amount of tension for the current task. It has been used since the 1920s[32] based on the theory that if we could relax voluntary muscles then the involuntary muscles would relax too.

PMR focuses on the process of tensing and relaxing muscles one muscle group at a time to promote relaxation and reduce some of the physical reactions to stress and pressure as well as improving economy of effort. By focusing on the process of gradually tensing each muscle group before relaxing them the athlete can learn to appreciate the differences in sensation between very tense and totally relaxed muscles as well as the levels of tension in-between. The strategy is used outside of the competition setting and the more it is practised the better the athlete learns how to feel the difference between different levels of tension. They can then use it to detect unwanted tension in any specific muscle groups and to reduce physiological arousal on demand so they feel less anxious.

How to do it

Initially athletes are learning to use the strategy so specific sessions may last up to 30 minutes but once they have mastered it they can run through the strategy alone much quicker.

The athlete needs somewhere to sit or lie down without disruption. Talk the athlete through the process, using a calm, relaxed voice. The script may begin something like this:

1 Take five slower, deeper breaths.
2 Let's start with the focus on our feet, the right foot first.
3 Notice the tension in the muscles of your right foot. Now increase the tension about halfway (medium) tension and then release that tension noticing how the muscles feel as you do.
4 Exhale as you let any tightness flow out of the tensed muscles. Repeat but with more tension this time, hold while you notice what maximum tension feels like then relax and notice the process of releasing tension to nothing. The muscles should then feel warm, heavy, or loose. Specifically try to notice the difference between the zero, minimum, medium and maximum levels of tension. Remain with the right foot relaxed for 15 seconds or so.

Then you move up the right leg to ankle, lower leg, upper leg (front and back) so each muscle group is involved. Repeat with the left foot and up the leg. For each group of muscles you want them to be repeating the tension-relaxation steps.

The muscle groups to include are:

- Foot – curl your toes downward and upwards.
- Ankle, lower leg and foot – tighten your calf muscle by pointing your toes away from you and then pull toes towards knee and notice tension on the front of the lower leg.
- Upper leg – engage front thigh muscles by pulling knee cap to hip and the back of thigh by straightening leg if

sitting or pulling heel back along the floor but not eating foot move.

- Hand – clench your fist then also spread fingers wide. Notice where the tension is and at what level.
- Entire arm – tighten your arm by drawing your forearm up towards your shoulder and 'make a muscle' while clenching your fist.
- Buttocks – tighten by pulling your buttocks together.
- Stomach – suck your stomach in – belly button to spine and then release.
- Chest – tighten by taking a deep breath and push hands together in front of chest.
- Upper back – draw shoulder blades together and down.
- Neck and shoulders – raise your shoulders up to touch your ears several times and then down so neck is very long.
- Mouth and jaw – open your mouth wide enough to stretch the hinges of your jaw and clench your teeth. Notice your tongue, press up into your palate then rest gently behind but not touching bottom teeth.
- Eyes – clench your eyelids tightly shut/open them wide.
- Forehead – raise your eyebrows as far as you can/frown.

Strategy 20 – deep breathing

When athletes get tense in a competition (or any potentially stressful situation) a natural response is to hold their breath. This increases muscle tension and restricts the movement we need to perform well. Instead we want athletes to breathe deeply, spending longer exhaling than inhaling as this deepens their relaxation and slows down their breathing overall. The in-breath should take over naturally. Deep breathing pushes us into breathing into our lower ribs and 'stomach' instead of upper chest. It gives athletes the ability to slow down their breathing, assess how they are doing and control it better. Using this strategy during longer breaks in competition (such as half time if they have one) helps the athlete maintain composure, reduce anxiety and stops them focusing on all the distractions around them.

How to do it

Use the following script to help your athletes learn to breathe deeply:

1   Slowly, slowly exhale (8–10 seconds) while slowly pulling in your abdomen and lowering your shoulders and chest.
2   Pause.
3   Imagine your lungs are divided into three sections; lower, middle and upper.
4   At the beginning of the in-breath fill the lower level of your lungs with air, pushing your diaphragm down and lower ribs out to the side towards your arms.
5   Over the next two seconds you fill the middle of your lungs by expanding your chest cavity and allowing your rib cage to continue expanding to the side.
6   Finally, fill the top of your lungs (expect your chest and shoulders to move a little).
7   Pause briefly before exhaling and inhaling.

Strategy 21 – competition planning

Some athletes may subconsciously fail to prepare for their competition as a way to persuade themselves they are not taking everything too seriously. This can reduce some of the pressure or expectation they have placed on themselves, but it can backfire as leaving everything to chance can increase the athlete's threat response as there will be a high number of elements where the athlete is not in control. It also acts as a form of self-sabotage where the more we stick our head in the sand and try to avoid preparing, the less time we give ourselves to do the preparation which would help us perform better. Alongside the self-sabotage we feel anticipatory stress, knowing we still have to do the competition and the preparation for it.

To increase the feeling of challenge instead of threat an athlete should look at the areas where they can be in control and make a strong plan around how to maximise their benefit in those areas. With this plan in place the athlete can then focus on the tasks included in it rather than ruminating over distracting worries or stressors.

The focus of the plan should always be on what the athlete has some control over (identified in Strategy 1) rather than things they can't, such as other competitors, who the referee is or the weather. The plan may not always be able to be followed through but should give the athlete enough options if something does change.

How to do it

1   The first step for the athlete is to gather all the information on the competition; venue, date, time, competitors, surface and anything sport-specific.
2   Then they add in their goal for competition, ideally something task- or process-related they can control (rather than a generic outcome goal such as 'to win').
3   Then consider any strengths in skills or mentality which will help reach that goal.
4   Next, they consider any specific barriers to successfully reaching goal; lack of recent training, poor fitness, still learning required skills, mental fatigue from heavy workload.
5   Working together you can develop a 'what if' plan (Strategy 29) to cover any potential fears, how the athlete can plan for them and what they will do if they happen.
6   Run through a timeline of the event to chunk it up (Strategy 36) into much smaller parts and include prior to and post event. In here they should ensure they include which strengths (Strategy 9) they have that can support them in each section. For each chunk they should have a strategy, a mindset to follow and specific actions or tasks to complete.
7   Pre-event they should think about the pre-performance routine (Strategy 40) they will follow.

The athlete can read through this competition plan whenever they get nervous in the build up to the competition.

Strategy 22 – confidence booster

An athlete's two most robust sources of confidence come from knowing they have the skills and experience they need and that they are fully prepared for the event ahead. Confidence and self-belief in their own abilities is a key ingredient for athletes to reach their potential[33] especially as they improve, take on a sporting identity and competitions become more important to them.[34] A confidence booster combines both of these to reduce nerves and give an athlete a visual reminder to increase their persistence and effort in achieving their performance goal.[35] It is designed to give athletes reassurance they are fully prepared and lots of positive things to remember if they start to get anxious in the build-up.

How to use:

The confidence booster should be created a few days before a competition so the athlete can get maximum benefit and look through whenever they get nervous. It covers their goal for the race, the mantra they will use, strengths which should be helpful, sessions they completed in the build-up and their mental and physical strategy.

Any time in the week before a key competition the athlete should get a piece of paper, get out their training diary and write down:

- Their goal for the competition (ideally something within their control).
- Their motivational mantra (Strategy 45) to use when it gets tough.
- Three strengths (Strategy 9) they will draw upon in the competition.
- Three key sessions they completed in their build-up which give them evidence they are well prepared.
- Their physical strategy.
- Their mental strategy.

They should keep this paper in their wallet, kit bag or by the side of their bed and when they feel the nerves creeping in, read through it and remind themselves how hard they have trained and how much they deserve to achieve their goal.

A nice version of this for younger athletes can be a letter to themselves telling them all about the preparation they have done and how hard they have worked. Writing this will be a positive boost and then reading back over the letter if their nerves start to take over will help them feel more confident.

Strategy 23 – confidence jar

We each have within us a negativity bias[36] where we give our negative traits greater weight in our evaluations than our positive ones.[37] From an evolutionary perspective there is good reason for this; it helps us learn and remember what to avoid so we stay safe. Unfortunately, in day to day life, it can make us feel pretty miserable. When we add this natural negative bias to the perfectionistic traits of many athletes, sport can sometimes feel like a stick to be beaten with.

To overcome this negativity, regular reminders of our efforts and achievements can be helpful. Friends, family and sporting supporters are great for this and boost an athlete's confidence through persuasion but they may not always want to share their fears widely and these other people are not with the athlete all the time. Instead, athletes need to find a way to capture the great stuff they recognise in themselves; the things they achieve or what is said to them by the people they love and respect. One way to do this is to record all their achievements physically in a confidence jar. This jar then acts as a visual reminder of how good they are and how hard they have worked.

How to do it

The athlete needs a jar (anything jam jar sized or smaller is great) and 24 thin strips of paper. They should write down:

- Anything they are proud of achieving.
- Anything they worked hard towards that was successful.

- Any strengths (Strategy 9) they have identified.
- New skills (Strategy 8) they have learnt.

Leaving the jar by the kettle or the side of their bed means that if prior to competition an athlete is lying awake ruminating and worrying they won't do well, they have all their evidence of skills and success to hand. They will be reminded, in their own writing and words, lots of really good reasons to be confident. They can also take their jar away with them to competitions giving them some great, visual evidence of their abilities, efforts and positive experiences when they feel anxious.

Strategy 24 – familiarisation training

Uncertainty can cause us to feel on edge and under threat. Bringing some familiarity to what an athlete is facing can reduce that threat response so they develop more of a challenge mindset. Studies have found that we recall information much better when our conditions resemble those we have been in before[38] so training in the same venue or location as where our event is taking place can be really beneficial training.

Familiarisation training facilitates this by taking the environmental aspects of a competition and immersing the athlete in as many potential scenarios as possible so they become known to the athlete, making them feel more comfortable. It could involve the competition venue or a race course, getting used to performing in different types of weather or being in front of different audiences. This increased comfortability should make the competition feel less intimidating and help the athlete not only pack the right kit but most importantly feel more in control on competition day.

How to do it

This activity can be completed after competition planning (Strategy 21) as then the athlete will have all the information about the venue or course they will be competing on and any notes of anything specific within that event which they fear. Specifically, it is helpful for them to consider the venue and the weather.

Venue: if there is a way they can go to the venue ahead of time to train in/on it this would be really valuable familiarisation. If this is a competitor's home ground or club it could be difficult so instead they could look on a mapping app to see what everything looks like, go through their website to see the facilities or ask someone who has already competed there what it was like. If the venue is open to anyone or is on open roads or land then build some time into the athlete's plan to visit and train on it. Something that athletes have found can make the environment they have practised on seem more welcoming and familiar when they go back for their competition is to name parts of it. The names don't have to be sensible and ones which make them smile will build the comfort. Ones previously used by athletes include; puddle corner (there is always a big puddle), jazz bend (a guy was playing the saxophone there) and windy way (big cross winds).

Weather: athlete and coach should spend some time working out all types of weather combinations and how that could impact competition. Extreme heat or rain are usually the most troublesome. Finding ways to practise in these will help with preparation. Sometimes these can be natural solutions (going out to train in heavy rain) but other situations can be created. Runners preparing for races in very hot places can run on a treadmill in heat chambers, polar explorers can spend time training in altitude tents, cyclists can do some work in wind tunnels. All of these help physically acclimatise the athlete with the environment they are heading into and mentally reassure the athlete they have coped in similar conditions before.

Strategy 25 – imagery

An amazing characteristic of our brain is the way it can bypass movement and physical activities and still simulate sensations, actions and experiences. Even without physically doing something, if we imagine it well enough, our neurons structurally modify themselves, making them more effective and supplementing our physical practice without the additional risk of injury or fatigue. It can also reduce an athlete's anxiety by familiarising them with the specific task or environment they will be in.

Imagery is something many athletes do inadvertently when they are daydreaming about their sport, thinking about their competitions going well or visualising themselves up on a podium. Doing this systematically however, with a specific purpose in mind, thinking of it as a mental rehearsal, learning to do it just as they would any other sporting skills can be a really beneficial strategy and one which can improve their performances.

Imagery allows an athlete to mimic real experience using different senses. Studies have found it can increase self-confidence,[39] works as way to maintain existing skills[40] and the types of imagery focused on skills development have been found to be as effective as physical practice.[41]

Using imagery effectively requires the engagement of as many senses as possible to create, imitate or recreate a sporting skill, experience or situation in an athlete's mind. It can be used at any time, in any place, before, during and after training or competition and helps athletes enhance their performance, either directly by improving their skills and strategies or indirectly through enhancing motivation, regulating arousal or increasing self-confidence.

Researchers trying to understand why it works suggest that, when we are using imagery, our neuronal groups interactively fire in defined patterns and structurally modify themselves in a way that makes them more effective. They suggest this means we gain a functional equivalence with the same areas of the brain firing whether a skill is actually performed or just imagined. So, while it can't replace physical practice, only supplement it, this functional equivalence means an athlete benefits from the extra 'imagined' practice but without the additional risk of injury or fatigue. The more vivid and realistic the images become, the more likely they are to be interpreted by the brain as identical to the actual event, which increases the effectiveness of mental practice and provides additional training without the physical impact on the body.

Cognitive imagery helps with skill and strategy rehearsal. It focuses on the motor skills and strategies an athlete may use. Motivational imagery will help an athlete immediately before a competition to increase arousal or self-confidence. It will focus on an athlete's goals and their overall performance.

There are five types of imagery:

1   To mentally rehearse race plans, strategies and routines. It gives general performance benefits.
2   To mentally rehearse specific sports skills so they enhance the performance of skills they already know and are learning.
3   To improve feelings of relaxation, stress, anxiety, affect, mood, emotions and arousal. Can be used to decrease anxiety or 'psych up' before a race.
4   To help an athlete feel in control, focused, mentally tough and confident.
5   To allow athletes to imagine goal achievement and accomplishments like winning.

Choosing the right type will ensure the athlete gets the biggest benefit based on their own strengths and weaknesses and their goal for that competition.

How to do it

To use imagery effectively it is suggested that a script is used. This allows the athlete to ensure the images and feelings they create in their mind are rich and realistic. They will need to write the script themselves so the images, senses and words they create really resonate and fully incorporate the feelings, situations and environments which are familiar to them so they can easily recall these details from memory. This will result in clearer and more vivid scenarios. They then record their script so they can listen to it.

To create their script and make it personal and meaningful the athlete needs to consider:

1   What is the purpose? To improve a skill or to motivate themselves? Picking the purpose from the five options will dictate the type of script they use.

2   Where and when they will listen to the recording? During training, relaxing in bed, pre-competition?

3   Which senses can they include: sight, sound, taste, touch or smell? To ensure the athlete's practice is high in functional equivalence the script needs to be as life-like as possible through the use of multiple senses.

4   Who will record it? Themselves or someone else? The voice, clarity, the tempo, tone, enunciation and pronunciation should help the athlete focus rather than detract from the imagery. If the sport they do includes music (such as gymnastics, trampolining or ice dance) then the recorded script should incorporate their music into the background.

5   Keeping it short. The first script should be no more than two minutes. It can then gradually be increased in length as the athlete develops their imagery skills.

6   Once the script is written and recorded they should practise over and over again. This helps embed the skill or motivation inside their head but imagery is a skill in itself so the more the athlete masters the skill of using it the more they will benefit.

7   Finally, the athlete should regularly evaluate and consider how the script is working and update and evolve it. Modifications will keep it fresh and effective.

Where the imagery is focused on developing or improving a motor skill then athletes should follow the seven point checklist in the PETTLEP model.[42] It should incorporate the relevant **physical** characteristics, the **environment** where the competition will take place, details relevant to the **task** at the appropriate mastery level and be done in 'real **time'** rather than speed up or slowed down. It should show the athlete continually **learning** and reviewing, trying to feel the same positive **emotions** they would feel while doing it and using the right **perspective** so the first person for some skills and third person (like watching yourself from above) for positioning skills.

Strategy 26 – mental tapering

Chapter 7 taught us that mental fatigue negatively impacts sporting performance. A big study on this asked participants to spend 90 minutes either watching a bland documentary or playing a demanding computer game. They then completed a time-to-exhaustion test on a bike.[43] The mentally tired participants, the ones who had been playing the computer game, reported higher levels of perceived effort and hit exhaustion on the bike 15% sooner than those who watched the documentary. The impact of mental fatigue has also been found in soccer,[44] swimming[45] and table tennis.[46]

Stress can have a similar impact on performance as the emotional regulation required to cope with it can cause mental fatigue. In one study cyclists were asked to watch something disgusting (a woman eating her own vomit) and not respond to it. This 'non response' requires emotional regulation. When the cyclists completed a 10k time trial on a bike after this emotional regulation they completed the time trial 25 seconds slower.[47] While having to not respond when someone does something disgusting is not a common issue for athletes, they do have to practise emotional regulation if they need to deal with the media or fans before a competition or are having to put on a game face around their competitors.

This suggests that avoiding cognitively challenging or stressful activities before a big competition by mentally tapering will positively benefit sports performance. Unfortunately, stressful and cognitively challenging activities are common in athlete's lives. Exams, school, house moves, work projects or difficult family issues can all arise so athletes need to understand mental fatigue, learn how to recognise it and, when they can, get clever about scheduling so big competitions and stressful life events do not clash.

How to do it

When preparing for a competition with an athlete take into account what they are likely to be doing in the week before and help them identify which elements of their week may increase their cognitive load. If it is likely to be high some ideas to suggest to help them reduce it could be:

- To make it clear that if they are physically tapering for their competition this is not an opportunity to fill that time with extra cognitive tasks. Instead they should be reducing what they do if possible, including on rest days.
- If they are in control of their own work or study schedule then to save some more of the more admin type tasks for close to competition day so they do not drain their mental energy on things with high cognitive load.
- To organise their competition packing, transport and logistics a long time prior to competition. Frantically packing the night before a very early start will not only see them sleep deprived but mentally tired.
- To increase the amount of sleep they have in competition week if they are likely to have unavoidable mentally fatiguing activities scheduled in.

Strategy 27 – overlearning skills

The term 'overlearning' comes from education where it has been used to describe training that leads to improved retention; either practising a skill to 100% accuracy[48] or at least beyond the point of immediate recall.[49] Overlearning creates fluency, and those with fluency get distracted less and can incorporate more complex skills.[50] Overlearning also develops automatic behaviours which gives the benefit of being able to do other things at the same time.[51] It means athletes cope better under pressure and have additional bandwidth and focus for thinking about the extras which will make that small (but critical) difference to their performance; a clever tactic, a higher shot or moving faster.

Overlearning means athletes are repeatedly executing the physical and mental skills they plan to reproduce in competition[52] giving them higher self-confidence[53] and lowering competition anxiety.[54] Some athletes combine overlearning skills with imagery (Strategy 25) so they can still reply the action or movement in their head but without risking overtraining or additional tiredness.

How to do it

Working with an athlete on their performance profile (Strategy 4) and their skills sheet (Strategy 8) should highlight some key skills or techniques that you both agree will make a difference to their future performances. To explain the approach of overlearning with athletes a phrase that often resonates well is: 'don't practice until you get it right. Practice until you cannot get it wrong'.

A way to help the athlete understand the value of this process is to explain how we learn skills. When we start to learn a skill we will be unconsciously incompetent at it (i.e. we don't know how bad we are). Over time we become consciously incompetent, we are still not good at using the skill but at least we realise this. With lots of practice we become consciously competent, so we get much better at doing the skill but we have to think about the process of doing it. When we are truly skilled we become unconsciously competent, we do it without even thinking about it. Overlearning skills achieves this.

With the skills the athlete is looking to overlearn it is important to set a goal around each one and record the number of physical repetitions successfully performed in training, and the number completed successful through imagery (Strategy 25) too. These figures will give the athlete a number to reflect upon ahead of competition which should give them evidence of their overlearning and boost their confidence.

Strategy 28 – simulation training

Simulation training is a much gentler process than adversity training (Strategy 12) which takes the athlete out of their comfort zone and into a place where they are having to mentally or physically over-reach. Simulation training aims to get the athlete used to things they will be dealing with in competition but which are not usually present in their training environment.[55] Athletes will be put under similar pressure and conditions to bring the feeling of competition to life but in a safe way so the athlete can build up their experience of the environment so competition day feels more comfortable and less intimidating. The aim is to physically and mentally simulate the competitive environment in a way that is as close to reality as possible so athletes are able to practice under similar conditions. It can help athletes develop realistic imagery[56] and prepare much more effectively for competition.

Examples of simulation training include Michael Phelps who practised swimming in a set of blacked-out googles to ensure he could still swim if something ever went wrong with his goggles in a race.[57] In the 2008 Olympics his goggles did fill with water and he couldn't see. But he still won the race. And set a new World Record.

Studies found that when cyclists in an indoor time trial were racing against an avatar (believing it was a competitor) they rode significantly faster than when they were asked to try to perform at their best but without a competitor.[58] This suggests that in simulation training to get someone working really effectively it is worth adding in a competitor or someone the athlete sees as a competitor.

How to do it

Coaches with the opportunity to lead training plans can schedule in 'practice' lead-up competitions to get the athlete working harder than they might otherwise in regular workouts. It gives them the pressure to work hard, and the feeling and atmosphere of competition to focus on what works and push themselves harder than they could on their own. Athletes without coaches scheduling training can look to find small local competitions to use as practice or agree with training partners (Strategy 64) to do a time trial or similar activity which will help put them under competition pressure.

Simulation training activities can include time trials, club races, penalty shoot-outs to bring the feeling of competition to life. Simulation conditions you may want to create could involve crowd noise, competitive rivals showing up or frustration or anger. All will give good experience for the athlete on race day.

Strategy 29 – 'what if' planning

One of the oldest and widest used sports psychology strategies, 'what if' planning, is brilliant for crisis prevention and planning. It is a process to firstly identify all the elements of competition an athlete is worried about, secondly to develop plans and strategies to prevent them occurring and thirdly to prepare what they would do if they were to happen. It is entirely focused on the athlete and what they fear so it is really personalised and helps them feel far more in control of the competition process. It can be used for a specific competition or to consider all the things that might derail an athlete over a season.

The first part helps an athlete to stop burying their head in the sand and face up to everything they are worried about. Getting this out on paper helps them be more reflective and honest with themselves about their fears.

The second part supports deep planning, to come up with a way to prevent their fears occurring. This brings confidence as if the activities and processes developed are being followed then the athlete will be far better prepared for their competition and likely to perform better.

Finally, the 'if … then' section allows the athlete to scenario plan for anything happening in their areas of fear. As athletes get energy depleted in competition they can start to lose their emotional control and make poor decisions. Having already completed the 'if … then' means they don't need to think about what to do when they come across a threat or a fear – all they do is follow the 'then' in their pre-prepared plan. It helps athletes know if one of their issues does occur in the competition they will be less flustered and more confident as they already have a logical and thought through strategy to deal with it. It improves confidence and their feelings of control.

How to do it

1   The first step is to sit down with the athlete and work out the purpose of the 'what if' plan; a specific goal, a season or a competition. If it is for a competition the

plan should be created about a month or so ahead of the competition so the prevention elements can be incorporated into everyday training and preparation. If it is for a season then it should be developed early on, just after completing their goal setting (Strategy 2).

2 The next step is to chat about all the worries they have about that event or period. What do they fear, what could hold them back? These don't need to be rational or even likely. But it is essential nothing is unsaid so it should be a complete brain drain (Strategy 16). If the athlete struggles to articulate their worries, then elements to prompt them about could be injury, poor decision making by an event official, seeing negative comments about themselves on social media, getting distracted, feeling ill, falling over or feeling pain mid-event, losing motivation, getting disqualified, starting to lose against someone who is lower ranked, or equipment failure.

3 Each scenario then requires the athlete to provide a couple of ways to prevent the fear from occurring.

4 Finally, the athlete works on their 'if …then' strategy for what they would do if any of the things they feared actually happened. There may be a few scenarios they can neither influence nor control so they can't prevent it happening but they can still have a plan for how they will approach it and respond if the worst case happened.

Notes

1 Jones, G. (2002). What is this thing called mental toughness? An investigation of elite sport performers. *Journal of Applied Sport Psychology, 14*(3), 205–218.

2 Galli, N., & Vealey, R. (2008). 'Bouncing back' from adversity: Athletes' experiences of resilience. *The Sport Psychologist, 22*, 316–335.

3 Trapp, T. K. (1989). Tactical soccer situations test for players and coaches. *Soccer Journal*, 33–34.

4 Nideffer, R. M. (1979). The role of attention in optimal athletic performance. In P. Klavora & J. V. Daniels (Eds.), *Coach, athlete and the sport psychologist* (pp. 99–112). Toronto: University of Toronto.

5 Wells, A. (2002). *Emotional disorders and metacognition: Innovative cognitive therapy*. Chichester: John Wiley & Sons.

6 such as Martens, 1989, Test of attentional shift – Martens, R. (1989). *Sport psychology workbook*. Champaign, IL: Human Kinetics.

7 White, R. W. (1959). Motivation reconsidered: The concept of competence. *Psychological Review, 66*, 297–333.

8 Bandura, A. (1986). Fearful expectations and avoidant actions as coeffects of perceived self-inefficacy. *American Psychologist, 41*(12), 1389–1391.

9 Duda, J. L. (1993). Goals: A social-cognitive approach to the study of achievement motivation in sport. In R. N. - Singer, M. Murphey, & L. K. Tennant (Eds.), *Handbook of research on sport psychology* (pp. 421–436). New York: Macmillan.

10 Forsterling, F. (1988). *Attribution theory in clinical psychology*. Chichester: Wiley; Marlatt, G. A., & Gordon, J. R. (1985). *Relapse prevention: Maintenance strategies in the treatment of addictive behaviours*. New York: Guilford Press.

11 Orbach, I., Singer, R. N., & Murphey, M. (1997). Changing attributions with an attribution training strategy related to basketball dribbling. *The Sport Psychologist, 11*(3), 294–304.

12 Orbach, I., Singer, R., & Price, S. (1999). An attribution training program and achievement in sport. *The Sport Psychologist, 13*(1), 69–82.

13 Sinnott, K., & Biddle, S. (1998). Changes in attributions, perceptions of success and intrinsic motivation after attribution retraining in children's sport. *International Journal of Adolescence and Youth, 7*(2), 137–144.

14 Sinnott, K., & Biddle, S. (1998). Changes in attributions, perceptions of success and intrinsic motivation after attribution retraining in children's sport. *International Journal of Adolescence and Youth, 7*(2), 137–144.

15 Benson, M. J. (1989). Attributional measurement strategies: Classification and comparison of approaches for measuring causal dimensions. *The Journal of Social Psychology, 129*, 307–323.

16 Prentice, W. E. (1998). Biofeedback. In W. E. Prentice (Ed.), *Therapeutic modalities in sports medicine* (4th ed., pp. 131–145). Boston: WCB/McGraw-Hill.

17 Hanin, Y. L. (2000). *Emotions in sport*. Champaign, IL: Human Kinetics.

18 Caird, S. J., McKenzie, A. D., & Sleivert, G. G. (1999). Biofeedback and relaxation strategies improve running economy in sub-elite long distance runners. *Medicine and Science in Sports and Exercise, 31*(5), 717–722.

19 Kavussanu, M., Crews, D. J., & Gill, D. L. (1998). The effects of single versus multiple measures of biofeedback on basketball free throw shooting performance. *International Journal of Sport Psychology, 29*(2), 132–144.

20 Petruzzello, S. J., Landers, D. M., & Salazar, W. (1991). Biofeedback and sport/exercise performance: Applications and limitations. *Behaviour Therapy, 22*(3), 379–392.

21 Prapavessis, H., Grove, J. R., McNair, P. J., & Cable, N. T. (1992). Self-regulation training, state anxiety, and sport performance: A psychophysiological case study. *Sport Psychologist, 6*(3), 213–229.

22 Blumenstein, B., Bar-Eli, M., & Tenenbaum, G. (2002). *Biofeedback applications in performance enhancement: Brain and body in sport and exercise.* New York: Wiley.

23 Bar-Eli, M., & Blumenstein, B. (2004). Performance enhancement in swimming: The effect of mental training with biofeedback. *Journal of Science and Medicine in Sport, 7*, 454–464.

24 Lehrer, P. M., Vaschillo, E., Lu, S. F., Eckberg, D., Vaschillo, B., Scardella, A., et al. (2006). Heart rate variability biofeedback: Effects of age on heart rate variability, baroreflex gain, and asthma. *Chest, 129*, 278–284.

25 Lagos, L., Vaschillo, E., Vaschillo, B., Lehrer P., Bates, M., & Pandina, R. (2008). Heart rate variability biofeedback as a strategy for dealing with competitive anxiety: A case study. *Biofeedback, 36*(3), 109–115.

26 Strack, B. W. (2003). Effect of heart rate variability (HRV) biofeedback on batting performance in baseball. *Dissertation Abstracts International: Section B: The Sciences and Engineering, 64*, 1540.

27 Ramirez, G., & Beilock, S. L. (2011). Writing about testing worries boosts exam performance in the classroom. *Science, 331*(6014), 211–213.

28 Marcora, S. M., Bosio, A., & de Morree, H. M. (2008). Locomotor muscle fatigue increases cardiorespiratory responses and reduces performance during intense cycling exercise independently from metabolic stress. *American Journal of Physiology-Regulatory, Integrative and Comparative Physiology, 294*(3), R874–R883.

29 Marcora, S. M., Staiano, W., & Merlini, M. (2015). A randomized controlled trial of brain endurance training (bet) to reduce fatigue during endurance exercise. *Medicine & Science in Sports & Exercise, 47*(5S), 198.

30 Khasky, A. D., & Smith, J. C. (1999). Stress, relaxation states, and creativity. *Perceptual and Motor Skills, 88*(2), 409–416.

31 Broucek, M. W., Bartholomew, J. B., Landers, D. M., & Linder, D. E. (1993). The effects of relaxation with a warning cue on pain tolerance. *Journal of Sport Behavior, 16*(4), 239.

32 Jacobson, E. (1929). *Progressive relaxation*. Chicago, IL: University of Chicago.

33 Connaughton, D., Hanton, S., & Jones, G. (2010). The development and maintenance of mental toughness in the world's best performers. *The Sport Psychologist, 24*(2), 168–193.

34 Jones, G., Hanton, S., & Connaughton, D. (2002). What is this thing called mental toughness? An investigation of elite sport performers. *Journal of Applied Sport Psychology, 14*, 205–218.

35 Feltz, D. L., Short, S. E., & Sullivan, P. J. (2008). *Sport: Research and strategies for working with athletes, teams, and coaches*. Champaign, IL: Human Kinetics.

36 Ito, T. A., Larsen, J. T., Smith, N. K., & Cacioppo, J. T. (1998). Negative information weighs more heavily on the brain: The negativity bias in evaluative categorizations. *Journal of Personality and Social Psychology, 75*(4), 887.

37 Anderson, N. H. (1965). Averaging versus adding as a stimulus-combination rule in impression formation. *Journal of Experimental Psychology, 70*(4), 394.

38 Matlin, M. W. (2002). *Cognition* (5th ed.). Fort Worth, TX: Harcourt College Publishers.

39 Garza, D. L., & Feltz, D. L. (1998). Effects of selected mental practice on performance, self-efficacy, and competition confidence of figure skaters. *The Sport Psychologist, 12*(1), 1–15.

40 White, A., & Hardy, L. (1998). An in-depth analysis of the uses of imagery by high-level slalom canoeists and artistic gymnasts. *The Sport Psychologist, 12*(4), 387–403.

41 Wright, C. J., & Smith, D. K. (2007). The effect of a short-term PETTLEP imagery intervention on a cognitive task. *Journal of Imagery Research in Sport and Physical Activity, 2*(1), 18–31.

42 Holmes, P. S., & Collins, D. J. (2001). The PETTLEP approach to motor imagery: A functional equivalence model for sport psychologists. *Journal of Applied Sport Psychology, 13*(1), 60–83.

43 Marcora, S. M., Staiano, W., & Manning, V. (2009). Mental fatigue impairs physical performance in humans. *Journal of Applied Physiology, 106*(3), 857–864.

44 Smith, M. R., Thompson, C., Marcora, S. M., Skorski, S., Meyer, T., & Coutts, A. J. (2018). Mental fatigue and soccer: current knowledge and future directions. *Sports Medicine, 48*(7), 1525–1532.

45 Penna, E. M., Filho, E., Wanner, S. P., Campos, B. T., Quinan, G. R., Mendes, T. T., & Prado, L. S. (2018). Mental fatigue impairs physical performance in young swimmers. *Paediatric Exercise Science, 30*(2), 208–215.

46 Le Mansec, Y., Pageaux, B., Nordez, A., Dorel, S., & Jubeau, M. (2018). Mental fatigue alters the speed and the

accuracy of the ball in table tennis. *Journal of Sports Sciences, 36*(23), 2751–2759.

47 Wagstaff, C. R. (2014). Emotion regulation and sport performance. *Journal of Sport and Exercise Psychology, 36*(4), 401–412.

48 Baldwin, T. T., & Ford, J. K. (1988). Transfer of training: A review and directions for future research. *Personnel Psychology, 41*(1), 63–105.

49 Ivarie, J. J. (1986). Effects of proficiency rates on later performance of a recall and writing behavior. *Remedial and Special Education, 7*(5), 25–30.

50 Binder, C. (1987). Fluency-building: Research background. As referenced in Dougherty, K. M., & Johnston, J. M. (1996). Overlearning, fluency, and automaticity. *The Behavior Analyst, 19*(2), 289–292.

51 Bloom, B. S. (1986). The hands and feet of genius. *Educational Leadership, 43,* 70–77.

52 Hardy, L., Jones, G., & Gould, D. (1996). *Understanding psychological preparation for sport: Theory and practice of elite performers.* Chichester, England: Wiley & Sons.

53 Hays, K., Maynard, I., Thomas, O., & Bawden, M. (2007). Sources and types of confidence identified by world-class sporting performers. *Journal of Applied Sport Psychology, 19,* 434–456.

54 Hanton, S., Wadey, R., & Mellalieu, S. D. (2008). Advanced psychological strategies and anxiety responses in sport. *The Sport Psychologist, 22*(4), 472–490.

55 Hardy, L., Jones, G., & Gould, D. (1996). *Understanding psychological preparation for sport: Theory and practice of elite performers.* Chichester, England: Wiley & Sons.

56 Jones, G. (1993). The role of performance profiling in cognitive behavioural interventions in sport. *The Sport Psychologist, 7,* 160–172.

57 White, D. (2012). London 2012 olympics: Michael Phelps sets mind's eye on triumphant role in final part of Lord of the Rings trilogy. *The Telegraph.* Retrieved from www.telegraph.co.uk/sport/olympics/swimming/9401518/London-2012-Olympics-Michael-Phelps-sets-minds-eye-on-triumphant-role-in-final-part-of-Lord-of-the-Rings-trilogy.html

58 Williams, E. L., Jones, H. S., Sparks, S. A., Marchant, D. C., Midgley, A. W., & Mc Naughton, L. R. (2015). Competitor presence reduces internal attentional focus and improves 16.1 km cycling time trial performance. *Journal of Science and Medicine in Sport, 18*(4), 486–491.

12

Strategies for performing in competition

Strategy 30 – smiling

Smiling is such a simple strategy yet increasingly research is finding benefits in doing so whilst in competition, especially in endurance sports.

One piece of research has found that runners who purposely smiled when struggling found their oxygen consumption and their perception of effort was lower.[1] It has been suggested this was a result of the smiling relaxing the athlete's emotional state and reducing their perception of effort, giving the athlete an improvement in speed for the same effort.

Separate research put 13 riders on exercise bikes in a lab and asked them to ride for as long as possible.[2] While riding, happy or sad faces were subliminally flashed incredibly quickly onto a screen. The cyclists weren't aware of the intervention and didn't know there were faces were being flashed but those who saw the smiles increased their endurance by 12% compared to those who were shown frowns. Based on an effort-based decision-making model anything which influences our perception of effort will then influence our performance. The idea is that visual cues, such as smiling, can again reduce perception of effort because it reduces our subjective appraisal of the demand required for the task ahead.

There is also an idea that smiling at your rivals, treating them in a way they completely do not expect, can throw them, and benefit us. There is a psychological concept called 'interpersonal complementarity' where we naturally follow the social cues around us. Someone smiles, we smile back.

Someone puts out their hand to shake it and we do the same. A Stanford psychologist, Brian Knutson, used this to his advantage when he realised he was in a difficult situation with a potential mugger barging into him aggressively.[3] Instead of offering an aggressive reaction back he pretended to know the guy, was overly friendly and completely caught him off guard, giving him time to escape safely. An athlete won't be mugged on the field of play but may well come up against raw aggression or sledging from competitors so smiling at them could put them completely off their guard.

How to do it

This knowledge can be used in competition by athletes in three ways:

- To smile when they feel they are struggling as a personal boost.
- To seek out those smiling at them in the crowd or field of play to feel more positive.
- To smile at rivals and put them off guard.

The process here is to explain to an athlete the benefits of smiling in a competition and letting them try it as a test, taking prompts from other competitors or anyone watching the competition. The smiling will directly help the athlete, and if they are close to those supporting or watching, then seeing the face of anyone smiling back at them will give a second boost. Athletes may also be able to use the smiling element as an instructional self-talk activity or a motivational mantra. Something like 'smile every mile' for endurance athletes is easy to remember and gives them a task-focused activity to do regularly.

Strategy 31 – acting confident

Our thoughts, feelings and behaviours all feed off each other. When we behave as if we are confident, then over time we can start to feel more confident. This 'fake it till you make it' idea sounds a little cheesy but it has validity as body language has been found to have an positive impact on how we feel about ourselves.

Prior to competition athletes should think about how they physically self-present. Using the right type of body language has been found to increase feelings of power, tolerance for risk and testosterone levels and decrease cortisol levels.[4] A simple place to start can be with power posing where we stand in a posture of confidence. A study of 54 peer-reviewed studies on power posing found that people who use open, expansive power poses *feel* more powerful.[5] The powerful body language also impacts how others see the athlete. With 50–70% of our communication being non-verbal[6] athletes can use this powerful body language to make competitors feel less confident and less likely to do well, giving themselves an improved likelihood of success.

Once an athlete has nailed their confident body position they can also be clever with how they dress for competition. Where athletes are able to choose their own kit they should research how the colour of the kit worn can influence mood, emotion and aggression. In research carried out over the 2004 Athens Olympics,[7] where athletes in combat sports were randomly assigned either a blue or red uniform, those wearing red won significantly more often than those wearing blue. It could be because judges are more drawn to certain colours, or the athletes themselves perform better when wearing colours which have specific psychological connotations. Red as a colour is considered to be powerful, dominant and physical and has been found to influence motivation.[8] The association with red has also carried over into team sports where research in football at the European Championships in 2004[9] found teams with red strips won more often than they statistically should have. Black is psychologically associated with being more threatening or intimidating and teams wearing black in NFL and ice hockey have significantly more penalties awarded against them.[10]

How to do it

To work on their body language a fun strategy to engage with a group of athletes is to ask them all to use just their body language to show how they are feeling. Acting as someone 'running scared' would involve making yourself as small as possible, shoulders slumped, head down, looking pained. Acting as a confident athlete would entail their head held high, their chest forward, shoulders back and down and thinking tall with a focused face will give a clear comparison.

The athletes can try:

- Sad
- Nervous
- Excited
- Terrified
- Happy
- Confident.

Once they have all shown 'confident' ask them to really consider their 'confident' stance. What about it made it obvious? Their hand position? How far apart their feet are? Where their shoulders are placed? The position of the head? Their facial expression? Where their eyes are looking? If they feel embarrassed to do this in front of others they can try this in the mirror.

The most common way to physically self-present as confident will be legs slightly apart, shoulders back, arms apart and relaxed and head up. A quick prompt for this with athletes could be to ask them to think: 'tall and wide'. This can be a useful mantra for them to use ahead of competition to help them feel more confident.

To adapt this for younger athletes you can turn it into a game of charades with two teams each getting a card with an emotion on and the other team has to guess which emotion they are showing.

Strategy 32 – alter ego

Alter egos have been used for many years in sport. They are designed to give an athlete all the characteristics and personality traits required to succeed in their chosen event. They are not usually creating an entire new persona but identifying a few traits (ones they feel don't currently feature strongly within their personality) which would help them perform better and building them into a character that they 'put on' when they compete.

A great example of an alter ego is Tiger Woods. He was actually born Eldrick Woods but is said to have been named Tiger by his father when he was three to emulate the way he needed to behave on the golf course. The Rock is another example. Dwayne Johnson, previously an American footballer, moved into wrestling and needed to distance himself from his true character which is shy and humble. He took The Rock as a name to highlight a character full of ego and empty of remorse.

Alter egos are most often used in sports where aggression is needed, particularly rugby, as the athletes competing in them may not have this aggression naturally. When athletes are already having to really step outside of their comfort zones and feel what they are doing is 'not really them', having an alter ego to call upon can make them feel more comfortable at competing effectively.

How to do it

Work with your athlete to create their performance profile (Strategy 4). This should highlight any areas they feel they need to improve in to become the athlete they want to be. Focus particularly on character traits and pick a couple of these to be used as a basis for their alter ego. With this in front of them they can start to develop their alter ego. This is not a completely new character, it is their personality with a few additional helpful characteristics mixed in.

To help them bring this to life they should consider:

- The name of their character.
- The music their character would listen to.
- The mental skills that character would use.
- What type of kit their character may wear (if they have choice over it).
- What strengths this character will give them.
- The mindset of their character.

They don't need to use their alter ego in every competition but practising using it will really help them feel more comfortable and efficient in switching it on and off so the more the athlete is able to add in the attributes they need to their performances the better mindset they will be in to back up their technical and fitness abilities.

A version for younger athletes can be 'be your own super hero', so helping them design their own sporting super hero and what characteristics that super hero would have to allow them to bring those characteristics into their competitions.

An important caveat for using this strategy is to ensure you are aware of any underlying mental health issues the athlete may have before using it. Athletes with any type of personality disorder or mental health condition should not be pushed into trying to create new personality traits for sport without having discussed this with their clinical psychologist or psychiatrist.

Strategy 33 – amping up or toning down

There is a prime level of arousal for each athlete when it comes to being in the right mental and physical place for performance. Athletes can learn through competition experience and post-competition analysis (Strategy 5) where their sweet spot is, that place where they feel they have just the right balance of nerves and excitement. Then they have to figure out what will get them there.

If an athlete finds themselves too amped up before the start of their competition they need to pick a tactic to calm themselves down. Pre-performance routines (Strategy 37) and colourful breathing (Strategy 18) are both helpful for this. If an athlete struggles to reach the excitement level they require then they are under-aroused and they need to amp themselves up to get adrenaline flowing and their heart rate higher. This is more common in sports where athletes are competing regularly so the threat or challenge of competition becomes more mundane.

A well-researched area around arousal in sport is the use of music. When music is used in the short period before competition it can help athletes get to their optimal arousal zone[11] by priming their body for the required action[12] perhaps as a result of music increasing the movement of dopamine (a chemical involved in pleasure) in the brain[13] which then enhances an athlete's mood and delays fatigue.[14]

How to do it

To physically tone down arousal an athlete can slow down their breathing. A good strategy for this is colourful breathing (Strategy 18) as they can do it in 12 seconds periods until they feel they have calmed enough.

To physically amp up arousal levels an athlete can behave energetically to physically wake themselves. They should complete a short simple warm up consisting of a short jog, bouncing up and down or tapping their legs. They can adapt this to match the level of arousal they are feeling. While doing this they should be acting confidently (Strategy 31). Athletes can also increase their breathing rate. Just as slowing breathing down can help to reduce arousal, increasing it can accelerate getting psyched up. The athlete needs to use short, deep breaths. Using a short phrase as they do it can be helpful. 'Energy in, tiredness out' might be one to try.

To use music effectively athletes should think about the purpose of the music – what do they want it to do for them; relax them, amp them up, make them smile, get focused, build energy? They should start with a long list of familiar tracks that cover their musical taste and then whittle them down taking into consideration tracks which:

- They love that get them fired up and ready to go.
- Have meaning or inspirational words which 'talk' to them and make them want to go out and perform at their best.
- Use strong rhythms.
- Invoke some positive memories or feelings.

Once the athlete is happy with the playlist suggest they put shuffle mode on. When an athlete listens to a playlist too often their brain is able to anticipate what comes next and they start to lose the dopamine benefit. Having the list on shuffle will deliver a bigger hit of dopamine and help the athlete feel rewarded.

While music works best when it is the music that the individual athlete connects with if you are working with a team having a team playlist to listen to on the way to competitions if they all travel together can be a really nice team bonding activity. If every athlete can pick their favourite track to put onto the list you'll have a great team chat and can learn from each athlete what it is about their track that gets them fired up.

Younger athletes can find this is a nice activity to do with their parents; choosing the purpose, selecting the playlist together, mixing up older and new tracks and making it a fun process.

Strategy 34 – associative attentional strategies

Associative attentional strategies are cognitive strategies for maintaining focus in competition. As we learnt in Chapter 4, what athletes focus on matters. If they focus on good strategy and effort levels then they will perform better. However, competition environments can be interpreted differently by athletes so there tends to be a split between those who like to focus on their bodies and use any pain they feel as feedback to adapt their strategy and style (associative attentional strategy) and those who like to completely distract themselves (dissociative attentional strategy) in order to get through the competition.

Attentional strategies are particularly well used in endurance sport where athletes are competing for very long periods of time without having a specific need to focus on objects or people (such as balls or team-mates). Research has found that while both types of strategy are used, often interchangeably within the same competition, elite athletes tend to use more associative attentional strategies[15] and those looking to complete rather than compete use more dissociative strategies.

There are a number of associative attentional strategies but a really popular one is body checking as it involves the athlete monitoring their body and adjusting pace, strategy or movement. It is particularly helpful in competition when athletes are competing in sports where they are responding to the environment around them (such as running or swimming) rather than a ball (football or rugby) or direct competitor (judo, fencing) but can be helpful for any athlete, whatever their sport, in training especially as research has found that those who focus on their body during exercise report more pleasure from the session.[16] Body checking helps the athletes to become hyper aware of their bodily actions and functions; heart rate, muscle tension, breathing rate and ensures they keep on top of the information they need to manage competition tactics.

How to do it

Working with the athlete on the perfect strategy for their biomechanics and their sport will give them a framework to follow when they need to focus either in competition or training. They will then be able to body check regularly while in motion; mentally thinking about each section of their body part by part and focusing on having good technique in each of them.

An example for a runner would be: monitoring their footstrike and stride pattern, ensuring their arms are swinging forwards and backwards rather than side to side and sticking to specific breathing patterns. Counting can also be helpful as it takes their mind off any body pain but keeps the athlete focused on the rhythm and pace they are aiming for.

Regularly practising this body checking in training helps the athlete be able to use it easily when under the pressure of competition and to be able to ask their coaches about ways to improve strategy if they notice it failing.

Strategy 35 – dissociative attentional strategy

Disassociation is simply the athlete finding ways to distract themselves from the way they are feeling during a competition. They aim to mentally focus on something unrelated to the process their body is going through in order to pass the time, reduce the level of boredom and make it to the end of their competition without dropping out. It keeps their mind off the effort their body is putting in, thus reducing the feelings of perceived exertion.

In some sports this strategy would be unsafe (such as downhill skiing or BMX) or cause a poor performance (in sports requiring intense concentration) so it is mainly in endurance sports, particularly in practice, where long hours of repetitive training and only low levels of situational awareness are required.

It is not a performance strategy though. A study of the United States Olympic Marathon trial contestants found while the top finishers used both associative and dissociative strategies, higher performing athletes preferred to spend time on associative attentional strategies (Strategy 34) with those finishing further back using dissociative strategies.[17]

How to do it

There are hundreds of ways to distract ourselves momentarily and each athlete needs to find the one that works best for them. This is usually through trial and error but will eventually become their own preference. Ideas to offer athletes wanting to use disassociation could involve:

- Doing maths and equations in their heads about the distance or time left till the finish.
- Counting how many other athletes they overtake.
- Counting up to 100 and back down again.
- Repeating a mantra in another language.
- Writing a competition report in their head.
- Thanking every volunteer or marshal.
- Thinking of the perfect tweet to summarise their competition.
- Planning their post-competition treat.
- In a race finding someone going the same pace as them and chatting to them.
- Making up the story of the person in front of them.
- Creating a competition in their head for the best banner or supporters sign spotted.

Strategy 36 – chunking

Chunking has two definitions in sport psychology. One refers to the chunking theory of memory which suggests ways that experts learn. The more relevant one for applied sport psychology focuses on the approach taken by athletes to break down a competition into much smaller chunks to make them it less intimidating and pressured. It is used by athletes to help them feel whatever is ahead of them is more manageable by breaking down large, and often scary, events or competitions into bite sized things that are easier to face. A long competition will be daunting. A small section of it is far less so. And each of those small sections which an athlete achieves will give them another piece of evidence that they can suffer for certain periods when required. This can be confidence boosting. Over time those periods can extend.

This strategy also facilitates an athlete having individual goals for each chunk of their competition, meaning they can be more strategic or tactical with the processes they follow at each specific point, increasing their chances of achieving their ultimate competition goal.

The process of chunking can work especially well for those in endurance sports whose competitions last for many hours and they may be completing distances they rarely reach in training. It may work due to the focus on reward and motivation which comes from increased dopamine (a brain chemical linked to reward). When we anticipate a reward dopamine is released. So breaking things down into smaller sections will help us get mini-surges of pleasure each time we achieve one of them. The more achievements we have, the more often we get our dopamine shot.

How to do it

To chunk down a competition the athlete should start about a week or so beforehand to create a timeline of the event. This timeline can then be broken down into natural breaks in the event; quarters or halves (for football rugby or cricket), distances (for running, swimming or cycling), number of attempts (for jumps or throws), disciplines (for multisport) or rounds or games (for tennis, golf or fencing). If the chunks still feel too big after these natural breaks are highlighted then the athlete can choose how to break them down further, until they get to a level where each chunk feels manageable. Once the chunks are clear the athlete needs to devise a physical and mental strategy for each section.

Strategy 37 – pre-performance routine

Burying our head in the sand just hoping a competition goes well is not an evidence-based strategy. It can give us a handy excuse for not doing well (and as such is a form of self-sabotage) but it rarely creates the ideal environment for a successful performance. What does give an athlete the best chance of success is meticulous planning so they arrive in plenty of time, have all the kit required, have taken in the right level of hydration and nutrition, have a well-executed warm up, know the mental skills which gets them into their performance mindset and all of this ensures they feel in control of all the controllables. Routines provide this security.

A pre-performance routine, a number of task relevant thoughts and actions used before a competition reduces anxiety,[18] pushes activation towards their optimal arousal level,[19] improves concentration and focus[20] and increases accuracy, form[21] and improves performance.[22] It gets athletes ready to compete both physically and mentally warmed up.

Pre-performance routines structure an athlete's thought processes and emotions so their attention stays in the present and on task-relevant activities rather than their mind wandering off into negative or unhelpful thinking territory. Knowing they have done all they need to reach the start with the best mental and physical preparation will create a sense of comfort and control knowing they have everything (kit, body and mind) in the right place, at the right time, so can feel confident.

How to do it

A pre-performance routine should be designed around the athlete's personality, the sport they are competing in and the logistics of their lives. Some athletes may benefit from a routine lasting 24 hours (particularly those who have to register or sign-in the day before a competition) others will want one which lasts just a few minutes. An athlete racing an Ironman triathlon (which lasts between eight and 17 hours) where they have to rack their bike and hand in their bags 24 hours before the race starts and is probably staying in a hotel beforehand will have a long routine. A footballer who plays every Saturday in a local league may be very comfortable in the environment and have low anxiety so their routine may just consist of their warm up, a specific drink they like and a mental skill, lasting just 20 minutes.

The more a routine is repeated (and practiced) the more beneficial it becomes.

Areas to consider and questions to help the athlete think about the routine they create include:

- Training: do I want to train or exercise the day before the race, and, if so, what shall I do?
- Kit and equipment: when will I pack my kit bag? Have I a list of everything I need? Have I recently used my kit to know it is not damaged? Will I be able to store it somewhere secure while I compete or do I need to make sure I don't take any valuables?
- Travel: how will I get to my competition? Have I checked the route? Am I sure I know where the venue is? Are there road/train works? Is there parking? What will I need to pay for?
- Food: what do I like to eat the night before a competition? What do I like for breakfast? Will I be able to get hold of it if staying away? What time should I eat breakfast? Will I take any nutrition before we start?
- Warm up: does my body like a warm up? Will I avoid people or chat to others? Will I listen to music while I do it?

- Mental skills: which mental skills will I use? Will I use my imagery (Strategy 25) to motivate myself? Will I repeat my mantra (Strategy 45)? Will I listen to my motivational music?

With all these answers they can build a timeline of what they will do and when. Something simple they can follow in the build up to their competition to focus on helpful tasks.

Strategy 38 – mid-competition routine

A mid-competition routine can be thought of as a crutch to lean on in a pressured situation which helps the athlete to regain focus on the important elements that impact their performance. Unlike a pre-performance routine, a mid-competition routine should be very brief. The construction of it will entirely depend upon the type of sport the athlete competes in and its required purpose but they are usually used to help an athlete regain an optimal level of arousal or focus. In football or rugby it will be something to get the athlete re-activated after half time, or to get focused for a penalty. In more fluid sports like endurance sports it may be something completed on the move to regain focus or positivity after a setback during the competition.

The actual elements of it will need to be designed by the athlete so they have full ownership and feel comfortable using it.

Routines can either be overt (practice swings, the setting or aligning of the feet or hands) or covert (such as focusing on the target or visualisation). Examples of these mid-competition routines include mental imagery and arousal control as a pre-shot strategy in basketball[23] and performing the swing mechanics of the shot ahead of actually hitting the ball in golf.[24]

How to do it

To develop the individual's mid-competition routine a discussion needs to take place about the key barrier to an athlete's success once the competition has begun. Is it a loss of temper when losing? A lack of patience when performing well? Frustration when the competition isn't going the way they had expected? Once the barrier is identified you can work out the purpose of the routine: to calm, to boost arousal, to refocus or to put into perspective.

There are four elements to then consider when building the routine:

1   The physical response – ideally one which ensures no-one else knows they are frustrated/angry/upset. An action that involves showing they are not frustrated (keeping shoulders down, face relaxed) helps tell their brain they are less frustrated too.
2   Gaining optimal arousal level – something to help the athlete relax (a breathing exercise to slow down activation) if required or bouncing up and down if the need is to amp up.
3   A reminder of the next action required and how that should go – often using positive, instructional self-talk (Strategy 42).
4   One move which starts off the required action and which everything else automatically follows on from.

An example in tennis would then be: shoulders down, one round of colourful breathing, repeating 'high serve' and bouncing the ball twice. This would take less than 20 seconds.

Strategy 39 – pain interpretation

Pain is something that many athletes are quite rightly fearful of. Not only does it hurt but it is often indicative of injury, and injury may mean time off, expense and missed competitions. Sometimes it is telling us we have an injury and need to stop. Other times it is coming from the discomfort of putting our body through something difficult. Athletes already have a higher pain tolerance compared to the general population[25] but when they are competing with other athletes this advantage is negated and so, when the pain is coming from the discomfort of high performance, they need to find other ways to cope with the pain and the fear of pain.

A study looking at how 204 athletes running 155 miles in stages across four deserts coped with pain identified adaptive strategies which involved ignoring pain, deciding it wouldn't bother them or trying to override it and maladaptive strategies involving catastrophising, fear or despondence.[26] Unsurprisingly those athletes completing the challenges were the ones focusing on using more adaptive strategies. Instead of seeing it as a barrier they were able to co-exist with the pain they felt. The researchers also found the more maladaptive coping an athlete was using the higher their perception of the impact of the pain, the more they thought about their pain and the less likely they were to finish the race. Therefore, the idea that pain is information (in sports where some level of hurt and discomfort is to be expected) and is transient is actually a great perspective to use.

It helps the athlete to restructure their thinking so they see pain and suffering as two separate things: (1) pain as an unpleasant sensory and emotional experience coming from some type of tissue damage and (2) the way we experience that pain in our brain, is suffering. Suffering is clearly impacted by the physical sensation of the pain but it is also affected by our mood, our coping skills and the context of the pain. The context is particularly important. When an athlete expects to feel pain, such as during a hard sprint, they are better prepared and so more able to cope with it. They feel the pain but suffer from it less.

How to do it

Most important is to establish why the pain is there. If investigations show it is coming from an injury then training and competing need to stop until recovery has begun. If it is discomfort caused by the physical challenge then the athlete can start to reinterpret it. Learning biofeedback techniques (Strategy 15) can help an athlete notice differences in injury pain and competition discomfort and keeping a training diary (Strategy 10) can help them note long-term niggles or potential injury issues.

One route to help an athlete reinterpret pain from discomfort is to suggest they embrace the information the pain receptors are giving them. So instead of suffering from pain or tiredness and interpreting this as a signal to stop they use it as a signal to take stock and mentally check through the physical sensations in their bodies. This associative attention strategy (Strategy 34) requires the athlete to mindfully focus on each body part, checking if it is being used with the strategy it should, relaxing anything that is too tense, concentrating on getting their breathing pattern consistent.

A further element to help the athlete acknowledge and even embrace the pain and suffering relationship can be to develop a story to narrate alongside any pain they feel. This process ensures the athlete, in having a chat with themselves, is creating some space between the physical sensation of pain and how they react to it. They are dispassionately observing their pain; seeing pain as information rather than a sensation that they must react to. They can use this when workouts or competitions start to get really tough. An example for a runner might be something like:

This is starting to hurt. But I was expecting it to. I am trying to get really fit so it was never going to be easy. But I am not my pain. We are separate so I know it will be ok and I will get through it.

Strategy 40 – pre-performance bubble

In the build-up to a competition the pressures for athletes can mount. Instead of relaxing and focusing on the excitement of the challenge ahead it is very easy for both external and internal expectations to creep in and take the athlete away from the processes and tasks they should concentrate on and onto how they 'must' or 'should' win or achieve a certain time.

For athletes to block out some of these expectations ahead of big competitions it can be helpful for them to go into a pre-performance bubble where they mentally build a bubble around themselves to keep out anything that could add on pressure or stress. It helps them stay in complete control of what they see and hear in the build-up and focus on just performance relevant activities.

A key element to exclude to help athletes feel protected within the bubble is social media. Partly to stop seeing any expectations about what others expect to see the athlete achieve but also to block out other competitors. There is a 'halo effect'[27] from other athletes where we can let the impression we have about them in one way (i.e. photos of them looking happy and relaxed) influence the way we feel about them in other areas so we make assumptions about other elements of their life or sporting abilities just because we know one positive thing about them, building them up out of all proportion. We also have an 'availability bias'[28] where we use the information close at hand when making decisions or opinions. Another athlete may come up time and time again with post training pictures but it may not mean they are actually training all the time; simply the algorithm is showing them regularly. In the athlete's head though they now seem unbeatable because they are training so seriously.

How to do it

Talking to an athlete about their perfect build-up to competition is a great place to start. Asking which elements they would incorporate, which type of people they like to be around and whether they find it helpful to see what sports and social media is saying about them or their competitors gives a base to start from. Discussing when they like to start to get into their competition mindset will establish a timeframe for their bubble.

The bubble can last as long or short as the athlete likes. Olympic athletes usually go for about 24–48 hours. It will be a lot shorter, perhaps just a few hours, for team athletes who play every week. Once the time has been picked the next stage is to agree how the athlete will protect themselves during this period. There are various options for the athlete to pick:

- Phone off.
- Phone on with internet off or using a non-smart phone.
- Phone on but messaging apps removed.
- Phone given to someone else so if there is an emergency they can let you know.
- Hanging out with others.
- Hanging out on your own.
- Having music which gets you amped up.
- Having music which calms you down.
- Having helpful routines such as a pre-performance routine (Strategy 37) which would include stretching, a warm up, breathing exercises or getting into their alter-ego (Strategy 32).
- Avoiding newspapers if it is a competition likely to be covered in them.
- Having a stack of DVDs to watch.
- For those travelling with teammates who struggle with engagement from others in the build-up then large headphones and music can help them to block out negative nervous talk from others.

Strategy 41 – respond, relax and refocus

In Chapter 5 we saw the importance of emotional control and reflected on the risks both for performance and reputationally if an athlete loses control. Their 'hot buttons' (the things that triggers a loss of emotional control) may be something fairly small, the opposition cheating, missing an 'easy' shot, starting to lose against someone they feel they should beat, but this minor irritation can build up until their inappropriate response (such as throwing a racquet, kicking a ball off the pitch, swearing at an official) becomes a habit. It can take a long time to turn around these habits to a more adaptive and helpful coping mechanism but it is an activity worth attempting especially if they want to compete at high levels.

The process is to follow the three Rs[29] where the first move is to respond. This is a positive action (such as walking to the edge of a court or pitch or snapping a band on their wrist) that the athlete has for whenever they feel themselves facing their hot button. The next step is to relax. This allows arousal levels to drop and space for the right decision (instead of the emotional one) to be made. Then attention moves to refocus, getting the attention back onto the how of the competition: how do I perform well?

With the three Rs written into a plan, those athletes who know they lose concentration or patience mid-competition will feel more confident they have a resilient strategy. The plan doesn't need to be in-depth or extensive – just some bullet points which highlight a couple of things the athlete can do when they notice they have lost concentration or emotional control.

This should be effective because it helps them deal with specific situations and adjust their behaviours, focus or mindset, to be more positive and proactive (they are doing something, rather than feeling like something is being done to them) and it helps them get back their focus onto a task which will help them perform better.

How to do it

1   The first goal is to identify all the athlete's hot buttons. You can talk in general about all the things in life which get them annoyed and then bring it to sport, to training and then finally competition. This means they should have really warmed up into it. The hot buttons are things which create negative and intense feelings.

2   Then the athlete needs to decide on a small action they will take to respond when they feel their hot button warm up. It can be very small; maybe squeezing their ear or bouncing up and down or walking to the edge of the competition zone and drinking some water.

3   The relax element will usually be one round of colourful breathing (Strategy 18) as this only takes 12 seconds.

4   Refocus may come with a cue word (Strategy 44) or some instructional self-talk (Strategy 42) to get them back on task.

The respond, relax, refocus can be practised really well using imagery (Strategy 25) so the athlete gets plenty of time to practise responding to their hot buttons in a more effective manner.

Self-talk

The next five strategies all focus on different elements of self-talk. Our self-talk is the internal chatter that reverberates around in our heads[30] and has a powerful influence on our behaviours, confidence, motivation, endurance, focus and performance. As one of the most well-researched and effective ways of improving sporting success it can be like receiving verbal persuasion from our coach standing alongside us as we compete, reminding us of the training we've put in and the skills we have mastered.

Many think of self-talk as being positive or negative but actually thinking in terms of whether it is helpful or unhelpful can help athletes to use it more effectively. Where it becomes really unhelpful is when athletes say things to themselves they would not dream about saying to others. This 'stinking thinking' will contain lots of unhelpful or negative phrases they repeat to themselves, lowering their confidence. This unhelpful self-talk has been associated poor performance.[31]

Studies of those using self-talk effectively though have found it can increase the time it takes an athlete to reach exhaustion,[32] to help them move from a threat to a challenge state,[33] to improve performance,[34] increase attention,[35] to boost confidence,[36] cognitive and emotional control[37] and positively benefit an athlete's automaticity of skill execution.[38]

Working on their self-talk to develop the most appropriate and helpful ways of thinking is a skill just like any other. It is important that the content within the self-talk route is about something the athlete has control of, is believable and realistic and focuses on the here and now. It also needs to be practised regularly to make it a habit.

There are a number of variants to try. Developing skills in each area means an athlete can pick and choose the most appropriate one for their current situation.

- Technical or instructional (Strategy 42)
- Thought stopping (Strategy 43)
- Cue words (Strategy 44)
- Motivational mantras (Strategy 45)
- Cognitive restructuring and reframing (Strategy 46).

Strategy 42 – technical or instructional self-talk

Technical self-talk is a way of teaching athletes to give them-selves specific instructions. The instructions are often around concentration or problem solving but can be around body position too. The statements the athletes use are usually around the process they need to follow in order to stay calm or continue to perform well. Instructional self-talk has speci-fically been found to improve performance[39] when athletes use it to work on strength, accuracy or fine motor skills.

The positivity the athlete puts into their technical self-talk is important. They need to be telling themselves to do some-thing rather than something to avoid[40] as ironic errors occur when we tell ourselves not to do something with the action playing on our mind making us more likely to actually do it.[41] An athlete telling themselves not to double fault in tennis is more likely to double fault. A golfer thinking they must not hit their ball into the bunker means their focus falls on the bunker and that is exactly where their ball is likely to go.

How to do it

Technical or instructional self-talk is usually a short sen-tence that can be repeated rhythmically while the athlete competes if they find their form or focus is failing. The specific statement chosen as the technical or instructional self-talk needs to come from the athlete but may well arise from a discussion around where the weaknesses lie in performance and which skills may fall apart when under pressure. These should make it clear what the purpose of the statement would be and what that phrase should be. Some athletes find it helpful to write the statement on their hand or water bottle so they are reminded to use it.

Strategy 43 – thought stopping

Thought stopping is when an athlete catches themselves having a negative or unhelpful thought and will purposefully tell themselves to STOP, click their fingers or ping something on their wrist to clear that thought from their mind.

How to do it

Mindfulness practice (Strategy 51) is a helpful way for an athlete to learn to notice all the thoughts they are having in a more purposeful way. It will help the athlete become aware of what they are thinking. When the athlete has mastered this it will be easier for them (pre- or mid-competition) to notice negative or unhelpful thoughts. Once accomplished they can use their preferred method (instruction to stop, band on wrist or finger click) to purposefully stop the thought and choose a more helpful thought to have instead. Often an athlete will then focus on a specific cue word or an instructional self-talk route to give attention to a thought which is more helpful.

Thought stopping can be a word, image or phrase that the athlete has on the tip of their tongue to use whenever they notice themselves using negative thoughts. It needs to really resonate with the athlete so they need to establish what it is themselves. They may need to try a number of different ones until they find something which works for them. Once established the athlete needs to proactively try to find a more positive thought instead to move them on and make the thinking process more productive.

Strategy 44 – cue words

Cue words are single words which help an athlete focus on something very specific. They click the athlete to attention. They may cover a behaviour that the athlete needs to display in order to be successful. For example, a gymnast may use the word 'power', a cheerleader the word 'sass' or a shooter the word 'target'. Cue words are particularly helpful if the athlete is trying to change their strategy or tactics in any way as they are a reminder they are to do something differently that has not yet embedded and become automatic.

How to do it

As the aim is to help the athlete focus attention the word must be simple and practised. The athlete should think of the one word they know their coach would be saying to them; focus, patience, high, power are all commonly used cue words. Once they have chosen their word they can write in on their hand or water bottle to ensure they remember it when required.

Strategy 45 – motivational mantra

A mantra is a short word or phrase to focus the mind which athletes can use to maintain motivation to compete their goal. It works best when it is really personal to the athlete and resonates deeply. Whenever the athlete has a dark moment repeating this over and over again will help them keep focused and working hard. It is really useful for athletes in sports where they have a lot of time to think and to talk themselves out of putting in the required effort as research has shown it increases perseverance. A mantra will either focus on the athlete's motivation for competing or on their goal, reminding themselves what they are hoping to achieve.

Good times to use a mantra are on the start line of a competition if feeling nervous, mid-competition when starting to struggle with a poor score, position or self-doubt and in training when struggling to master new skills or speeds.

How to do it

The first task is to decide with the athlete the type of mantra they want to develop: goal-focused or motivational-driven? Then ask, in an ideal world, what would they want someone else to say to them when they start to struggle in competition. The mantra chosen doesn't need to be set in stone. Some athletes choose one mantra which really works for them for every competition and others may mix and match their mantra depending on the type or level of competition or time in their season.

The mantra which will work best will be the one which makes them slightly emotional. It gives the athlete a bit of a lump in their throat thinking it. To be most effective it needs to be positive, purposeful, memorable and short. Some athletes use metaphors such as 'I'm strong like an ox' or 'I'm as fast as a fox'[42] to enhance the chance of remembering it and to incorporate some positive imagery.

Strategy 46 – cognitive reappraisal and reframing

As we see when an athlete completes their control mapping (Strategy 1) a lot of the actions that occur during competition are outside of their control. What they do have control of, is the meaning they give to them. Whether it is a setback, hopes, ambitions, wins or losses, over time, as the emotion of the situation fades, they can become better able to change the meaning they ascribe to each outcome, and become better able to recognise which thoughts are helpful or unhelpful and aim to see them more dispassionately so they can utilise a reframing strategy to deal with the unhelpful ones.

Rather than trying to simply suppress the thought (which rarely works) the athlete learns to dispute the negative thought patterns and reframe them into something more positive.[43] This is known as cognitive reappraisal (or reframing). It is very helpful for athletes struggling with negative thoughts or dealing with setbacks as the unhelpful statements often centre around irrational or stress inducing ideas; fear of failure, judgement from others, losing to athletes they feel they shouldn't lose to or fear of disapproval. By providing some space to step back and change the meaning they ascribe to each thought they can find a more helpful route to success.

When researchers got 24 runners to complete three 90-minute treadmill runs[44] they gave them one of three different options for each run; no specific instructions to follow, cognitive reappraisal or distraction. The cognitive reappraisal strategy was found to be the one where the runners felt they were exerting the least amount of effort and felt best able to cope emotionally.

How to do it

To begin it is important to get the athlete to talk about the unhelpful thoughts they are having. Asking them to keep a diary for a couple of weeks noting down all the unhelpful or negative thoughts they have while training and competing will give an extensive framework to start from. This helps the athlete acknowledge the thoughts they are having and makes it possible to identify any themes arising.

With this list in place you can look through each statement and discuss how it could be appraised differently to reframe it into something more helpful, motivating or focused on their goal.

The reframed statement needs to be realistic and truthful. We are not trying to create new realities here – just to give the athlete the space to come up with a different perspective and to practise it enough for it to become a habit. Some example reframes could be:

- 'I'm not good enough to be here' into 'I'm using this as preparation for competing in the future so I will use the opportunity to learn as much as possible'.
- 'The wind is making this impossible' into 'all my rivals are battling the wind too, I'll use it to my advantage'.
- 'I can't do this' into 'I can't do this yet, but I'm going to have a go'.
- 'I hate climbs' into 'every hill I climb makes me stronger'.

It takes some practice and may feel a little awkward to begin with but once the athlete has the hang of it, this strategy can work wonders for their confidence and mindset. If the athlete struggles to see their statement from any other perspective perhaps ask them what their coach or training partner might see. This will help them step away from their own thoughts to see a different angle. If athletes still struggle it may help to ask them to think of themselves like a commentator. This should help them to create a more positive commentary without feeling so awkward.

With younger athletes a group activity to do can be to get each athlete to write down three negative thoughts they have when performing on three cards. Then they all get shuffled up and each athlete gets three cards back. On the other side of the card they write a way that it could be reframed. Shuffle the cards again and each person gets three cards to read out. This should give lots of examples for athletes to relate to and use themselves.

Strategy 47 – sensory management

Sensory management is a really simple strategy which helps an athlete feel a little bit safer and more protected from everything going on around them. It can be part of a pre-performance bubble (Strategy 40) or pre-performance routine (Strategy 37) or simply a way for athletes to physically block out as many of the physical elements of a competition which cause them anxiety as they can. This can be done by wearing sunglasses, having big headphones on or purposely staying away from other athletes during warm up or in a changing or call room.

How to do it

If an athlete talks about feeling anxious when they get to their competition venue have a conversation about any elements in particular which prompt that anxiety. Is it other athletes? Seeing the course or pitch or court or venue? Is it the noise or the smell of the venue?

Break each area down into what could dull the images or senses they are struggling to cope with. If it is the lights and medals or supporters then sunglasses can tone everything down. If it is the noise or other athletes wanting to talk (even in a friendly manner) then headphones playing either amping up or a relaxing playlist would be good or even just ear defenders to block out a noise. If it is specific competitor or group of competitors then finding a quiet place away from the hubbub to warm up would help reduce the feeling of threat.

Asking the athlete to think of each element they add as a sort of sensory shield to protect them from stimulation or stresses from anyone else around them should help them to feel more in control and less confronted by everything going on around them.

Notes

1 Brick, N. E., McElhinney, M. J., & Metcalfe, R. S. (2018). The effects of facial expression and relaxation cues on movement economy, physiological, and perceptual responses during running. *Psychology of Sport and Exercise, 34*, 20–28.

2 Blanchfield, A., Hardy, J., & Marcora, S. (2014). Non-conscious visual cues related to affect and action alter perception of effort and endurance performance. *Frontiers in Human Neuroscience, 8*, 967.

3 Knutson, B. (2011). Brian Knutson: Anti-complementarity. Psych to the rescue. *British Psychological Society Research Digest*. Retrieved from: https://digest.bps.org.uk/2011/11/03/brian-knutson-anticomplementarity/

4 Carney, D. R., Cuddy, A. J., & Yap, A. J. (2010). Power posing: Brief nonverbal displays affect neuroendocrine levels and risk tolerance. *Psychological Science, 21*(10), 1363–1368.

5 Cuddy, A. J., Schultz, S. J., & Fosse, N. E. (2018). P-curving a more comprehensive body of research on postural feedback reveals clear evidential value for power-posing effects: Reply to Simmons and Simonsohn (2017). *Psychological Science, 29* (4), 656–666.

6 Burke, K. L. (2005). But coach doesn't understand: Dealing with team communication quagmires. In M. Anderson (Ed.), *Sport psychology in practice* (pp. 45–59). Champaign, IL: Human Kinetics.

7 Hill, R. A., & Barton, R. A. (2005). Psychology: Red enhances human performance in contests. *Nature, 435*(7040), 293.

8 Elliot, A. J., Maier, M. A., Moller, A. C., Friedman, R., & Meinhardt, J. (2007). Color and psychological functioning: The effect of red on performance attainment. *Journal of Experimental Psychology: General, 136*(1), 154.

9 Hill, R. A., & Barton, R. A. (2005). Psychology: Red enhances human performance in contests. *Nature, 435*(7040), 293.

10 Frank, M. G., & Gilovich, T. (1988). The dark side of self-and social perception: Black uniforms and aggression in professional sports. *Journal of Personality and Social Psychology, 54*(1), 74.

11 Bishop, D. T., Karageorghis, C. I., & Loizou, G. (2007). A grounded theory of young tennis players' use of music to manipulate emotional state. *Journal of Sport and Exercise Psychology, 29*(5), 584–607.

12 Lane, A. M., Davis, P. A., & Devonport, T. J. (2011). Effects of music interventions on emotional states and running performance. *Journal of Sports Science Medicine, 10*(2), 400–407.

13 Blood, A. J., & Zatorre, R. J. (2001). Intensely pleasurable responses to music correlate with activity in brain regions implicated in reward and emotion. *PNAS, 98*(20), 11818–11823.

14 Salimpoor, V. N., Benovoy, M., Larcher, K., Dagher, A., & Zatorre, R. J. (2011). Anatomically distinct dopamine release during anticipation and experience of peak emotion to music. *National Neuroscience, 14*(2), 257–262.

15 Masters, K. S., & Ogles, B. M. (1998). Associative and dissociative cognitive strategies in exercise and running: 20 years later, what do we know? *The Sport Psychologist, 12*(3), 253–270.

16 Jones, L., Karageorghis, C. I., Lane, A. M., & Bishop, D. T. (2017). The influence of motivation and attentional style on affective, cognitive, and behavioral outcomes of an exercise class. *Scandinavian Journal of Medicine & Science in Sports, 27*(1), 124–135.

17 Silva, J. M., & Appelbaum, M. I. (1989). Association-dissociation patterns of United States Olympic marathon trial contestants. *Cognitive Therapy and Research, 13*(2), 185–192.

18 Hazell, J., Cotterill, S. T., & Hill, D. M. (2014). An exploration of pre-performance routines, self-efficacy, anxiety and performance in semi-professional soccer. *European Journal of Sport Science, 14*(6), 603–610.

19 Mesagno, C., & Mullane-Grant, T. (2010). A comparison of different pre-performance routines as possible choking interventions. *Journal of Applied Sport Psychology, 22*(3), 343–360.

20 Shaw, D. (2002). Confidence and the pre-shot routine in golf: A case study. In I. Cockerill (Ed.), *Solutions in sport psychology* (pp. 108–119). London: Thomson.

21 Heishman, M. F., & Bunker, L. (1989). Use of mental preparation strategies by international elite female lacrosse players from five countries. *The Sport Psychologist, 3*(1), 14–22.

22 Le Lobmeyer, D., & Wasserman, E. A. (1986). Preliminaries to free throw shooting: Superstitious behavior. *Journal of Sport Behavior, 9*(2), 70.

23 Wrisberg, C. A., & Anshel, M. H. (1989). The effect of cognitive strategies on the free throw shooting performance of young athletes. *The Sport Psychologist, 3*(2), 95–104.

24 Lee, D. (2009). The effect of pre-shot routine on performance of a drive in golf. Thesis. Retrieved from: http://cardinalscholar.bsu.edu/handle/123456789/193793

25 Tesarz, J., Schuster, A. K., Hartmann, M., Gerhardt, A., & Eich, W. (2012). Pain perception in athletes compared to normally active controls: A systematic review with meta-analysis. *Pain, 153*(6), 1253–1262.

26 Alschuler, K., Kratz, A., Krabak, B., Jensen, M., Pomeranz, D., & Lipman, G. (2018). Pain is inevitable but suffering is optional: Predictors of pain in multi-stage ultramarathon runners. *The Journal of Pain, 19*(3), S50–S51.

27 Nisbett, R. E., & Wilson, T. D. (1977). The halo effect: Evidence for unconscious alteration of judgments. *Journal of Personality and Social Psychology, 35*(4), 250.

28 Tversky, A., & Kahneman, D. (1973). Availability: A heuristic for judging frequency and probability. *Cognitive Psychology, 5*(2), 207–232.

29 Lauer, L., Gould, D., Lubbers, P., & Kovacs, M. (2010). *USTA mental skills and drills handbook*. Monterey, CA: Coaches Choice.

30 Van Raalte, J. L., Vincent, A., & Brewer, B. W. (2016). Self-talk: Review and sport-specific model. *Psychology of Sport and Exercise, 22*, 139–148.

31 Tod, D., Hardy, J., & Oliver, E. (2011). Effects of self-talk: A systematic review. *Journal of Sport & Exercise Psychology, 33*, 666–687.

32 Blanchfield, A. W., Hardy, J., De Morree, H. M., Staiano, W., & Marcora, S. M. (2014). Talking yourself out of exhaustion: The effects of self-talk on endurance performance. *Medicine and Science in Sports and Exercise, 46*(5), 998–1007.

33 Moore, L. J., Vine, S. J., Wilson, M. R., & Freeman, P. (2014). Examining the antecedents of challenge and threat states: The influence of perceived required effort and support availability. *International Journal of Psychophysiology, 93*(2), 267–273.

34 Tod, D., Hardy, J., & Oliver, E. (2011). Effects of self-talk: A systematic review. *Journal of Sport & Exercise Psychology, 33*, 666–687.

35 Galanis, E., Hatzigeorgiadis, A., Zourbanos, N., & Theodorakis, Y. (2016). Why self talk is effective? A review on the self-talk mechanisms in sport. In M. Raab, P. Wylleman, R. Seiler, A. M. Elbe, & A. Hatzigeorgiadis (Eds.), *Sport and exercise psychology research: from theory to practice* (1st Eds., 181–200). London: Elsevier.

36 Wadey, R., & Hanton, S. (2008). Basic psychological skills usage and competitive anxiety responses: Perceived underlying mechanisms. *Research Quarterly for Exercise and Sport, 79*, 363–373.

37 Theodorakis, Y., Hatzigeorgiadis, A., & Chroni, S. (2008). Self-talk: It works, but how? Development and preliminary validation of the functions of self-talk questionnaire. *Measurement in Physical Education & Exercise Science, 12*, 10–30.

38 Hardy, L., Jones, G., & Gould, D. (1996). *Understanding psychological preparation for sport: Theory and practice of elite performers*. Chichester, UK: Wiley.

39 Cutton, D. M., & Landin, D. (2007). The effects of self-talk and augmented feedback on learning the tennis forehand. *Journal of Applied Sport Psychology, 19*(3), 288–303.

40 Singer, R. N., & Janelle, C. M. (1999). Determining sport expertise: From genes to supremes. *International Journal of Sport Psychology, 30*, 117–151.

41 Wegner, D. M., Ansfield, M., & Pilloff, D. (1998). The putt and the pendulum: Ironic effects of the mental control of action. *Psychological Science, 9*(3), 196–199.

42 Hanin, Y. L., & Stambulova, N. B. (2002). Metaphoric description of performance states: An application of the IZOF model. *The Sport Psychologist, 16*(4), 396–415.

43 Beck, J. S. (2011). *Cognitive behavior therapy: Basics and beyond*. New York: Guilford Press.

44 Giles, G. E., Cantelon, J. A., Eddy, M. D., Brunyé, T. T., Urry, H. L., Taylor, H. A., & Kanarek, R. B. (2018). Cognitive reappraisal reduces perceived exertion during endurance exercise. *Motivation and Emotion, 42*(4), 482–496.

13

Strategies for self-awareness

Strategy 48 – value mapping

To feel authentic and comfortable with what we do in sport, and in life, our actions should be aligned with our values. Our values highlight who we are at our deepest level so we can build that authenticity in all we do. If an athlete is able to identify their values and from that ensure their sporting life is aligned around those then they should feel more comfortable when performing in their sport. Despite being so fundamental to our journey in life actually discussing our values seems to happen only rarely so it needs a purposeful activity to get athletes thinking about them.

An athlete who really values trust, communication and creativity would struggle to feel comfortable with a coach who had very rigid rules and told the athlete what they thought they wanted to hear rather than what they actually thought. However, an athlete whose values were discipline, dependency and happiness may be quite happy with this approach.

Values are not just helpful for ensuring the athlete has the right sporting set-up but also when they have to confront unethical issues within their sport; both the obvious like doping but also the more everyday issues such as the opponent who is cheating on line calls in junior tennis, a fencer purposefully taking too long between calls, someone cutting corners in a road race, sledging going on between cricketers or an athlete drafting in a non-drafting triathlon. An athlete sure of their own values can feel more secure with the position they take on any contentious issues knowing it is based on who they feel they are as a person.

How to do this

Two routes to try when helping athletes map their values are asking some questions and asking them to prioritise pre-suggested values. Four questions you can ask to help athletes reflect upon their values and what really matters to them:

1   What do you want to be remembered for?
2   When you look back over this year what will you need to achieve to feel proud?
3   When have you felt disappointed in your behaviour?
4   What are the three values that matter most to you?

We are helping them consider the 'then, now and the future' and within this understanding better their values so they can more proactively and consciously shape the narrative around their sporting performances.

If an athlete struggles to think about their values in this way you may want to offer them this list of different values to consider. Writing the values on cards and asking them to prioritise helps them to really consider each value in turn. We would like them to filter until they have four or five values and then ask them to explain why they have chosen each one. This can be completed as part of becoming a self-expert (Strategy 52) as it helps the athlete understand themselves at a deeper level. Younger athletes may need some terms explained to them or some more child-friendly terms to consider.

Strategy 49 – know your why

We are all motivated differently. Our personality traits, upbringing, previous actions, current environment and value systems all play a part. Understanding where our personal motivation comes from and being aware of how it manifests

Achievement	Effectiveness	Honesty	Quality
Affection	Efficiency	Hope	Recognition
Ambition	Empathy	Humour	Respect
Autonomy	Equality	Independence	Risk-Taking
Beauty	Excitement	Innovation	Security
Challenge	Faith	Integrity	Service
Communication	Family	Intelligence	Simplicity
Competence	Flexibility	Love	Spirituality
Competition	Forgiveness	Loyalty	Strength
Courage	Freedom	Open-minded	Success
Creativity	Friendship	Patience	Teamwork
Curiosity	Growth	Pleasure	Trust
Decisiveness	Happiness	Politeness	Truth
Dependability	Harmony	Power	Variety
Discipline	Health	Productivity	Wealth
Diversity	Helpful	Prosperity	Wisdom

when we are thinking and performing in our sport can be really valuable, especially if we are underperforming or struggling. A simple way to start this classification of our 'why' is through intrinsic and extrinsic motivation.

Intrinsic motivation is when the athlete competes for personal satisfaction; their love of using the skills or the sensations in their bodies. When this is in place their motivation can remain sustainable even if they go through difficult periods as it is the process they love, not the outcome. If their 'why' comes from a more externally driven focus; from the medals, awards or prize money won, to socialise with others, the accolades given, or to keep others happy then they will be fine when they are competing well but when they suffer a setback (as almost every athlete inevitably will) and their rate of improvement slows then they may really struggle. At this point training will feel like a chore and they may well drop out. To counter this, if those working with athletes can appreciate what motivates them they can focus on those elements and help the athlete put in place relevant support.

How to do it

A great way for the athlete to assess their 'why' is free writing. The athlete will need a pen, notebook and 20 minutes where they won't be disturbed. They should answer the question: I compete in [my sport] because …

If they struggle to write freely from that some questions you could suggest are:

- What feelings do you have ahead of competition day?
- What to do you want to feel as you cross the finish line or the whistle blows?
- What outcome from a competition makes you happy?
- When you have those days when you feel flow, what is in your mind?
- What gives you your buzz in your sport?
- If you were told you couldn't do your sport at all for the next month how would you feel?

Once they have this they can start to identify which are extrinsic reasons; the trophies or medals, the praise from others, the accolades from friends, and which are intrinsic motivations; the fundamental processes of their sport. You can then use these in your communications with them as they head into competition.

With younger athletes this can be a nice activity to do in a group session. If they have the chance to listen to their peers talking about their own reasons for doing their sports they will get a variety of angles to think about.

Strategy 50 – metacognition

Much of our behaviour is determined not by how things are, but how we think things are. Therefore metacognition, the process where we think about our knowledge or cognitions[1] and use our own mind to monitor and control itself[2] is a valuable skill.

Using metacognitive processes can enhance performance and equip athletes with the strategies, beliefs and self-understanding to excel in their performances. Researchers argue that these metacognitive processes and inferences play a central role in an athlete developing expertise in their sport and that the more an athlete is able to recognise and use their metacognition then the more expert within their sport they are likely to be.[3] In competition, when our cognitive system is challenged with large amounts of information, the expert athletes will be those able to sort and understand the implications of each piece of information and make use of the information they need, incredibly quickly so they can perform at a higher level.

There are several benefits to purposefully using metacognition in sport. It helps athletes realise what they don't yet know so they can identify their own knowledge and development gaps. It also means they can prepare much more effectively for competition. Without being able to see the bigger picture of something we tend to rush in without thinking. Being aware of the whole event, from start to finish means we can see where it is most important to invest our time and effort so we can pace and prepare better.

How to do it

Many of the mental skills strategies that athletes are advised to use are improved if the athlete has a high level of metacognition[4] as they don't just use the skills but regularly reflect and refine them based on their continual analysis of their effectiveness. In this way it helps athletes to think about their own learning, development and performance more explicitly. Many of the mental skills strategies listed included within this book contribute to this.

1   Goal setting (Strategy 2) helps athletes think about what they want to achieve and how to do that. Regularly taking the athlete back to the goals they have set and talking through them will help keep their thoughts about their goals and how closely they are sticking too them front of mind.

2   Asking good questions such as in a training diary (Strategy 10) helps athletes think more about the actions they take and how they may do them differently next time. Athletes can also use this knowledge to

monitor their performance better and choose at different times whether to use dissociative (Strategy 35) or associative (Strategy 34) attentional strategies to focus on. Reflecting regularly on the training diary and which skills have been used will increase their metacognition.

3   If the athlete is struggling with negative or unhelpful thinking metacognition helps the athlete recognise this, reflect on the impact it has on their performance and can help them to reframe it (Strategy 46). To help athletes develop this reflection process you can ask them at the start of training sessions to do the session with the intention of 'catching' thoughts and emotions. Simply focusing on noticing the thoughts and feelings which are getting in the way of their goals helps them to assess and understand them better and hinder them less or help them more. Once practiced at catching their thoughts they can direct them towards more helpful alternatives. The alternatives won't be false, they will still be true, just a more beneficial version.

Strategy 51 – mindfulness

Mindfulness is a form of awareness and attention where the athlete's focus is on the present moment in a way that is entirely non-judgemental.[5] It can be thought of as self-regulation of attention and being open to our experiences and as either a trait (so within an athlete's disposition) or a set of skills which can be learnt.

Mindfulness interventions aim to change the relationship to thoughts and emotions rather than the content of them. Mindfulness training has been found to be helpful for performance enhancement and to help athletes enhance their activation skills,[6] become more aware of bodily sensations, sift relevant information and make better tactical decisions,[7] get into a flow state[8] to improve attentional and perceptual-cognitive skills[9] to increase our levels of acceptance[10] and helps athletes have better control over their behaviours.[11]

During mindfulness practice an athlete will become more aware of the thoughts they are having but not trying to squash or block out those thoughts. Instead, using that awareness and trying to accept the thoughts for what they are; just thoughts, and only later deciding what to do about them. Over time they will get far more expert at recognising the thoughts, labelling them and taking action if they have a strategy already worked out.

In noticing their thoughts the athlete is offering themselves a non-judgemental way of accepting the things in their head which may otherwise distress them. In consciously paying attention to the things which are worrying them but refraining from engaging with them they can pare back their overthinking and make better decisions. Mindfulness leads well into many of the mental skills strategies discussed within this book such as progressive muscle relaxation (Strategy 19), metacognition (Strategy 50) and thought labelling (Strategy 56).

Mindfulness is used in professional sport. A study run on seven members of the USA BMX team[12] saw mindfulness training improve their self-awareness, the awareness of body sensations, helped them feel more present in competition and when their brains were scanned they were responding differently to physical stress. Performance-wise their coach was clear they were able to get out of the gates faster on competition day.

How to do it

Mindfulness and acceptance may present different advantages for different sports, depending on the characteristics which lead to optimal performance (such as physical, technical, psychological or tactical). This will need to be considered when mindfulness training is adapted for athletes.

Mindfulness training can be developed from the principles of Mindfulness-Based Cognitive Therapy[13] or by using the Acceptance and Commitment Therapy tools.[14] Examples, analogies and exercises can be incorporated to help the approach resonate with athletes.

Elements will gradually build over a period of a few months:

- Introduction to mindfulness – focusing on awareness of breathing and different body sensations.

- Mindfulness training – more specific elements of breathing, body sensations and movement.
- Mindfulness and acceptance training – athletes becoming more aware (but not judgemental) of thoughts and emotions
- Mindfulness, acceptance and commitment training – to use the acceptance element to commit to a relevant object of attention.

Practice between sessions is vital to build up skills especially if mindfulness is being run as a group class as some athletes may struggle to truly relax in an environment where they are with their friends.

Some athletes also struggle with the stillness that mindfulness often asks for so one exercise which can work really well for athletes is a 'body scan',[15] a short exercise, where the athlete learns to notice their own sensations and cognitions. It feels closer to their sport and more purposeful to their performance than simply sitting or lying still for a period. Some athletes who find their levels of arousal before competition get too high can then incorporate the mindful activities which have worked well for them into pre-performance routines.

Strategy 52 – self-expert

As an athlete develops in their sport it is not just their sport they become an expert in but how they personally behave within their sport. Becoming an authority on themselves helps them so they become far more self-aware of their likes, dislikes, preferences and fears so they can design or adapt their competition environment to maximise their performance preferences and avoid those elements which reduce their enjoyment and potential success.

How to do it

There are a huge number of areas to assess for preferences. Just a few are featured here but running through each area with your athletes will help prompt them to consider in depth their personal preferences.

Engagement with others

Athletes may not be able to change much about their environment, but they can influence those in it, especially their own supporters. Considering whose presence puts pressure on them and who helps them to thrive is helpful. Considering how supporters would behave in the athlete's ideal world helps to open up those helpful communication channels.

Circadian rhythm

Knowing which type of biological clock the athlete has is helpful as although studies have found for many their circadian rhythm means they are best completing cognitive tasks in the morning and gross motor skills in the afternoon, an athlete's chronotype will impact the fluctuation of their cognitive performance throughout the day. Larks are sharpest in the morning and owls better in the later hours. This then matches when they like to sleep and train and whether they may need more of a boost for competitions at specific times of the day or extra strategies to get to training if it falls at a difficult time for them.

Logistics

Whether an athlete likes to be very planned with their organisation and time management or turn up at the last minute hoping it all goes ok will impact on how they prepare for competitions and whether they need prompts to consider organisation in more depth.

Nutrition

Nutrition is incredibly personal to each athlete but their preferences around nutrition, foods they like before or after training or during competition will need to be considered and incorporated into their performance planning.

Mental skills

Understanding an athlete's motivation and their 'why' (Strategy 49) is important for the athlete and the coach so that they are able to get themselves going again after a setback. Similarly, if there are mental skills the athlete has learnt to use effectively they can be employed quickly when going through a tough time.

Training preferences

Does an athlete prefer to train alone, in groups, in short bursts of concentration or in a steady manner? Do they like to have training partners (Strategy 64)?

Attentional strategies

How does the athlete prefer to behave in the hour or so before a competition? Some love to chat to others to manage their nerves, others like their own space and quietness. If chatting to team-mates or friends before their competition will add to their anxiety they may want to wear headphones to indicate to others they need their own space. Those who feel overly nervous before competitions may want to stay away from others who also feel nervous as they can make each other feel worse.

Coping methods

What coping mechanisms does the athlete like to use mid-competition? Many of these will be contained within Chapter 12. They may include colourful breathing (Strategy 18), chunking (Strategy 36), associative (Strategy 34) or dissociative (Strategy 35) strategies or respond, relax and refocus (Strategy 41).

Injury

How does the athlete cope with injury? Hiding away or spending time with sporting peers? Do they write off the season, find other ways to stay active, use the time to learn more about their sport? How do they most effectively return from injury; throw themselves back in, step back in cautiously or get lots of expert help? How do they take steps to prevent getting injured again?

Personality traits

Understanding an athlete's personality traits and the way these impact on their sport can be a really beneficial short cut to designing effective training that will help them reach their athletic endeavours. Those high in extroversion often need the external stimulation of working with a team or training for a race. They are more likely to stick to plans if there is a social element to it. Those high in introversion can feel overwhelmed by too much external stimulation making them keener to exercise alone. Those with high levels of openness will be more willing to try new exercises or options; maybe making them early adopters of new technologies or gadgets. Those high in perfectionism may work very hard in their training but struggle with the pressure of competition. Those with an external locus of control may believe that things will happen to them and that others control outcomes – this may reduce the amount of impact they feel they have on the outcome of a competition, feeling any success is down to luck rather than their efforts.

A fun version of this process for junior athletes to use is a 'self-awareness washing line'. Give them a piece of string, some mini pegs and some small pieces of paper. As they notice the elements of their sport that they prefer, they write them down, peg them up and help them make their strategies for competition and decisions for their sport in line with their preferences.

Strategy 53 – self-identity mapping

At their core, how an athlete feels about their sport often comes down to where it sits within their self-identity. Our self-identity is important as we look at everything through the lens of our different identities and interpret all new information through those lenses. If the overriding self-identity is as an athlete then that will be the dominant lens. They will strongly identify with that role and look for others to acknowledge that too. They may have grown up with a very specific idea of what an athlete looks like, how they behave, what type of person they are and shape their expectations of what they can and can't do.

This athletic self-identity can manifest externally as well as internally. When an athlete takes part in their sport they are making a social statement about who they are. The more time they spend doing their sport, the more skills and strategies they learn, the stronger that statement becomes. If they are competing in races or competitions then that social statement sits in black and white on results pages for them, and anyone else, to see.

A strong self-identity as an athlete can be helpful to their performance as it helps maintain their motivation to train, helps them work consistently, prepare well and pushes them to make the right choices for their sport in the rest of their lives (i.e. eating healthily, getting enough sleep). If their self-identity is too fragmented they may struggle to maintain positive sporting behaviours or feel like they don't fit in. On the other hand having too strong a sporting self-identity can be difficult if an athlete gets injured, has a performance setback, retires or struggles to maintain previous performance levels due to the aging process. It is particularly difficult when they retire as shown by research across football, rugby and cricket which found that the loss of identity contributed to over half of retiring athletes struggling with their mental health when they retired.[16] This is also influenced by the manner of their retirement. An athlete with a number of self-identities who has planned their next steps and is choosing to retire because they have met their ambitions will be in a very different place mentally than one who has a very strong sporting identity and is being forced to retire due to injury or being dropped from a team. Therefore, understanding the facets of an athlete's self-identity can be realty helpful to support them when they go through difficult periods.

How to do it

Draw two large circles on a piece of paper. In the first circle ask the athlete to split the day into a 24-hour clock. They can gradually fill the clock with what they do on a -typical day. This will show all the physical elements of an athlete's life; school or work, eating, travelling, caring for others, playing games or watching TV, chatting to friends, a partner or children, hobbies and their sport. In the second circle take out the time they sleep and with the rest ask the athlete to focus on what they think about; splitting the pie chart to show what percentage of their thoughts are focused on each of those elements above (or others). This should highlight any obvious discrepancies between time spent and mental focus and highlight how strong an athlete's self-identity towards their sport is.

If the athlete's sporting self-identity is too strong then athletes can be advised to grow their support network and interests outside of sport. This will mean when they retire or have a setback they will have the support they need from friends who care about them, rather than their sporting endeavours. With a particularly strong sporting identity the athlete may also need some support in separating out their sporting successes and failures from their feeling of worth as a person. They will need help to see that sporting failure is not the same as personal failure.

If the athlete has too many self-identities and their sporting self-identity is relatively weak then perhaps a chat about how seriously they want to take their sport would be helpful. If they are frustrated that they are not performing better maybe a focus on goals they really want to achieve in their sport and the time and effort required to do so would be good. If they are happy with their balance then the issue can be left alone.

Strategy 54 – stressor identification

The more destructive stresses we have in our lives the more coping mechanisms we need to employ and the greater our risk of making errors or feeling under threat. The stressors are not just big events like moving house, exams or divorce but the small daily hassles, those things which can be considered as the 'chronic strains of everyday life'[17] which make us feel tense, grumpy and out of sorts. Added up, these hassles can start to impact our physiological responses to training or our mental reactions when in a competitive or pressurised situation.

These hassles and pressures can be both magnified when an athlete is aiming to perform at a high level and occur alongside athlete and sport specific stressors. In fact, 93 distinct stressors have been identified for elite athletes[18] which break down into:

- Performance (preparation, injury, pressure, opponents, self, event superstitions).
- Environmental (selection, finances, training environment, accommodation, travel, competition environment, safety).
- Personal (nutrition, injury, goals and expectations).
- Leadership (coaches, coaching style).
- Team (atmosphere, support, roles, communication).

Spending time working out strategies to diminish some of these hassles and stressors to make an athlete's life easier can be really beneficial for a number of reasons. Firstly, research has found that these stressors increase our risk of illness[19] and injury.[20] Secondly, many hassles create distractions away from what the athlete would ideally be focused on. Some will be real, some will be perceived, and some will be personal pressures which are self-amplified. In becoming more aware of these hassles and distractions the athlete can analyse which ones are preventing them from performing at their best. Deeply assessing the hassles and stressors an athlete is dealing with in their lives increases their emotional self-awareness to know where their frustrations or anxieties are coming from and may help them focus on identifying different coping strategies.

How to do it

The athlete should spend some time working out all the little things in their life and sport which have the potential to cause them stress and think about how they can manage them better. Even if they can't fix them this will make the athlete more aware of what is impacting them and consider how to deal with it, either to confront the stressors or to learn coping mechanisms to deal better with them.

The first step is for the athlete to note down all the hassles and stressors they are confronting over the course of a week. Once they have their list they should highlight all those where they can do something; the ones where they have some control or influence. With this they can work on a plan to deal better with each so they can train and compete more effectively.

If an athlete struggles to identify their hassles some prompts to use[21] could include:

- Home life (misplacing or losing things, too many responsibilities, keeping home clean and tidy, meal planning or preparation, living in a challenging area, noise).
- Family (aging parent care, childcare, problems with children, overwhelmed by family responsibilities).
- Social life (fear of confrontation, difficult neighbours, social obligations, loneliness, use of alcohol, discrimination or prejudice).
- Health (health fears, not being able to afford things to improve health, fear of injury, health of those you love, fertility, medical treatment, poor quantity or quality of sleep, not enough energy to do everything, pollution).
- Future (fear of failure, not sure of future needs, retirement planning, crime).
- Money (loans, debt, not earning enough to live comfortably, bills rising, not enough in savings, travel costs, housing costs).
- Work (not liking colleagues, threat of redundancy, insecurity in role, bored in job, difficult boss, difficult customers, harassment, feeling exploited, not enough time to get things done).
- Sport (performance, environmental, logistics, personal, coaching or team).

Strategy 55 – thinking aloud

Complementary to self-talk (Strategies 42–46) is thinking aloud. It involves athletes (usually while in training but sometimes in low-level competitions) stating out loud everything running through their head. It shows the athlete and the coach exactly where their focus and attention is and allows both to become more aware of the athlete's thoughts and thought processes. Developing this greater self-awareness means both athletes and coaches are able to see where potential negative or distracting thoughts may be hindering their performances so they can use reframing (Strategy 46) to structure their thoughts in a more effective way.

If completed in training the session is usually run by a coach or a psychologist so that they can understand what the athlete is focussing on and attending to. Then work can take place to see if those thoughts are helpful or the elements being focused on are ones which impact positively on performance.

The process can also act as a tool to support reflection to help an athlete look deeper into key incidents or periods in training where they struggled and could have performed better. Feedback to a coach after a competition or key training session can often be clouded by the result or comments given, biasing the feedback and reflections so having verbalised thoughts mid-session can give a less subjective picture to the coach. A further benefit was found in a study using thinking aloud where cyclists verbalised their thoughts while completing a ten-mile time trial. They found thinking aloud helped them to stay focused on their performance[22]

How to do it

To use thinking aloud with athletes a recording device is needed. It is possible for the coach to write down the thoughts as the athlete says them but this is difficult in a very active session and will break up the sporting fluidity. Additionally, if an athlete can listen back to their spoken thoughts they may resonate more.

Once recorded and then listened to, sitting down together with the athlete to talk about patterns of thoughts, the direction of them (helpful/unhelpful) and when in the process the patterns appear can help to shape their understanding of how their self-talk is currently being used. You can then go into a more formal process of identifying self-talk strategies (Strategies 42–46) to replace unhelpful thoughts within specific periods of the competition.

Strategy 56 – thought labelling

Competitions can induce emotions. Athletes who have invested lots of time and energy in their event or who have a limited number of self-identities may take even small losses very personally so focusing on increasing emotional control will be beneficial. One specific tactic to increase emotional control is thought labelling. Some athletes worry that putting negative feelings into words will intensify them but research has found that writing down what you are feeling, a process known as 'affect labelling' can actually reduce the level of emotion.

Neuro-imaging studies using MRIs found the process of thought labelling diminished the response of the amygdala (the area we learnt about in Chapter 1 which sets off our threat emotions).[23] This suggests that consciously recognising emotions reduces their impact on us. Ideally then, when an athlete names or labels their thoughts, the emotion attached to them reduces so they feel more comfortable and able to discuss them. A study analysing nearly 75,000 tweets found that when someone tweeted something negative about their feelings, further tweets over the next six hours became less emotional, indicating that getting their negative thoughts out reduced the impact of their feelings.[24]

How to do it

The first step is to use a mindfulness programme (Strategy 51) to help athletes notice and then recognise their thoughts. Doing this process regularly can help the athlete become much more self-aware of which thoughts arrive regularly, especially those which are helpful and those which are sabotaging their goals.

The more sensations an athlete is able to recognise within their thoughts the better they will be able to describe and label them. Therefore, you can ask the athlete not just to describe the thought they are having but the sensations they feel when having it. Then ask them to label that feeling. What would they call it? Once they have labelled their most common competition thoughts they can filter them into helpful and unhelpful. Sometimes a thought may be negative can still be helpful. Once the thought is labelled they can make a better decision on how to deal with it, perhaps through thought stopping (Strategy 43), a motivational mantra (Strategy 45) or cognitive reframing (Strategy 46).

A more visual way for younger athletes to take on this activity is to ask them to think of their mind as a comment box and that the slips of paper that are dropped into it are their thoughts. They can consider each of these thoughts but they are not required to act on them. They are just comments or suggestions which they need to sort into named piles.

Notes

1 Flavell, J. H. (1979). Metacognition and cognitive monitoring: A new area of cognitive-developmental inquiry. *American Psychologist, 34*, 906–911.

2 Van Overschelde, J. P. (2008). Metacognition: Knowing about knowing. In J. Dunlosky & R. A. Bjork (Eds.), *Handbook of metamemory and memory* (pp. 47–71). New York: Psychology Press.

3 MacIntyre, T. E., Igou, E. R., Campbell, M. J., Moran, A. P., & Matthews, J. (2014). Metacognition and action: A new pathway to understanding social and cognitive aspects of expertise in sport. *Frontiers in Psychology, 5*, 1155.

4 Moran, A. P. (1996). *The psychology of concentration in sport performers: A cognitive analysis*. Hove, East Sussex: Psychology Press.

5 Kabat-Zinn, J. (1994). *Wherever you go, there are you: Mindfulness meditation in everyday life*. New York: Hyperion.

6 Gardner, F. L., & Moore, Z. E. (2007). *The psychology of enhancing human performance: The Mindfulness-Acceptance-Commitment (MAC) approach*. New York: Springer.

7 Bernier, M., Thienot, E., Codron, R., & Fournier, J. F. (2009). Mindfulness and acceptance approaches in sport performance. *Journal of Clinical Sport Psychology, 3* (4), 320–333.

8 Kee, Y. H., & Wang, C. K. J. (2008). Relationships between mindfulness, flow dispositions and mental skills adoption: A cluster analytic approach. *Psychology of Sport and Exercise, 9*, 393–411.

9 Chambers, R., Lo, B. C. Y., & Allen, N. B. (2008). The impact of intensive mindfulness training on attentional control, cognitive style, and affect. *Cognitive Therapy and Research, 32*, 303–322.

10 Hayes, S. C., Strosahl, K., & Wilson, K. G. (1999). *Acceptance and commitment therapy: An experiential approach to behavior change*. New York: Guilford.

11 Coffey, K. A., Hartman, M., & Fredrickson, B. L. (2010). Deconstructing mindfulness and constructing mental health: Understanding mindfulness and its mechanisms of action. *Mindfulness, 1*, 235–253.

12 Haase, L., May, A. C., Falahpour, M., Isakovic, S., Simmons, A. N., Hickman, S. D., … Paulus, M. P. (2015). A pilot study investigating changes in neural processing after mindfulness training in elite athletes. *Frontiers in Behavioral Neuroscience, 9*, 229.

13 Segal, Z. V., Williams, J. M. G., & Teasdale, J. D. (2002). *Mindfulness-based cognitive therapy for depression: A new approach to preventing relapse*. New York: Guilford Press.

14 Hayes, S. C., & Strosahl, K. D. (2004). *A practical guide to acceptance and commitment therapy*. New York: Springer.

15 Segal, Z. V., Williams, J. M. G., & Teasdale, J. D. (2002). *Mindfulness-based cognitive therapy for depression: A new approach to preventing relapse*. New York: Guilford Press.

16 *BBC*. (2018). State of sport study 5th February 2018. www.bbc.co.uk/sport/42871491 (Retrieved on 10/1/19).

17 DeLongis, A., Coyne, J. C., Dakof, G., Folkman, S., & Lazarus, R. S. (1982). Relationship of daily hassles, uplifts, and major life events to health status. *Health Psychology, 1*(2), 119.

18 Hanton, S., Fletcher, D., & Coughlan, G. (2005). Stress in elite sport performers: A comparative study of competitive and organizational stressors. *Journal of Sports Sciences, 23*(10), 1129–1141.

19 Holmes, T. H., & Rahe, R. H. (1967). The social readjustment rating scale. *Journal of Psychosomatic Research, 11*(2), 213–218.

20 Hanson, S. J., McCullagh, P., & Tonymon, P. (1992). The relationship of personality characteristics, life stress, and coping resources to athletic injury. *Journal of Sport and Exercise Psychology, 14*(3), 262–272.
21 adapted from DeLongis, A., Folkman, S., & Lazarus, R. (1988). The impact of daily stress on health and mood: Psychological and social resources as mediators. *Journal of Personality and Social Psychology, 54*, 486–495.
22 Whitehead, A. E., Jones, H. S., Williams, E. L., Rowley, C., Quayle, L., Marchant, D., & Polman, R. C. (2018). Investigating the relationship between cognitions, pacing strategies and performance in 16.1 km cycling time trials using a think aloud protocol. *Psychology of Sport and Exercise, 34*, 95–109.
23 Lieberman, M. D., Eisenberger, N. I., Crockett, M. J., Tom, S. M., Pfeifer, J. H., & Way, B. M. (2007). Putting feelings into words. *Psychological Science, 18*(5), 421–428.
24 Fan, R., Varol, O., Varamesh, A., Barron, A., van de Leemput, I. A., Scheffer, M., & Bollen, J. (2019). The minute-scale dynamics of online emotions reveal the effects of affect labeling. *Nature Human Behaviour, 3*, 92–100.

14

Strategies for providing support

Strategy 57 – verbal persuasion

Verbal persuasion is one of four sources of self-efficacy, the psychological characteristic that influences an athlete's behaviours, thought patterns and reactions.[1] It can come in the form of statements at training, in feedback conversations, in team talks or speeches or in a single comment ahead of a competition. It can boost an athlete's confidence to know someone else believes they have the ability or effort levels they need and takes the time to tell them as encouragement. It is a reminder to the athlete that they have what it takes to perform well.

The encouragement can come from a coach or other involved expert or from others within the athlete's support network but must be authentic so related to something they have expertise in. Sometimes that expertise will be in the athlete themselves (such as being able to remind them of the many times they worried and yet performed well) or in the sport (such as highlighting a course or competition is suited to them). It can play a key part in the athlete's confidence as it is not only a great source of confidence but can be more effective the more it is tailored to the athlete.

How to do it

This is a really simple strategy but the person offering the verbal persuasion should follow four rules:

- The persuasion should come from someone the athlete trusts.
- The statement given should be based on facts and logic – it has to be believable to the athlete.
- The statement should link to the athlete's current skills or recent experiences.
- The ambition must be within the athlete's capabilities.

Statements offered can focus on a key strength of the athlete, a technical point they would do well by following or something that reminds them they have the skills or experience to perform well.

Strategy 58 – feedback preferences

Feedback is essential for athletes to understand how to improve. Researchers have found that the better the quality and quantity of feedback from coaches the higher the athlete's perception of their competence, self-esteem and enjoyment will be.[2] The way a coach gives feedback can make a big difference to how the athlete takes it on board with delivery being most effective is when it is sincere, specific and focused on behaviour or effort rather than on something uncontrollable like talent.

The two types of feedback to incorporate into a tool kit to support athletes are:

- Motivational feedback – this enhances confidence, inspires greater effort and energy investment and creates a positive mood. This can reinforce things the athlete should know about themselves already. It can also help them focus on some of the goals they have set, particularly process goals.
- Instructional feedback – this covers specific behaviours they demonstrate and how well they are achieving them at this stage in their development. Breaking down complex skills into much smaller component parts will give more information to the athlete on how to perform the skill and confidence they can perform it well. There is a difference between 'great start – you were really fast' and 'great

start – you pushed off strongly with your back leg.' The first doesn't help the athlete to replicate it. The second shows why it was effective and helps the athlete to remember to continue doing it.

How to do it

Keeping a diary of how athletes respond to different types of feedback and where you can see the biggest improvements will help to highlight any preferences they have and where they will respond best. Then each time you need to give feedback to an athlete you can phrase it in the most effective way.

To do this effectively (and pick the right type of feedback at the right time) it is really valuable to understand the goals they have set for themselves (Strategy 2) and to have chatted through with them work they have complete on developing their own self-awareness such as their strengths audit (Strategy 9) and their self-expert reflections (Strategy 52).

Strategy 59 – managing difficult conversations

As anyone working with athletes will know, supporting them effectively in their sport is so much more than setting a training plan and running practice sessions. At its core it is about being able to effectively and knowledgably communicate theories, strategies, tactics and expected behaviours to athletes, in a way they will understand, process and incorporate. And this is where it sometimes goes wrong.

If the communication is shared in poor conditions or where either party is under stress or emotional then the communication is open to misinterpretation and resentment and additional, unnecessary stress can set in. Proactively addressing the difficult relationship can be hard, and really daunting for coaches, but also really beneficial.

How to do it

Some things to think about when preparing for and having a difficult conversation:

- You will each have your own version of the truth so it will be rare that a difficult conversation ends with a simple outcome but, if you know your boundaries and where you are prepared to flex them in advance, you won't feel under pressure if you are pushed back.

- Your physical positioning is important. Rather than sitting face to face with someone which can feel rather confrontational, being side by side can feel much easier and can take some of the emotion and threat out of the situation. Side by side during a walk or car journey can work well.

- Listening. Athletes and coaches need to feel their views have been listened to and acknowledged as valid. Only once this has happened will they be open to working on a solution together. Making space for this to happen at the start of a difficult conversation can actually speed up the process and get you both to a resolution much quicker.

- Have notes. It can be helpful to write yourself a short note of what you want from a conversation. This helps if you get flustered and can keep the tone positive and proactive, rather than becoming an opportunity to score points. Use this 'goal' as your mantra to keep you on track if you get tempted to pour out everything you are feeling.

- Timings. Make sure there is enough time for the conversation needed. The worst thing is for it to be squeezed into a small gap and the athlete to get called away and you have gone through that worry and preparation and not got an outcome. Ideally the conversation is held early on in a session so you don't spend the whole session feeling anticipatory stress.

- Summarise. Close the conversation with one key thing to work on and an agreement over when to catch up next to assess how everything is working.

Strategy 60 – payback points

To be effective in their sport and to perform well athletes often need to be fairly selfish in taking what they need from others – advice, time, transport, childcare, flexibility, coaching or money – and during competition season may have little time or bandwidth to give back to those people. It can create a fairly misbalanced relationship. Their friends and family often recognise and accommodate this but may not necessarily welcome it. It can cause conflict when they have watched their athlete compete, driven them to competitions, had important days interrupted with training or competitions and continually feel they come second to their loved one's sport.

When the athlete does have capacity during off-season or injury they can feed back into these relationships not only to secure further long-term support but also to ensure those important to them know how much their investment means and is valued. It can be thought of as paying back. It is an opportunity to give loved ones full attention and (self-ishly) it also helps reduce the impact of post-competition blues or injury stress.

How to do it

A nice process to go through with athletes as the end of season nears is to look at where their support throughout the season has come from. They can consider what help they got and then be prompted to think about ways to pay that support back.

Firstly, consider who helped them; partner, parents, siblings, coaches, team mates, colleagues or peers, friends, wider family.

Secondly, consider ways to pay each back. The best and most appropriate ideas will come from the athletes themselves but elements they could consider may be:

- Finding a creative way to thank them for their support.
- Supporting them in something to do with the supporter's hobby or passion.
- Taking them out to celebrate end of season as a thank you for the part they played in it.
- Helping out at the club as a coaching assistant or giving fun sessions to younger athletes.
- Asking their supporters how they can thank them and booking that in as a treat.

- Seeing friends they don't get to see much and worry they have neglected.

Strategy 61 – reality checking

Individuals can get very self-critical when they compare themselves to others and athletes have far more opportunities than most to compare themselves; their bodies are on display (usually in tight clothing), their performances are timed or measured and compared, tracking or achievement data is posted online, not just after competitions but sometimes after every training session and the media and other athletes may discuss these elements in public, in detail, whether the athlete likes this or not. Not only is this superficial (and without context) but athletes may well be comparing their true 'warts and all' self to someone else's instagrammed, glossy version; one that is probably set up and filtered purposefully to give a stage-managed vision of themselves. A set of studies have found that people actually think they are more alone in their emotional difficulties than they actually are[3] so they are bound to feel low and self-critical in comparison when they imagine everyone else has it better, easier or is happier.

Additionally, the harder we are on ourselves the harder it is to regain our motivation and we are less likely to achieve the goals we do set. This means the more we compare, the worse we will do,[4] so setting in place some reality checking can benefit an athlete greatly.

This reality checking can involve the athlete comparing themselves with where they were previously. The focus on temporal comparison where the athlete is reflecting on their past and their future selves can help them set clear steps and plans to get where they want to go. This process will help them feel more in control, more self-aware and more in tune with their motivations and ambitions. If this is tied in with their values (Strategy 48) it should help the athlete feel their progression is different to others for very good reasons. A training diary (Strategy 10) is a really good way to do this as the athlete can see in their own writing what they have achieved already and how far they have come.

How to do it

To help athletes reality check and keep their focus on themselves and their own sporting journey they need to be asked the right questions at the right times.

- For newer athletes spending a lot of time comparing themselves with more experienced rivals asking them to compare themselves now with themselves 12 months ago is a good way for them to see how far they have come.
- For more experienced athletes you can ask them to consider their own journey and bumps in that journey so they can see the context in which their development has taken place be reminded the journey is neither smooth nor linear.
- Some athletes find it helpful to look up their competitors in advance and see who they are competing against, what sort of times or distances or skills they have been achieving and watch YouTube videos to see what tactics they use. This helps them feel prepared. For other athletes this will be harmful and just cause anxiety and stress, sometimes making them feel they will lose before they even reach competition day. Asking your athletes how they respond when they know lots about those they are competing against will help you either hold back starting information or offer it up so they can research effectively.
- A further tactic, which is particularly good for younger athletes, is to work with them on their athlete journey. They can spend some time studying athletes in their sport who have done well and that they admire and learn about the route they took to get there where their blips came. They can be asked to discuss the things they may have in common with their athlete and the things which are different. This allows a discussion about how we are our own journey, as is everyone else.

Strategy 62 – support team identification

Support is vital in sport. Studies have found that the more support an athlete perceives they have the lower their likelihood of burnout and stress,[5] the higher their motivation[6] and the better they are able to overcome adversity.[7] There are numerous experts an athlete can call upon to support their performance goals but the 'team' around an athlete doesn't have to be formal experts or people paid to give advice. As well as coaches and technical experts, support may also come from friends, parents, wider family, colleagues, teammates or even people online and each can play a role in an athlete's development and performance. It is usually found that coaches and teammates tend to provide support which requires expertise in sports. Friends, parents and others offer complementary support.[8]

Support will include the formal elements that people may be employed for, especially in technical jobs such as psychologists, coaches, strength and conditioning experts or physios. They will offer technical appreciation and challenges coming from a level of sporting or professional expertise. Identifying who all these people are can help an athlete feel better supported and means when in a difficult situation they immediately know who to go to. They may not have yet even used this person but having this database of support means there is a little less panic when they stumble upon a setback and can identity the right support quickly.

There will also be people around the athlete with no formal 'role' but who are vital in offering emotional support and share the athlete's reality[9] by providing the space to vent feelings, get reassurance and to reduce uncertainty during times of stress.[10]

Understanding where all these potential sources of support come from can be particularly helpful for young athletes who will go through lots of transitions as they develop and age. The pressures these athletes will face; relationships, feelings, stress and of course injury all impact on their performances and if they have a 'go-to' person for each area of their worries they will be a better and healthier athlete; both mentally and physically.

How to do it

Run through a list with them of who they go to for each thing (the same person may pop up more than once):

- Sporting strategy advice
- Fitness advice
- Training advice
- Competition preparation advice
- Nutrition advice
- Injury advice
- Health advice
- Mental approaches to their sport
- Advice or support about family, friend or romantic relationships
- When they need cheering up
- When they need school or career advice
- When they want to have fun
- When they need to talk about something personal.

If there are big gaps in these answers support the athlete to identify people in their training group they may be able to approach. Have a list yourself of local specialists in nutrition, psychology, physio and medicine you can suggest they add into their network. Before handing over the list though ask the athlete to consider which skills or characteristics they would be hoping to find in the expert they seek so they begin to develop an idea of what works for them in a support team.

Strategy 63 – technology strategy

Technology is becoming more invasive in sport. Sport used to be one area safely tucked away from technology but it is now fully integrated, from VAR in football to route and data tracking for endurance and adventure athletes. The pros and cons of using it will be very personal so for some athletes it can be very helpful; allowing athletes to focus, to amp up or tone down their arousal levels or to get data feedback on their performances, for others it causes significant harm; prompting exercise addiction, facilitating self-sabotage or reducing sporting enjoyment.

Understanding each athlete's relationship with technology, how they like to use it, how helpful it can be in their individual sport and how they can benefit rather than suffer from it will be a positive exercise. Once they understand the benefits and risks of integrating technology into their sport athletes can write a technology strategy to ensure it improves their performance while still protecting their wellbeing.

A specific area for athletes to consider is social media. Does sharing sporting information on here harm or help the athlete? Some athletes enjoy the online community support they get. Others worry about being judged. Online groups or forums can boost an athlete's resilience and provide fantastic support but can turn harmful if the athlete feels judged and mentally painful if they become injured and their online friends are inadvertently providing constant reminders of what they cannot do.

How to do it

1   A technology strategy would begin by an athlete considering all the types of technology the athlete uses and then considering the areas where technology is impacting their sporting life. Technologies to consider:

- Smart phone
- GPS watch (or other measuring devices)
- Biofeedback apps or equipment (such as Heart Rate Monitor or Powermeter)
- Music player
- Laptop.

2   Looking at the goals the athlete has set (Strategy 2) an analysis of how these different technologies could help them fulfil each goal can take place followed by the ways technology could undermine each goal. Some of this will depend upon the personality of the athlete so will be different in every case. Ways that technologies or apps can help support include:

- Helps stick to goals
- Helps tracks speed/distance/height/time trained accurately without judgement
- Develops supportive online communities
- Provides honest feedback
- Facilitates biofeedback.

Ways technologies or apps can push the athlete off track:

- Online challenges or competitions becoming more important than ones taking place in real life
- Online judgement or bitching
- Jealously and comparisons with other athletes
- Isolation when injured.

3   A negative element for everyone is that if we spend too much time when training plugged into technology we can find it becomes hard to read our own body. So even if an athlete loves using technology they will benefit by picking a couple of sessions a week where they train 'naked' without any tech. In these sessions they should do some body checking; following a basic move from their sport mentally checking and listening to the signals each part is giving. Estimating their overall Perceived Rate of Exertion (PRE) and learning how this relates to the statistics or readings from their gadgets will help them be able to judge effort when having to perform without any technology.

Strategy 64 – training partners

Purposefully finding other athletes to train with can be really beneficial for athletes.

Athletes with a training partner have been found in research to have better adherence to training (as it makes training more enjoyable and increases accountability), improved technical skills and to enjoy training more. It also boosts confidence as training with others provides loads of opportunities to give praise and to receive it. Specifically developing a training partnership with another athlete has been found to improve work ethic,[11] pain tolerance[12] and accountability.[13] The accountability study is particularly interesting because it involved the role of spotters in bench press performance who found that not only did lifters manage more reps when they thought spotters were watching them but the effort levels when watched felt lower too.[14]

The physicality of these benefits can be highlighted in technical sports. Research has found trampolinists mirror and learn from each other, becoming each others' performance analysts[15] and that our physical interactions with others can change and improve our own motor behaviour[16] so one athlete's good technique rubs off on the other.

For all these benefits though there are risks. Research on distance runners found that when 12 male distance runners did three 6.4k runs on an outside trial; one alone, one with one training partner and one with two training partners, the runners enjoyed the run most when they were in the group but they actually ran slower. This may be because the athletes spent more time chatting rather than focusing on their training or rushing to complete the session.

A further risk can come if one starts to improve at a much greater rate than the other. Jealousy, resentment or over-competitiveness may appear. This was found when researchers looked at what influenced 424 masters swimmers to keep on training. They found that pressures from training partners actually reduced the likelihood of them wanting to continue to commit.[17] Finally, training partners also need to remember their partner will know them really well; their hopes and fears, their strengths and weaknesses and may use this against them in competition.

Despite these concerns, finding a training partner can be a particularly helpful tactic when an athlete is unmotivated due to the time in the season, poor form or difficult environmental conditions.

How to do it

The key to a successful training partnership is finding the right training partner. There are six elements to consider if trying to set up an athlete with a training partner.

- Ideally, to really benefit, the partners will physically train alongside each other. The first place to look will often be within their own club.
- The focus for most shared sessions should be on recovery, fitness or technical sessions.

- While it has worked successfully in the past, trying to force close rivals together in a partnership may not bring out great results. They need to be comfortable working together to bring out the best in each other.
- Sometimes a couple of training partners can be helpful. They can be utilised if one is injured, on holiday or tapering for a different competition or if they are of different abilities or specialisms.
- Ideally the athlete picks someone more experienced than them who can help them push themselves a little bit more, pick their brains about training strategies and use them a little bit like a mentor.
- Personality traits need to be considered. If someone is always late they may not suit someone who is always early. An introvert may struggle to train for hours alongside an extrovert. If athletes are to spend significant amounts of time together they need to get on and enjoy each other's company.

Then rules need to be agreed up front. Two which will be key are:

- For the athletes to agree they are in sessions to train and not compete. They should be pushing each other but not trying to beat each other.
- How they behave on competition day if they are individual athletes competing against each other.

Notes

1 Bandura, A. (1997). *Self-efficacy: The exercise of control.* New York: Freeman.
2 Smoll, F. L., & Smith, R. E. (2002). Coaching behavior research and intervention in youth sports. *Children and Youth in Sport: A Biopsychosocial Perspective, 2*, 211–234.
3 Jordan, A. H., Monin, B., Dweck, C. S., Lovett, B. J., John, O. P., & Gross, J. J. (2011). Misery has more company than people think: Underestimating the prevalence of others' negative emotions. *Personality and Social Psychology Bulletin, 37* (1), 120–135.

4   Powers, T. A., Koestner, R., & Zuroff, D. C. (2007). Self–criticism, goal motivation, and goal progress. *Journal of Social and Clinical Psychology, 26*(7), 826–840.

5   Albrecht, T. L., & Adelman, M. B. (1984). Social support and life stress: New directions for communication research. *Human Communication Research, 11*(1), 3–32.

6   DeFreese, J. D., & Smith, A. L. (2013). Teammate social support, burnout, and self-determined motivation in collegiate athletes. *Psychology of Sport and Exercise, 14*(2), 258–265.

7   Morgan, T. K., & Giacobbi Jr, P. R. (2006). Toward two grounded theories of the talent development and social support process of highly successful collegiate athletes. *The Sport Psychologist, 20*(3), 295–313.

8   Rosenfeld, L. B., Richman, J. M., & Hardy, C. J. (1989). Examining social support networks among athletes: Description and relationship to stress. *The Sport Psychologist, 3*(1), 23–33.

9   Rosenfeld, L. B., Richman, J. M., & Hardy, C. J. (1989). Examining social support networks among athletes: Description and relationship to stress. *The Sport Psychologist, 3*(1), 23–33.

10 Albrecht, T. L., & Adelman, M. B. (1984). Social support and life stress: New directions for communication research. *Human Communication Research, 11*(1), 3–32.

11 Desender, K., Beums, S., & Van den Bussche, E. (2015). Is mental effort exertion contagious? *Psychonomic Bulletin & Review, 23*(2), 624–631.

12 Cohen, E. E., Ejsmond-Frey, R., Knight, N., & Dunbar, R. I. (2009). Rowers' high: Behavioural synchrony is correlated with elevated pain thresholds. *Biology Letters, 6*(1), 106–108.

13 Sheridan, A., Marchant, D., Williams, E. L., Massey, H., Hewitt, P. A., & Sparks, S. A. (2017). Presence of spotters improves bench press performance. *Journal of Strength and Conditioning Research.*

14 Sheridan, A., Marchant, D., Williams, E. L., Massey, H., Hewitt, P. A., & Sparks, S. A. (2017). Presence of spotters improves bench press performance. *Journal of Strength and Conditioning Research.*

15 Lund, O., Ravn, S., & Christensen, M. K. (2014). Jumping together: Apprenticeship learning among elite trampoline athletes. *Physical Education and Sport Pedagogy, 19*(4), 383–397.

16 Ganesh, G., Takagi, A., Osu, R., Yoshioka, T., Kawato, M., & Burdet, E. (2014). Two is better than one: Physical interactions improve motor performance in humans. *Scientific Reports, 4*, 3824.

17 Young, B. W., & Medic, N. (2011). Examining social influences on the sport commitment of masters swimmers. *Psychology of Sport and Exercise, 12*(2), 168–175.

Index